GLOBALIZATION, INTERNATIONAL LAW, AND HUMAN RIGHTS

GLOBALIZATION, INTERNATIONAL LAW, AND HUMAN RIGHTS

JEFFREY F. ADDICOTT
MD. JAHID HOSSAIN BHUIYAN
TAREQ M.R. CHOWDHURY

OXFORD
UNIVERSITY PRESS

OXFORD
UNIVERSITY PRESS

Oxford University Press is a department of the University of Oxford.
It furthers the University's objective of excellence in research, scholarship,
and education by publishing worldwide. Oxford is a registered trademark of
Oxford University Press in the UK and in certain other countries

Published in India by
Oxford University Press
YMCA Library Building, 1 Jai Singh Road, New Delhi 110001, India

ISBN-13: 978 019 8074151
ISBN-10: 019 807 4158

Typeset in Adobe Garamond Pro 11/13
by BeSpoke Integrated Solutions, Puducherry, India 605 008
Printed in India at Rakmo Press, New Delhi 110 020

Contents

Preface

Since humans are organized into separate national entities or States, the matter of human rights deals with the relationship between the individual and the national entity. In contrast to the situation a few generations ago, when the sovereignty of the State was the fundamental principle upon which international law was based, the rapid development of certain human rights norms and standards now require the sovereignty of the State to be weighed and measured against what might be called the freedom of the individual.

Given that the corpus of human rights is still developing in the international community, the term human rights is often used in a variety of ways and given a variety of meanings. Indeed, as reflected in various chapters of this book, human rights can encompass an expansive category of issues, many not deemed to be legally binding in the context of either domestic or international law. Nevertheless, the debate concerning whether human rights should expand from restricting the behaviour of government in the context of infringing individual freedoms, such as life, liberty, and the pursuit of happiness, to mandating that the government provide certain benefits to individuals, such as education, food, or healthcare, is sure to continue in a world under the increasing pressures of globalization.

The contributors to this book provide commentary and insights on various issues associated with the evolution of human rights law in the context of globalization. We express our heartful gratitude to the contributors for their thought-provoking inputs. It has been a pleasure to work with the staff of Oxford University Press in the preparation of this book. We are grateful to Faithe Campbell of St. Mary's University School of Law, United States of America for her valuable assistance. We hope that the book would be a valuable addition to the scarce literature on globalization, international law, and human rights.

Jeffrey F. Addicott
Md. Jahid Hossain Bhuiyan
Tareq M.R. Chowdhury

Abbreviations

ACHPR	African Charter on Human and Peoples' Rights
ACIA	Arctic Climate Impact Assessment
ACP	Africa, Caribbean and Pacific Group of States
AIDS	Acquired Immune Deficiency Syndrome
AJIL	American Journal of International Law
ANC	African National Congress
ASIO	Australian Security Intelligence Organisation
BITs	Bilateral Investments Treaties
CEDAW	Convention on the Elimination of All forms of Discrimination Against Women
CEO	Chief Executive Officer
CERD	Committee on Elimination of Racial Discrimination
CESCR	Committee on Economic, Social and Cultural Rights
CESR	Centre for Economic and Social Rights
CFRN	Constitution of the Federal Republic of Nigeria
CIA	Central Intelligence Agency
CIEL	Center for International Environmental Law
CPRs	Civil and Political Rights
CRC	Convention on the Rights of the Child
CSR	Corporate Social Responsibility
DIA	Defense Intelligence Agency
ECHR	European Convention for the Protection of Human Rights and Fundamental Freedoms
EEC	European Economic Community
EFA	Education for All

ESC	European Social Charter
ESRs	Economic and Social Rights
EU	European Union
FIPA	Foreign Investment Promotion and Protection Agreement
GA	General Assembly
GATT	General Agreement on Trade and Tariffs
GYIL	German Yearbook of International Law
HIV	Human Immunodeficiency Virus
HJIL	Heidelberg Journal of International Law
HRC	Human Rights Committee
HRCion	Human Rights Commission
HRLR	Human Rights Law Review
HRQ	Human Rights Quarterly
IACHR	Inter-American Commission on Human Rights
ICC	International Criminal Court
ICC	Inuit Circumpolar Council
ICCPR	International Covenant on Civil and Political Rights
ICERD	International Covenant on the Elimination of Racial Discrimination
ICESCR	International Covenant on Economic, Social and Cultural Rights
ICLQ	International and Comparative Law Quarterly
ICRMW	International Convention on the Protection of the Rights of All Migrant Workers and Members of Their Families
ICSID	International Centre for the Settlement of Investment Disputes
IFIs	International Financial Institutions
IJIL	Indian Journal of International Law
ILO	International Labour Organization
IMF	International Monetary Fund
ISO	International Standards Organization
ITK	Inuit Tapiriit Kanatami
LEAT	Lawyers' Environmental Action Team
MDBs	Multilateral Development Banks
MDGs	Millennium Development Goals
MEAs	Multilateral Environmental Agreements

MNCs	Multinational Corporations
NAFTA	North American Free Trade Agreement
NAMCO	North Atlantic Marine Mammal Commission
NCP	National Contact Point
NGOs	Non-governmental Organisations
OAS	Organization of American States
OAU	Organisation of African Unity
OECD	Organization for Economic Cooperation and Development
ONA	Office of National Assessment
OPSC	Child Prostitution and Child Pornography
RITs	Regional Investment Treaties
SERAC	Social and Economic Rights Action Center
SPD	German Social Democratic Party
SRSG	Special Representative of the Secretary-General on the issue of human rights and transnational corporations and other business enterprises
TAC	Treatment Action Campaign
TBT	Technical Barriers to Trade
TBT	Agreement on Technical Barriers to Trade
TGNP	Tanzania Gender Networking Programme
UBE	Universal Basic Education
UDHR	Universal Declaration of Human Rights
UN	United Nations
UNCITRAL	United Nations Commission on International Trade Law
UNDP	United Nations Development Programme
UNESCO	United Nations Educational, Scientific and Cultural Organization
US	United States
USSR	Union of Soviet Socialist Republics
WTO	World Trade Organization
WW II	World War II

Introduction

International Implications of Globalization on Emerging Notions of Fundamental Human Rights

Jeffrey F. Addicott
Md. Jahid Hossain Bhuiyan
Tareq M.R. Chowdhury

Strictly viewed from an international legal perspective, any discussion of the concept of globalization and its impact on humans must be juxtaposed against the concept of the utility and function of international treaties and binding covenants between nation-states as the central cornerstone of advancing greater freedoms and human rights. Globalization may mean that the world is getting 'smaller,' but the emerging problems can only find solution within the framework of existing international laws.

From the creation of the United Nations in 1945, to the 1949 Geneva Conventions, to the 1996 International Covenant on Civil and Political Rights, the world has recognized the necessity of approaching desires for world peace and human rights by binding nation-states in such a manner to inhibit both the external and, to a lesser degree, the internal dimensions of State sovereignty. The unfettered power of States to pursue activities and policies that threaten international peace and human rights can only be squarely addressed in terms of the rule of law commonly called international law. While many argue that the utility of the nation-state has lost significance in an ever shrinking world due to the impact of globalization, the rule of law, that is, how to deal with problems associated with globalization, is still primarily understood in terms of the nation-state and whether it is bound by legally enforceable mandates via specific intent (entering into an international treaty) or customary principles (accepted widespread international practice). Accordingly, since the sovereignty of each State still remains as the primary basis for entering into international agreements, the issue of globalization is best understood against the backdrop of the existing legal structure of the world body. In other words, globalization is occurring at a rapid pace, but the international legal framework remains firmly cemented in the nation-state.

Of course, before one can discuss an issue it must be defined. Nowhere is this task more difficult than in terms of globalization. While the term globalization rolls off the tongue with great ease, the primary frustration is that there is no universally accepted definition. Even among scholars, the term is a moving target and can be used to discuss political, social, or economic phenomena mostly associated with how these various forces are breaking down national borders and minimizing the importance or impact of the nation-state. Nevertheless, perhaps the most common understanding that most attach to the term globalization is in the context of the far reaching impact of economic issues, for example, the rise of multinational corporations, coupled with the spread of information systems (by 2011 over 2 billion humans will use the Internet). Globalization recognizes an ever increasing interconnectivity and dependency not only between nation-states, but between common people regardless of where they reside.

In any event, in terms of evaluating a legal framework to address the concept of globalization, one must recognize that even the most brilliantly crafted legal framework is useless without an enforcement mechanism. In terms of halting unlawful aggression, for example, the drafters of the UN Charter established an extensive and flexible international framework for responding to those rogue nations which might choose to violate the provisions of the UN Charter and engage in unlawful aggression. Chapter VI of the UN Charter authorizes the Security Council to investigate any situation that might endanger the maintenance of international peace and security and to make recommendations for the peaceful resolution of such disputes. Chapter VII of the UN Charter authorizes the Security Council to determine the existence of a threat, a breach of peace, or act of aggression, and to take appropriate measures in response.

Accordingly, if one hopes to effectively address mattes related to globalization and its impact on universally recognized human rights (as well as on emerging human rights concepts associated with social issues), it is clearly a matter that must find solution at the highest levels of international discourse and agreement. Indeed, a central element of promoting human rights that are impacted by globalization demands the creation of a new legal structure that can work in the real world—new rules and legal standards of behaviour recognized and practiced between civilized States in the context of the community of nations.

The endeavour of the editors is to present a variety of thematic explanations under the broad rubric entitled: '**Globalization, International Law, and Human Rights**,' with the primary objective of examining the patterns of State responses to what have otherwise been seen as emerging notions in the realm of certain categories of human rights paradigms. In the course of selecting each of the thematic explanations for inclusion, the editors are confident that a self-explanatory answer as to their relevance and utility will quickly emerge. Not only do these works demonstrate the ingenuous efforts of the select group of authors to promote their vision of emerging developments in human rights related to government and corporate obligations to perform certain categories of actions, but also their zeal in promoting a wide range of trends in the relationship between the patterns of internationalized State responses and the innately fundamental rights of human beings.

In the first chapter of the book, entitled: '**Corporate Human Rights Obligations under Economic, Social, and Cultural Rights**,' the authors explore a contemporary debate in relation to the safeguarding of certain human rights and the controversy between the State and non-state actors, i.e., corporate organizations. Taking the base line argument that the increasingly powerful personality and influence of corporations must carry the additional responsibility of human rights promotion, the authors critically examine and evaluate the associated corporate responsibilities. With special reference to health, social welfare, and natural environment concerns, for example, water, the article traces out certain human rights obligations emanating from national and international legal systems. While examining the interface between corporate obligations and human rights owed to individuals, the authors examine the theme as to whether the voluntary commitments of corporate organizations have any linkage with human rights of obligations. With the help of a variety of case studies, the authors encourage the reader to ponder this ongoing debate. In addition, the authors also examine the role played by regional human rights enforcement and monitoring structures. In summary, the authors explore the interface related to the obligations of State and non-state entities in upholding certain individual human rights while expressing concern over corporate responsibilities; they argue for the solution to be based on the larger interests of the community.

Interestingly, in the second chapter of the book, entitled: **'Globalization, Climate Change, and Indigenous Peoples in the Arctic: An Interface between Free Trade and the Right to Culture**,' the author places the onus of his discussion on a region that may suffer greatly from 'climate change.' At the threshold, the author addresses the fundamental premise that those responsible for economic development related to globalization must mitigate the costs associated with the adverse environmental impact upon the said region, particularly in the long term. Thereafter, the chapter clearly examines the nature of activities being carried out in this region and the implications to the people of this region, both from the external and internal factors of influence. Based on the inter-relationship between globalization and harm to the region the author examines the restrictions on free trade which generate economic loss to the indigenous community as well as the latest State practices in relation to conflict resolution before international dispute resolution bodies. The depth of information matches the analysis on the part of the author as he discusses the issue of increased shipping and trading activities as it impacts on the delicate ecological balance of the given territory and the environment. Examination of the scope of the right of people to 'culture' and the State's policies in the context of indigenous people versus the European Union's import ban policy is a key issue of this work.

The third chapter examines issues of religion and human rights from a territorial and cultural perspective. '**Freedom of Religion in a Globalized World: The European Experience**' begins with the core emphasis of the basic tenets of every major religion—namely tolerance and pluralism. Addressing the responses of States in the European context related to religious sentiments and religious expressions, the author examines the resurgence of religion as a dominant power in the administration of Nations and its influence on the law making process in the regional context of Europe. In this discussion of religion, the author also examines the roots of secularism as it relates to the permissiveness and tolerance on the part of the State. The author critically evaluates a series of instances of State actions and judicial interpretation of the interface of the values of secularism and the State's endeavour to keep religion as a support mechanism. In turn, this interface poses a question as to what extent the action of the State finds legitimacy in the context of free religious practices and choices by persons. While the author's ardent analysis of the judicial process and the struggle of the affected to pass through the different tiers of the judicial process may cause one to wonder as to the systemic apathy of the innate sensitive notions of an individual and his practices, the analysis nevertheless reminds the reader that a system has to be appreciated for the systemic relevance. The author's in-depth effort related to conflict resolution by the jurisprudential approaches finds its noteworthy analysis in the elaborative effort of the comparative approaches of the courts in other countries in Europe. Raising the analysis from the nationalistic notions to regional jurisprudential approaches, the author provides far fetching questions of analysis to the reader, namely: (1) How far does the European Convention go to address religious pluralism?, and (2) how far the State's practices are in conformity, in the real sense, with the innate meaning of secularism?

In a title that is self explanatory, the author in the fourth chapter of the book, entitled: '**Globalization, Terrorism, and Human Rights: The Mouse that Roared**,' places before the reader a fundamental issue of debate—the mounting incidence of intolerance when it is not confronted in a pluralistic context. Adopting the premise that some States in the world, led by America, overreacted to the threat of global terrorism following the attacks on the United States on 11 September 2001, the author views those responses as a setback to the promotion of human rights. The author explores the impact of globalization on the responses of States and examines the relationship between the notion of human rights and activities related to the use of violence. The author also explores the impact of the International Criminal Court, the UN Security Council, and other international entities on this matter. Through a series of reflections, the author supports many of his assertions related to the Iraq War and War on Terror, in his view, emerging from an atmosphere of fundamentalist political and religious intolerance. The author provokes the reader to ponder over what changes in United States foreign policy settings are needed before it can again claim a leadership role in the enhancement of human rights.

Keeping at the forefront the fundamental relevance of the 'right to education' in the context of human rights jurisprudence, the fifth chapter of the book, entitled: '**Globalization and Its Effects on the Emerging Jurisprudence on the Right to Education in South Africa and Nigeria**,' explores the matter from the point of view of South Africa and Nigeria. Through a wide canvas of international instruments the authors portray the scope of the right to education as encompassing education in a formal sense and in an informal sense so as to address the cultural and pluralistic notions. Placing emphasis equally well on the applicable regional human rights instruments, the authors begin the critical inquiry of the national legislative parameters and the recognition of the right to education at various levels. Interesting to the reader's appreciation is the authors' contemporary journey through the national legal regimes of South Africa as well as Nigeria. This simultaneous coverage makes the reader appreciate the similarities and contrasts at the same time, without being confused by overlaps. Shifting the attention on what globalization really means to these two nation's policies and efforts of implementation in making the right to education a practically endeavoured right, the authors bring to the forefront another interesting analysis on the impact of globalization. Terming it to be a process of positive and negative implications, the authors provoke the reader as to whether the very face of education in itself has been reshaped, for globalization always finds its dominant concern for trade at the forefront if not as the incidental demands of its stakeholders. Aptly, the authors refer to the roles of the international stakeholders, who must transform from the role of guardians of values to the role of promoters of a level playground. Examining the development model and its implications as against the third world countries economies in a holistic sense, the author places before the reader a question—whether, in such a transformed situation, access to free education remains as the cherished reality set out by the framers in the international instruments, when it was so conceived? Addressing the need on the part of the State to assert and keep education as a primary goal with proper resources as intrinsic to the very process of governance, the authors place a demand for a reoriented approach on the part of the State and warn of the negative implications if the State does not allow larger community interests to prevail in policy planning in the name of trade driven globalization processes.

A chapter of vital importance to individuals and their communities related to trade concerns, the sixth chapter is entitled: '**Emergence of the Human Right to Water in an Era of Globalization and Its Implications to International Investment Law**.' The author examines the conflicting concerns of community survival verses community growth and development. Bringing to the forefront an analysis of the utility of public/private investment partnerships and their trade related notions, the first question that is placed by the author is whether the emphasis of the Millennium Development Goals on the fundamental needs of the human population is required to be seen from a realistic perspective. Juxtaposed to the State's obligations to fulfil the said aspirations of the community as well as the corporate world's trading concerns, the author places before the reader a variety of international developments including the policies and practices that emerged under the aegis of a number of international organizations. Yet, the author does not limit the scope of the State's obligations only to one side of the community, but the author looks into and evaluates the emerging notions of international investments and their importance in the context of the State's proactive policies involving strong social players. Understanding that the players are both national and foreign national, the author examines the complexities being handled by the States in the fulfilment and realization of the fundamental right of people, namely access to water. In exploring the critical issues of water rights, the author is concerned with presenting a balanced approach including the State and international players.

In an interesting examination of what are contemporarily being termed as 'third generation human rights'—the obligation of the State to provide certain composite things to the individual—the seventh chapter of this book is entitled: '**Interface between the Third Generation Human Rights and the Good Governance in a Globalized World**.' The author contrasts first and second generation human rights as both 'negative' human rights (freedom from government action) and civil liberties, with third generation human

rights which deal with 'solidarity' rights, requiring the State to provide things to people such as a clean environment, peace, education,
healthcare, etc. Terming third generation human rights like development, education, health, and food as community oriented, the author
traces the evolution of the said terminology to the African Charter on
Human and People's Rights and provides a clear linkage to the subsequent international instruments that have spoken about the said
rights including the Millennium Goals Declaration. While enumer-
ating the dimensions of third generation human rights, the author
also examines the uncertainties surrounding these rights including,
the ownership, claimants, and scope of redress. Tracing the existence
of third generation human rights, the author builds on the premise
as to why these rights may go to the very root of governance so that
the institutions of governance should plan their policies and shape
their implementation measures accordingly. Subtly commenting on
the nuances of globalization, the author reiterates why concerns of
communities cannot be comprised to the concerns of a few trading
interests and thus concludes with emphasis on the examination of
human rights in the specific context.

The introduction to this work cannot be completed without
examining the intrinsic value of the final chapter of the authorial
contribution, namely '**The Place of Capitalism in the Pursuit of
Human Rights in the Globalized Relationships of States**.' The
authors examine the developments of the Post World War II period
and the impact of economic ideologies on the development of various
societies. In so doing, the authors offer a theoretical explanation as
to the gap which exists between various States and peoples based on
class privilege and human solidarity. The authors use South Africa as
a case study on the thematic accounting of economic superstructures
and their role in the actualisation of certain inseparable human rights
which serve, to a large extent, as a significant historical insight to the
premise. To a great extent, the authors build the explanation on the
much publicized divide of the human rights notions of the twentieth
century but quickly offer the explanation in terms of their ultimate
convergence with the developments of the final phase of the twentieth century. The authors take the inseparable interface of the two
facets of inalienable rights in the human context as the foundational
basis finding its place in the analysis of the South African realities of
employment opportunities and the extent of employment equality.

Looking at the new paradigm of the South African Constitution that adapted a new regime of civil and political rights to be placed on a par with economic and social rights, the authors attempt to look at other country explanations as to the differential priority offered to these invaluable facets and what these models could mean to South African needs. What keeps the reader's attention at hold is the examination of the case of South Africa and implications of the 'progressive realization' being adopted. The authors express their approval of the Cuban experiment, in theory, with an obvious inclination towards the political choice and option in favour of the consolidation of human solidarity through the proper enforcement of socio economic rights without eliminating the need to uphold the right of every one to live with human dignity.

In conclusion, these carefully selected chapters demonstrate the concern and efforts of the editors of the book to provide expression of a variety of human rights implications regarding globalization associated with national policies and with a realization of the imperative needs of human communities of societies.

1

Corporate Human Rights Obligations under Economic, Social, and Cultural Rights

Brigit Toebes
Jernej Letnar Černič

Introduction

Over the past decades, globalization has stirred a number of positive and negative developments in national and international environments. An important feature of globalization is the rise of the economic, social, and political power of corporations. Corporations account for forty-five of the 100 largest economies in the world, or ninety-one of the 150 largest.[1] Human rights scholars and activists are increasingly pointing at the human rights responsibilities of businesses. They argue that corporations are bound by human rights laws and that they should be held accountable for violations of these laws.[2]

The precise scale of human rights violations by or involving corporations remains difficult to ascertain. The Office of the UN High Commissioner for Human Rights reported in 2007 more than 300 allegations of corporate human rights abuses.[3] In July

---

[1] 'Compare World's Largest Corporations (Global 500)', *Fortune*, 21 July 2008, available at http://money.cnn.com/magazines/fortune/global500/2008/full_list/; 'World Development Indicators: Gross Domestic Product', 2007, available at http://siteresources.worldbank.org/DATASTATISTICS/Resources/GDP.pdf (accessed 15 January 2009).

[2] *Inter alia,* Nicola Jägers, *Corporate Human Rights Obligations: In Search of Accountability* (Antwerp: Intersentia, 2002).

[3] UN High Commissioner for Human Rights, 'Corporate Responsibility to Respect Human Rights', Summary report on Geneva Consultation, Geneva.

2005, John Ruggie, a professor at the John F. Kennedy School of Government of Harvard University who was closely involved with the process of the UN Global Compact, was appointed special representative of the UN secretary general. The special representative was given a mandate to identify and clarify standards of corporate responsibility and accountability. He submitted his interim report in 2006, the second report in February 2007 and the final report in June 2008. He found that the extractive sector—oil, gas, and mining—dominated the account of reported abuses with two-thirds of the total.[4] The International Council on Mining and Metals, in 2008, noted thirty-eight allegations against mining companies in twenty-five countries. Ruggie's final report observed that approximately 60 per cent of reported cases accounted for direct forms of company involvement in the alleged violations, meaning that the company had allegedly committed violations through its own acts or omissions.[5]

The status of corporations under international law has been examined thoroughly, and more and more convincing arguments have been brought forward for assuming that corporations have legal obligations under human rights law.[6] This chapter focuses on the responsibilities of corporations under the so-called economic, social, and cultural rights, sometimes also denoted by the slightly outdated term 'second generation rights'.

Economic, social, and cultural rights include the rights to housing, food, education, water, and health. This set of rights complements the so-called civil and political rights, also sometimes addressed as

---

4–5 December 2007, is p. 2, available at http://www.reports-and-materials.org/Ruggie-Geneva-4-5-Dec-2007.pdf (accessed 15 January 2009).

[4] SRSG, 'Interim Report of the Special Representative of the Secretary General on the Issue of Human Rights of Transnational Corporations and Other Business Enterprises', paras 24–27, delivered to the Commission on Human Rights, UN Doc. E/CN.4/2006/97, 22 February 2006 (hereafter, 'Interim Report of the Special Representative'). The special representative of the secretary general surveyed sixty-five instances of abuses reported by NGOs in twenty-seven countries.

[5] See J. Ruggie, 'Corporations and Human Rights: A Survey of the Scope and Patterns of Alleged Corporate-related Human Rights Abuse: Interim Report of the Special Representative', A/HRC/8/5/Add.2, 23 May 2008, pp. 3, 14–15.

[6] For a recent publication on this matter see Salomon, Arne Tostensen Salomon, and Wouter Vandenhole (ed.), *Human Rights, Development and New Duty-Bearers* (Antwerp: Intersentia, 2007).

'first generation rights', including the right to life, the right to a fair trial, and the right to freedom of expression. Despite claims that both sets of rights are of equal importance and are interdependent, civil and political rights are more solidly established under international and national laws. Corporations play an important role in the realization of the economic, social, and cultural rights of their employees, and of society as a whole. For example, they are responsible for guaranteeing adequate labour conditions to their employees, and they may be involved in the provision of water services to communities. They can become violators of economic, social, and cultural rights, for example, where their activities lead to environmental pollution, or where their products are detrimental to the health of consumers.

This chapter will start with a general overview of the human rights responsibilities of corporations and of the laws from which such claims can be derived. Subsequently, it will focus on economic, social, and cultural rights more specifically. To make the analysis more concrete, special attention will be paid to two important rights: that is, the right to health and the right to water. A set of obligations to 'respect, protect, and fulfil' is defined in relation to both rights.

We are fully aware that the primary responsibility for realizing human rights lies with national governments and that recognizing the responsibility of non-state actors should never undermine this responsibility. Yet, given the powerful position that corporations increasingly possess, we argue that corporations carry an additional responsibility under human rights law. This chapter seeks to contribute to the further delineation of this responsibility, in particular when it comes to responsibilities in the areas of health, social welfare, and the environment.

LEGAL BASIS FOR HUMAN RIGHTS RESPONSIBILITIES OF BUSINESSES

Before we can focus on the analysis of corporate responsibility for economic, social, and cultural rights, we need to discuss the legal basis for corporate human rights responsibility more generally. It is submitted that human rights obligations of corporations derive from three levels of legal sources.[7] Human rights obligations derive, first,

---

[7] J. Letnar Černič, *Human Rights Law and Business* (Gronigen: Europa Law Publishing, 2010).

from national legal orders; second, they derive from the international level, and, third, from unilateral voluntary commitments by corporations themselves.

In national legal orders, human rights obligations of corporations can be found in constitutions or under ordinary legislation, which are the main written sources of domestic positive law in most countries. In other words, the fundamental human rights obligations of corporations within the various national legal orders can be readily identified in most instances. Most commonly, all natural and legal persons must act in compliance with national constitutional laws. Constitutional rights can arguably be translated into human rights obligations of corporations. In other words, constitutional protections of fundamental human rights apply to both natural and legal persons. While the majority of European countries include human rights in their constitutions, the inclusion of human rights in the national constitutions of non-European countries is much more limited. The majority of constitutions in Africa, and North, and South Americas include, however, fundamental human rights, and lend support to the substantive fundamental human rights obligations of corporations. However, only a few Arab and Asian countries include any provisions on security and human dignity of persons. It must be recognized, however, that only a handful of constitutions contain explicit provisions that the constitutional protection of fundamental human rights applies to both natural and legal persons.

With regard to national legislation, there are numerous examples of human rights obligations of corporations deriving from national legal orders. Human rights obligations derive from ordinary criminal legislation, civil law legislation, consumer protection laws, company law, and national law covering the extraterritorial operations of corporations, such as, for example, the United States Federal Alien Torts Claims Act, 1789, which grants rights to aliens to seek civil remedies in American courts for certain violations of their human rights inside and outside the USA.[8]

Human rights obligations of corporations may secondarily derive from the international level. Several international treaties include state obligations to protect fundamental human rights in relation to the activities of corporations. It appears that international legal

---

[8]   28 U.S.C. § 1350.

obligations to respect fundamental human rights bind corporations to the extent that further national and international measures are taken. Most of the international treaties only indirectly regulate corporations as states are their primary addressees, which are then required to translate such international legal obligations into national legislation. In this context, Article 2 of the Organization for Economic Cooperation and Development (OECD) convention on Combating Bribery of Foreign Public Officials in International Business Transaction states that 'each Party shall take such measures as may be necessary, in accordance with its legal principles to establish the liability of legal persons for bribery of a foreign public official'.[9] Reading the international treaties together, M.T. Kamminga correctly notes that 'there are no reasons of principle, why companies cannot have direct obligations under international law'.[10]

When it comes to international *human rights* treaties more specifically, it can be observed that the first three international human rights treaties, the International Covenant on Civil and Political Rights (ICCPR), 1966, the International Covenant on Economic, Social, and Cultural Rights (ICESCR), 1966, and the International Covenant on the Elimination of Racial Discrimination (ICERD), 1969, do not include any express references to corporations or any other legal persons. Rather, they impose general obligations on states to regulate private conduct in relation to the enjoyment of rights. Article 2(1)(d) of ICERD stipulates, for example, that each state party shall prohibit and bring to an end racial discrimination by any *persons, group*, or *organization* (emphasis added). Similarly, Article 4 of ICERD provides that 'States parties condemn all propaganda and *all organizations*

---

[9] OECD Convention on Combating Bribery of Foreign Public Officials in International Business Transactions, 18 December 1997, S. Treaty Doc. 105-43 (1998), 37 ILM, entered into force 15 February 1999. Paris Convention on the Third Party Liability in the Field of Nuclear Energy, 29 July 1960, 956 UNTS 251. Brussels Convention Relating to Civil Liability in the field of Maritime Carriage of Nuclear Material, 17 December 1971, 974 UNTS. International Convention on Civil Liability for Oil Pollution Damage Article 1(1), 29 November 1969. COE Convention on Civil Liability for Damage Resulting from Activities Dangerous to the Environment, 21 June 1993.

[10] M.T. Kamminga, 'Corporate Obligations under International Law', Paper presented at the 71st Conference of the International Law Association, Plenary Session on Corporate Social Responsibility and International Law, Berlin, 17 August 2004, p. 4.

which are based on ideas or theories of superiority of one race or group of persons of one colour or ethnic origin, or which attempt to justify or promote racial hatred and discrimination in any form'. However, human rights treaties adopted at a later stage address more explicitly corporate activities. Article 2(e) of the Convention on the Elimination of All Forms of Discrimination Against Women (CEDAW), for example, asks states to 'take all appropriate measures to eliminate discrimination against women by any *enterprise*'.[11] The Optional Protocol to the Convention on the Rights of the Child (CRC), 1990 on the Sale of Children, Child Prostitution and Child Pornography (OPSC), 2002 requires states to prohibit practices such as the sale of children, child prostitution, and child pornography, including taking action against legal persons where appropriate, in Article 3(4). Furthermore, Article 16(2) of International Convention on the Protection of the Rights of All Migrant Workers and Members of their Families (ICRMW) stipulates that migrant workers and members of their families are entitled 'to effective protection by the state against violence, physical injury, threats and intimidation, whether by public officials or by private individuals, groups or institutions'. It appears that the trend is moving towards the direction of explicitly recognizing state obligations in this context.

As noted, international treaties do not bind only states. Clapham notes that it 'makes sense to talk about the parties to a human rights treaty rather than use the expression of states parties, which indicates that states are exclusive members of every human rights regime'.[12] Second, other international human rights treaties address corporate human rights obligations in a similar way. It appears that the positive legal obligations of corporations to observe fundamental human rights derive also from international treaties that are not directly addressed by corporations. What remains clear is that international norms may also have applicability to corporations even if there is no international mechanism established for enforcing this norm.

Third, it can be argued that human rights obligations derive from unilateral voluntary commitments by corporations themselves. The

---

[11]   Convention on the Elimination of All Forms of Discrimination Against Women, GA Res. 34/180, 34 UN GAOR Supp. (no. 46), Article 2 (e).

[12]   A. Clapham, *Human Rights Obligations of Non-State Actor* (New York: Oxford University Press, 2006), p. 91.

voluntary commitments of corporations can be most often found in internal human rights polices or codes of conduct. The OECD defines codes of conduct as 'commitments voluntarily made by companies, associations or other entities, which put forth standards and principles for the conduct of business activities in the marketplace'.[13] Similarly, the International Labour Organization (ILO) defines a code of conduct as 'a written policy, or statement of principles, intended to serve as the basis for a commitment to particular enterprise conduct'.[14] Codes of conduct are voluntary initiatives adopted by companies in order to improve their public reputations and to answer to demands for more responsibility in their activities. They include the normatively non-binding obligations/commitments of corporations. In other words, codes of conduct create at the most moral, not legal, obligations. They are drafted by corporations themselves because it is in their interests to adopt them. The codes of conduct include principles, standards, or guidelines.[15] A number of corporations have formally and publicly acknowledged responsibility for ensuring that their actions are consistent with human rights, starting with the Universal Declaration of Human Rights (UDHR), 1948. Shell, for example, notes that 'operating companies … have a responsibility to identify existing and potential human rights issues which may arise in their area of operations'.[16] For instance, the following corporations all refer in one way or another in

---

[13] OECD Directorate for Financial, Fiscal and Enterprise Affairs, 'Codes of Corporate Conduct: Expanded Review of their Contents', May 2001, Working Papers on International Investment, November 2001/6.

[14] International Labour Organization Governing Body, Working Party on the Social Dimensions of the Liberalization of International Trade, 'Overview of Global Developments and Office Activities Concerning Codes of Conduct, Social Labelling and Other Private Sector Initiatives Addressing Labour Issues, Executive Summary', GB 273/WP/SDL/1, 273rd Session Geneva, November 1998.

[15] S.D. Murphy, 'Taking Multinational Corporate Codes of Conduct to the Next Level', *Columbia Journal of Transnational Law*, 43(2), 2005, pp. 389–433, 2005; M.B. Baker, 'Promises and Platitudes: Toward a New 21st Century Paradigm for Corporate Codes of Conduct?', *Connecticut Journal of International Law*, 23, 2007, pp. 123–63.

[16] See Shell, 'Business and Human Rights: A Management Primer', p. 23, available at http://www-static.shell.com/static/responsible_energy/downloads/management_ primers/business_and_human_rights_primer.pdf.

their policies to human rights protections: Wal-Mart Stores[17], Exxon Mobil[18], British Petroleum[19], General Motors[20], Toyota, Chevron[21], Daimler–Chrysler[22], Conoco–Philips[23], and Total[24]. As noted, nearly 125 corporations refer to the UDHR, whereas a further seventy-two have explicit human rights policies.[25] More than 5000 corporations have expressed commitment to the so-called UN Global Compact, a corporate social responsibility initiative at the UN level.[26]

Taken together, while national legal orders and international systems impose human rights obligations on corporations, voluntary commitments may offer further evidence of such obligations. In this light, the sources of human rights obligations of corporations should be treated as mutually complementary rather than as mutually exclusive. The fact that international jurisdictions for legal persons are yet to be developed does not imply that a corporation does not have any legal obligations. This is because the human rights obligations of corporations primarily derive from national legal orders. On the contrary, it would be to futile to argue that a

[17]   See Wal-Mart, 'Requirements for Suppliers', <http://walmartstores.com/Suppliers/248.aspx>; See Equal Opportunity Practices (accessed 20 February 2009).

[18]   See Exxon Mobil, available at http://www.exxonmobil.com/Corporate/community_local_rights.aspx (accessed 20 February 2009).

[19]   See British Petroleum, 'Human Rights: A Guidance Note', 2005, p. 12.

[20]   See General Motors, available at http://www.gm.com/corporate/responsibility/reports/00/vision/social/human.html (accessed 20 February 2009).

[21]   See Chevron Corporation, 'Human Rights Statement', available at http://www.chevron.com/globalissues/humanrights (accessed 20 February 2009).

[22]   See Daimler-Chrysler, available at http://www.daimler.com/dccom/0-5-880434-1-881989-1-0-0-0-0-0-8-876574-0-0-0-0-0-0-1.html (accessed 20 February 2009).

[23]   See Conoco-Philips Corporation, 'Human Rights Position', available at http://www.conocophillips.com/social/values_policies/humanrights/index.htm (accessed 20 February 2009).

[24]   See Total Corporation, 'Code of Conduct', p. 10.

[25]   See Business and Human Rights Resource Centre, http://www.business-human-rights.org/Documents/Policies. For a detailed account see the work of research fellows under the direction of UN Special Representative, John Ruggie, Michael Wright, and Amy Lehr, *Business Recognition of Human Rights*, Mossavar-Rahmani Center for Business & Government, Kennedy School of Government, Harvard University, 12 December 2006.

[26]   UN Global Compact, available at http://www.unglobalcompact.org/ParticipantsAndStakeholders/index.html (accessed 20 February 2009).

substantive obligation only arises when joined with a jurisdiction that can enforce it. Otherwise, corporations would only be obliged to *pro forma* observe the human rights of individuals. This not only matters at the normative level but also beyond the form, beyond the pure normative, when corporations are *de facto* faced with a decision as to what kind of business policy to adopt.

ECONOMIC, SOCIAL, AND CULTURAL RIGHTS

It has been just argued that corporate responsibility for human rights violations derives from national law, international law, and voluntary mechanisms. The economic, social, and cultural rights will now be dealt with, particularly in the way they are set forth under the international human rights treaties that contain such rights explicitly. However, additional foundations for such arguments can be found in national legal orders and in the voluntary corporate codes of conduct as already explained. National legal orders can provide an important additional and complementary source of legal obligations of corporations in the area of economic, social, and cultural rights. For example, national legal orders in a number of countries include a governmental obligation to provide everyone with access to clean water. The 1996 South African Constitution (Chapter 2, Bill of Rights), for instance, provides in Section 27 (1) that 'Everyone has the right to have access to (b) sufficient food and water'. Similarly, the Constitution of Ethiopia notes in Article 90(1) that 'every Ethiopian is entitled, within the limits of the country's resources, to … clean water'.

Before embarking upon a discussion of corporate responsibility for economic, social, and cultural rights, we need to discuss the character and legal status of economic, social, and cultural rights more generally. As mentioned in the Introduction, a distinction is generally made between 'generations' or 'types' of rights: first generation, or civil and political rights; second generation, or economic, social, and cultural rights; and third generation, or collective/solidarity rights. Examples of civil and political rights are the rights to life, prohibition of torture, freedom of expression, and freedom of religion. Examples of economic, social, and cultural rights are the rights to food, housing, and education; and examples of collective rights are the rights to self-determination, peace, and development.

The term 'generations of rights' refers to the different historical phases during which the rights emerged, predominantly in the West. Roughly speaking, while civil and political rights were first claimed during the age of Enlightenment, social rights were first asserted during the social rights movement of the nineteenth century. Collective rights were stressed during the decolonization process after the Second World War. Some authors have criticized the term 'generations of rights', asserting that the history of human rights at the national level does not make it possible to identify clear-cut stages during which the various types of rights emerged.[27] As such this terminology ignores the existence of diverse perspectives on human rights from different, non-Western parts of the world. As we will argue now, the identification of different generations of rights may also undermine the holistic nature of human rights: in other words, the 'inter-relatedness and interdependence' of both sets of rights, civil and political rights on the one hand, and economic, social, and cultural on the other.

The most important set of international documents that stipulates human rights is the United Nations' International Bill of Human Rights, comprising the UDHR, ICCPR, and ICESCR. While the UDHR contains a comprehensive range of all the aforementioned types of rights, the ICCPR, and ICESCR were adopted under Western pressure, the first containing civil and political rights and the second containing economic, social, and cultural rights.[28] Some of the objections raised against placing all the rights in one covenant were that while civil and political rights are 'absolute', 'immediate', and 'cost-free', economic, social, and cultural rights are 'programmatic' in character, often costly, and can only be realized gradually.[29]

Since the adoption of the two covenants in 1966 there has been extensive debate about the perceived differences between civil and political rights, and economic, social, and cultural rights. Several

---

[27] Asbjørn Eide and Allan Rosas, 'Economic, Social and Cultural Rights: A Universal Challenge', in *Economic, Social and Cultural Rights*, 2nd edn, A. Eide *et al.* (eds) (Dordrecht/Boston/London: Martinus Nijhoff Publishers, 2001), p. 4.

[28] ICCPR, including Optional Protocol, concluded 16 December 1966, entered into force 23 March 1976, 999 UNTS 171; ICESCR, concluded 16 December 1966, entered into force 23 March 1976, 999 UNTS 195.

[29] Asbjørn Eide, 'Economic, Social and Cultural Rights as Human Rights', in *Economic, Social and Cultural Rights*, A. Eide *et al.* (eds) (Dordrecht/London: Martinus Nijhoff Publishers, 2001).

scholars have tried to demonstrate that there are considerable similarities in state obligations with regard to both sets of rights.[30] It is argued that while civil and political rights are not necessarily cost-free, economic and social rights are not necessarily costly. The typical example concerns the civil and political right to a fair trial, which requires substantial investments on the part of states (for example, ensuring that there is legal assistance and that there are courts). On the other hand, respecting the freedom of education is a low-cost element of the economic and social right to education. To strengthen their arguments, scholars have argued that inherent in every human right are (negative) obligations to 'respect' as well as (positive) obligations to 'protect' and 'fulfil' human rights, a concept which will be defined later in this chapter. There has also been a gradual move towards the recognition of the equal importance and legal status of both sets of rights. At the World Conference on Human Rights in 1993, the Vienna Declaration and Programme of Action was adopted, which stresses that all rights are 'interdependent, interrelated and of equal importance'.[31] Moreover, several of the more recent human rights treaties contain both sets of rights.[32]

Nevertheless, while both sets of rights are now equal 'on paper', in practice the debate continues. And while an extensive body of case law has come into existence in relation to civil and political rights, courts are still very reluctant to adjudicate cases on the basis of economic, social, and cultural rights. This refers to the question of the so-called 'justiciability' of economic, social, and cultural rights, or the question of whether these rights are enforceable before a court of law.[33]

---

[30] Ibid.

[31] World Conference on Human Rights: Vienna Declaration and Programme of Action, UN Doc. A/CONF.157/23, Part I, para. 5.

[32] For example: Convention on the Elimination of All Forms of Discrimination Against Women, concluded 18 December 1979, entered into force 3 September 1981, 1249 UNTS 13; and the Convention on the Rights of the Child, concluded 20 November 1989, entered into force 2 September 1990, 28 I.L.M. 1456 (1989). Regional human rights treaties, however, show the old divide: for example, the European Convention on Human Rights (1950, ETS No. 5) and the European Social Charter (1961, ETS no. 35) of the Council of Europe.

[33] Fons Coomans, *Justiciability of Economic, Social and Cultural Rights* (Antwerpen/ Oxford: Intersentia, 2006). For examples of cases see also http://www.escr-net. org/caselaw/ (accessed April 2009).

BUSINESSES AND ECONOMIC, SOCIAL, AND CULTURAL RIGHTS

Examples of Violations

A number of allegations have been made against corporations in relation to violations of economic, social, and cultural rights. This section concentrates on the violations of the rights to health and water.

As regards health, corporations have been responsible for infringing upon people's health in multiple ways. As health is such a broad notion, it is impossible to give a complete overview of the all the types of violations that have occurred. Nonetheless, some examples of violations will give an idea of the type and scale of violations. A case in point is the position of the Ogoni people, an indigenous population that lives in the Niger Delta in Nigeria, who have suffered from environmental degradation due to oil extraction in the area where they live.[34] In 1996, a complaint was lodged by two non-governmental organizations (NGOs) with the African Commission on Human and Peoples' Rights.[35] The commission decided that the Nigerian government had violated, *inter alia*, the rights to health and to a healthy environment provided for in the African Charter.[36] Other instances where court cases were instituted include the construction of an access road by an oil company in a national park in Ecuador[37] and the (well-known) chemical disaster in a carbide plant near the city of Bhopal in India.[38] Although these cases were primarily directed at governments, corporations were indirectly involved. Therefore, it would be worthwhile to explore the corporate responsibility for such violations

---

[34] *Inter alia*, Frank Horn, *Economic, Social and Cultural Rights of the Ogoni*, (Finland: University of Lapland, 1999).

[35] Social and Economic Rights Action Center (SERAC) and Centre for Economic and Social Rights (CESR).

[36] Articles 16 and 24 of the African Charter on Human and Peoples' Rights. Communication 155/96, available at http://www.achpr.org/. See also Fons Coomans, 'The Ogoni Case before the African Commission on Human and Peoples' Rights', available at http://www.righttoenvironment.org/ip/uploads/downloads/OgoniCaseProf.Coomans.pdf (accessed August 2009).

[37] See Inter-American Commission on Human Rights (IACHR), 'Report on the Situation of Human Rights in Ecuador', Doc. 10 rev 1, 24 April 1997, pp. 106–7.

[38] Bhopal Gas Disaster Case, *Charan Lal Sahu* v. *Union of India*, 1990 (1) SCC, p. 613.

further. Furthermore, when it comes to health, we can refer to the issue of product safety and the marketing of unhealthy products by corporations. A clear example would be the aggressive marketing of powdered milk by multinationals, which, because it overlooked the lack of clean water needed to reconstitute the milk, led to an increase in infant mortality.[39] Finally, in relation to health we can refer to the acts of (private) healthcare providers (hospitals and health workers) and suppliers (producers of medical equipment and pharmaceutical companies). This is a vast area in itself, as these actors are directly involved in the promotion and protection of health. Briefly, 2 billion people lack access to essential medicines. As such, it is being increasingly argued, the pharmaceutical industry has a responsibility to address the structural lack of access to essential medicines in Africa and South-East Asia.[40] Other potential violations are the selling of counterfeit drugs,[41] the lack of research into the so-called 'neglected diseases', and the appropriation and patenting of traditional medicines without compensation to the original knowledge holders.[42]

As to water, the World Health Organization (WHO) estimates that 1.7 billion people do not have access to clean water and 2.3 billion people are subjected to water-borne diseases each year.[43] The private sector may have a responsibility for these high numbers. For instance, FIAN International, an NGO, in 1999, reported that a private company allegedly contaminated water in the river Chambira basin in Peru.[44] It also reported that in 2001, two Coca-Cola bottling plants in

---

[39] Nicola Jägers. *Corporate Human Rights Obligations,* p. 87.

[40] Special Rapporteur on the Right to the Highest Attainable Standard of Health, Paul Hunt, 'The Human Rights Responsibilities of Pharmaceutical Companies in Relation to Access to Medicines', in General Assembly, 'The Right to Health', note by the secretary general, UN Doc. A/63/263, 11 August 2008.

[41] See Brigit Toebes, 'Human Rights and Health Sector Corruption', in *Global Health and Human Rights: Legal and Philosophical Perspectives,* J. Harrington *et al.* (eds), (Routledge, 2009).

[42] 'Report of the Special Rapporteur on the Right to the Highest Attainable Standard of Health', Paul Hunt, Mission to the World Trade Organization, UN Doc. E/CN.4/2004/49/Add.1, 1 March 2004, para. 42.

[43] Food and Water Watch, available at http://www.foodandwaterwatch.org/water/world-water/right.

[44] FIAN International, 'Identifying and Addressing Violations of Human Right to Water—Applying the Human Rights Approach', available at http://www.menschen-recht-wasser.de/downloads/violations_human-rights-water.pdf, p. 10.

Kerala and Tamil Nadu in India were allegedly involved in the deple-
tion and contamination of groundwater.[45] In 2005, an oil pipeline
network funded by a German state-owned bank allegedly destroyed
access to water and livelihoods in Ecuador.[46] On many occasions, both
the public and the private sectors have been involved. For example, in
2000, the price of water rapidly increased after water privatization in
Cochabamba in Bolivia.[47] In 2003, the Indian government decided to
divert water meant for 20,000 peasant families to a water theme park
in India.[48] Elsewhere in India, in 2008, in Jai Bhim Nagar in Meerut,
several thousands of people allegedly suffered from lack of safe drinking water supply. Construction of dams has also led to large-scale
deprivation of water. In 2004, in Ghana, many thousands of people
were allegedly deprived of their access to water due to the damming
of the river Subri. The project proceeded on the basis of an investment agreement between Newmont Mining Corporation and the
Government of Ghana.[49] Further, the Baba dam project in Ecuador
is likely to affect the right to water of more than 20,000 women and
men, farming, fishing communities and indigenous people settled in
this basin.[50] The International Fact Finding Mission, an international
NGO, has concluded that extreme violations of the human right to
water have taken place due to bauxite mining in Rayagada and Koraput
districts of Orissa in India.[51] Several domestic courts have responded
to these violations. For example, Indian courts have held that the right
to life in Article 21 of the Constitution of India includes the right to
safe and sufficient water.[52] And an Argentinian court ruled in
2004 that public water services must be extended to outlying poor
communities.[53]

---

[45] Ibid.
[46] Ibid., p. 12.
[47] Ibid., p. 11.
[48] Ibid.
[49] Ibid., p. 14.
[50] Ibid., p. 16.
[51] FIAN International, 'Investigating Some Alleged Violations of the Human Right
to Water in India', Report of the International Fact Finding Mission to India,
January 2004, available at http://www.menschen-recht-wasser.de/downloads/
report_komplett.pdf, pp. 9–13.
[52] The Right to Water, 'Legal Redress: The Right to Water under the Right to Life:
India', available at http://www.righttowater.org.uk/code/legal_3.asp
[53] Ibid., p. 13.

All in all, businesses can have a substantial impact on economic, social, and cultural human rights. We argue that such acts can potentially lead to violations of human rights in general, and of economic, social, and cultural rights more specifically. We will also attempt to demonstrate how such violations can be addressed and prevented, by translating human rights into clear-cut obligations of corporations.

However, we first need to identify which rights we are talking about when we speak of economic, social, and cultural rights. The question arises: Can corporations affect all these economic, social, and cultural rights, or only some? As argued by the UN High Commissioner on Human Rights on the Responsibilities of Transnational Corporations, J. Ruggie, 'businesses can affect virtually all internationally recognized human rights'. And, as such, 'any limited list will almost certainly miss one or more rights that may turn out to be significant in a particular instance, thereby providing misleading guidance'.[54] In line with Ruggie's assertion, we argue that corporations can potentially have an impact on all economic, social, and cultural rights, although some (elements of) rights are more relevant than others. We also reiterate that this responsibility needs to be considered separately from the primary human rights responsibility of governments, and that it should never undermine the primary duty of states under human rights law.

General Outline of Obligations

As already mentioned, scholars have attempted to prove and underline that economic and social rights are more equal to civil and political rights than was previously assumed. They have introduced a so-called 'tri-partite typology of state duties', which defines state obligations to 'respect, protect and to fulfil', inherent in each human right. This typology was first introduced by Henry Shue, and later refined by several other scholars.[55] While an obligation to 'respect'

---

[54] UN Doc. A/HRC/8/5, 7 April 2008, para. 6.
[55] H. Shue, *Basic Rights, Subsistence, Affluence and U.S. Foreign Policy* (New Jersey: Princeton, 1980). Eide, 'Economic, Social and Cultural Rights as Human Rights', pp. 21–41; and G. J. H. van Hoof, 'The Legal Nature of Economic, Social and Cultural Rights: A Rebuttal of Some Traditional Views', in *The Right to Food*, P. Alston and K. Tomaševski (eds) (Utrecht: SIM, 1984), pp. 97–111.

is a negative (state) obligation to refrain from action, an obligation to protect is a positive (state) obligation to protect individuals from harmful acts of third parties, and the obligation to 'fulfil' is a positive (state) obligation to ensure access to or provide a certain service. This so-called 'tri-partite typology of state obligations' will be applied to identify the obligations of corporations in relation to economic, social and cultural rights. It is increasingly argued that this tri-partite typology also applies to corporations. Nicola Jägers, for example, identifies a set of corporate duties based on the aforementioned tri-partite typology.[56]

But before we attempt to make such an analysis we need to place our model in the context of Ruggie's analysis. In his 2008 report, Ruggie proposes a three-pillar framework for corporate account-ability for human rights, which he describes as 'protect, respect and remedy'. The framework 'rests on differentiated but complementary responsibilities',[57] which include: the state duty to protect against human rights violations by or involving corporations; the corpo-rate responsibility to respect human rights; and effective access to remedies. Ruggie also confirms that 'the corporate responsibility to respect exists independently of states' duties'.[58] Ruggie does not attempt to explain how his proposed framework relates to the gen-erally accepted framework under international human rights law, where state obligations are usually classified into the three categories already mentioned: the obligation to respect, the obligation to pro-tect, and the obligation to fulfil. Ruggie's framework easily leads to the conclusion that corporations merely have 'negative' obligations not to harm individuals. Yet, as Ruggie explains in his 2008 report, 'Finally, "doing no harm" is not merely a passive responsibility for

---

[56] Nicola Jägers. *Corporate Human Rights Obligations*, ch. IV.

[57] UN Human Rights Council (HRC), Promotion and Protection of All Human Rights, Civil, Political, Economic, Social and Cultural Rights, Including the Right to Development, 'Protect, Respect and Remedy: A Framework for Business and Human Rights', UN Doc. A/HRC/8/5, 7 April 2008 (prepared by John Ruggie), available at http://www.reports-and-materials.org/Ruggie-report-7-Apr-2008.pdf. See also Ruggie's more recent report of 22 April 2009 (UN Doc. A/HRC/11/13). See also Olufemi Amao, 'Protect, Respect and Remedy: A Framework for Business and Human Rights', a review of 'Interim Report of the Special Representative'.

[58] Ruggie's 2005 report, para. 55.

firms but may entail positive steps—for example, a workplace anti-discrimination policy might require the company to adopt specific recruitment and training programmes.'[59]

In effect, we may assume that Ruggie's 'duty to respect' goes further than a mere negative obligation for companies not to do harm. As such, we assert that the tri-partite typology to 'respect', 'protect', and 'fulfil' can be read into Ruggie's 'duty to respect'.

RIGHT TO HEALTH

'Health' is an important condition for leading a dignified life and, as such, a key element of the concept of 'human dignity', the core notion underlying human rights law. As a result, references to the protection of health are plentiful under international human rights law and also under national constitutional law.[60] While international human rights law recognizes the 'right to health', many national Constitutions contain a similar right or a reference to the duty of governments to enhance and promote the health of their population. We also find numerous references to health in other international treaties, for example, in the conventions of the ILO. Specifically, the right to health can be derived from international human rights law and national (constitutional) law, and from international law more generally,

It must be admitted that the 'right to health' is very general in character and that as such is difficult to define. Over the course of the past twenty years attempts have been made to clarify the meaning and implications of this human right.[61] An important milestone was the adoption of a General Comment in 2000 on the right to health

---

[59] Ibid., para. 55.

[60] In addition to Article 12 of ICESCR, the right to health is recognized by provisions in a number of other international human rights instruments, including Article 25 of the UDHR; Article 5 (e) of ICERD); Articles 11.1 and 12 of CEDAW; and Article 24 of CRC. At the regional level, we come across the right to health in Article 11 of the (revised) European Social Charter (ESC), in Article 16 of the African Charter of Human and Peoples' Rights, and Article 10 of the Additional Protocol to the American Convention on Human Rights in the Area of Economic, Social and Cultural Rights. Furthermore, over a hundred national constitutional provisions include the right to health.

[61] See, *inter alia*, Toebes, *The Right to Health as a Human Right in International Law*.

under Article 12 of ICESCR, the most important international provision that stipulates the right to health.[62] The document explains that the right to health is not a right to be healthy, but rather a broad human right extending not only to access to healthcare services but also to the underlying determinants of health, including access to safe and potable water, and adequate sanitation, healthy occupational and environmental conditions, and health-related education and information.[63] As such, the right to health has two dimensions: right to healthcare services and right to a broad set of underlying conditions for health. The document defines a set of state obligations to 'respect, protect and fulfil' human rights and also describes potential violations of states in relation to the right to health. Although strictly speaking not legally binding, this document is the most authoritative document on the right to health.

The General Comment clearly recognizes that the right to health in Article 12 of ICESCR is directly applicable to the private business sector: 'While only States are parties to the Covenant and thus ultimately accountable for compliance with it, all members of society—individuals, including health professionals, families, local communities, intergovernmental and non-governmental organizations, *as well as the private business sector*—have responsibilities regarding the realization of the right to health'[64] (emphasis added). On the basis of this statement, Jägers asserts that the right to health can be applicable in the legal relations of corporations.[65]

Based on the foregoing assumptions, we can now turn to the definition of the set of corporate obligations to 'respect, protect and fulfil' the right to health. In this enumeration we will make a distinction between 'internal' and 'external' obligations. While internal obligations are obligations that a company has under its direct sphere of influence (mostly within the company), external obligations are obligations that a corporation has in relation to the public as a whole

---

[62]   Committee on Economic, Social and Cultural Rights, 'The Right to the Highest Attainable Standard of Health', UN General Comment No. 14 (2000), UN Doc. E/C12/200/4, 11 August 2000.

[63]   General Comment 14, paras 8 and 11.

[64]   Committee on Economic, Social and Cultural Rights, 'The Right to the Highest Attainable Standard of Health', UN General Comment No. 14 (2000), UN Doc. E/C12/200/4, 11 August 2000, para. 42.

[65]   Jägers, *Corporate Human Rights Obligations,* p. 69.

or towards the community that lives in the area where it operates. Furthermore, these obligations will cover the following areas: workplace health and safety, environmental health, product safety, and the provision of healthcare services and drugs. The following set is non-limitative:[66]

*Obligations to respect: corporations are to **refrain from***:
Internal obligations:

- taking measures that negatively affect workplace health and safety

External obligations:

- taking measures that negatively affect the environment and health of communities
- the production and marketing of products that are detrimental to the health of consumers
- the production, marketing, and provision of unsafe and counterfeit drugs and medical equipment

*Obligations to protect: corporations are to **adopt regulations and other measures in order to***:
Internal obligations:

- protect the health and safety of workers in their corporations, and in the corporations of their contractors and business partners

External obligations:

- protect the environment in the area in which they operate
- ensure the safety and quality of the products that they and their business partners as well as subcontractors produce
- ensure the quality, accessibility, affordability, and safety of the drugs and medical equipment that they and their business partners and subcontractors produce

*Obligations to fulfil: corporations are to **take active measures to ensure the availability of***:
Internal obligations:

- a healthy and safe working environment, based on effective health and safety standards

[66] Ibid., pp. 87–88.

External obligations: where government services are not available (for example, in remote areas)

- a proactive strategy for the protection of the environment in the area in which they operate
- healthcare services and drugs for the family of the workers and/ or the public as a whole in the area in which they operate
- Specific external obligations for pharmaceutical companies
- ensure that research goes into 'neglected diseases' to enhance the health of vulnerable populations
- promote the availability, affordability, geographic accessibility, and quality of the drugs that they produce to vulnerable populations.

We are fully aware that some of the obligations are more self-evident and easy to realize than others. For example, while it is generally accepted that a company has regulations in place to ensure workplace health and safety, it is less evident that a company has to provide healthcare services to the family members of its workers. We argue that the aforesaid obligations represent a sliding scale of obligations, which need to be realized depending on the financial capacity of the company and its location, for example, whether the company operates in a remote or ecologically vulnerable area. The obligations of healthcare providers and pharmaceutical companies constitute a separate issue, as health services and medicines are 'products' that are closely connected to the realization of the right to health.

RIGHT TO WATER

A billion people do not have access to clean and safe water. Access to safe drinking water and sanitation is increasingly being considered as a fundamental human right. In view of this, this section attempts to identify whether corporations have obligations relating to the right to water, in national law and international law. The Office of the UN High Commissioner for Human Rights notes that 'international human rights law entails clear obligations in relation to access to safe drinking water'.[67] The Institute for Business and Human Rights

---

[67] Report of the United Nations High Commissioner for Human Rights on the scope and content of the relevant human rights obligations related to equitable

suggests that 'business has three potential responsibilities concerning water: as a user or consumer, as an enabler of access to water and as a provider or distributor of water'.[68] It must be observed as a note of caution that obligations of corporations in relation to the right to water are not identical to those of a state. Some commentators argue that corporations cannot have obligations that pertain exclusively to the state apparatus, such as the right to a nationality, the right to asylum, or the right to have a fair hearing, but surely corporations are obliged to respect the right to water.[69] In this regard, while their obligations may be construed as an obligation to respect, protect, and fulfil, some authors accept that such an obligation will also include the obligation to promote the right to water in relation to contractors and subcontractors.[70] An obligation 'to promote' includes dissemination of information concerning corporate obligation deriving from the right to water. The aim of this section is also to examine the nature and the scope of the fundamental human rights obligations of corporations.

A number of national legal orders provide for a right of access to water. For instance, municipalities in Spain are obliged to offer access to water and sewer services.[71] Consequently, public and private corporations have obligations to provide such access. In France, legislation provides that 'each person, for its own supply and for hygiene, has the right of access to drinking water at economically accepted conditions for all'.[72] In Belgium, water is a right across all the regions. The Waloon Region provided in its decree that 'every

---

access to safe drinking water and sanitation under international human rights instruments, 16 August 2007. Available at http://daccessdds.un.org/doc/ UNDOC/GEN/G07/136/55/PDF/G0713655.pdf?OpenElement, para. 47.

[68] Institute for Business and Human Rights; Business, 'Human Rights & Right to Water, Challenges, Dilemmas, Opportunities, Roundtable Consultative Report', January 2009. Available at http://www.institutehrb.org/Downloads/Draft% 20Report%20-%20Business,%20Human%20Rights%20and%20Water.pdf, p. 3.

[69] J. H. Knox, 'Concept Paper on Facilitating Specification of the Duty to Protect', prepared for UN SRSG on Business and Human Rights, 14 December 2007.

[70] Amy Hardberger, 'Life, Liberty, and the Pursuit of Water: Evaluating Water as a Human Right and the Duties and Obligations it Creates', *Northwestern University Journal of International Human Rights*, 331, 2005.

[71] Municipal Law 7/28, Article 26. 1.

[72] Law of 30 December 2006.

person has the right to make use of drinking water of a quality and in quantity appropriate for nutrition, domestic needs and health'.[73] A large number of countries in every continent, from Latin America to Asia, include the right to water in their constitutional laws and national legislations.[74] Consequently, it may be argued that corporate obligations arising from the right to water are well established and recognized in national legal orders.

International human rights treaties also protect the right to water. Everyone is entitled to 'sufficient, safe, acceptable, physically accessible and affordable water for personal and domestic uses' and 'access to adequate sanitation' under Articles 11(1) and 12 (1) of ICESCR. Article 14 (2) of CEDAW notes that:

> States parties shall take all appropriate measures to eliminate discrimination against women in rural areas in order to ensure, on a basis of equality of men and women, that they participate in and benefit from rural development and, in particular, shall ensure to women the right: (h) To enjoy adequate living conditions, particularly in relation to housing, sanitation, electricity and water supply, transport and communications.

Similarly, Article 24(2)(c) of CRC states that 'States parties shall take appropriate measures' to 'combat disease and malnutrition, including within the framework of primary healthcare, through, inter alia, … the provision of adequate nutritious foods and clean drinking water'. Consequently, the right to water is also part of the right to health. Further, the Convention on the Rights of Persons with Disabilities provides in Article 28 for an adequate standard of living and social protection, and that states parties 'must ensure equal access by persons with disabilities to clean water services, and ensure access to appropriate and affordable services, devices and other assistance for disability-related needs'. On a regional level, the Committee of Ministers of the Council of Europe adopted the European Charter on Water Resources in 2001, (Rec. [2001]14), which in Article 5 provides that 'Everyone has the right to a sufficient quantity of water for his or her basic needs', and that 'International human rights instruments recognise the fundamental right of all human beings to be free from hunger and to an adequate standard of living for themselves and their families'. It is quite clear

---

[73] Decree, 15 April 1999.
[74] Unitarian Universalist Service Committee, A bibliograhy of primary and secondary sources of law on the human right to water, Unitarian, 2008, pp. 16–21.

that these two requirements include the right to a minimum quantity of water of satisfactory quality from the point of view of health and hygiene. Further, the ESCR Committee, the treaty-monitoring body of the ICESCR, asserts in paragraph 33 of General Comment 15 on the right to water that:

> ... steps should be taken by states parties to prevent their own citizens and companies from violating the right to water of individuals and communities in other countries. Where states parties can take steps to influence other third parties to respect the right, through legal or political means, such steps should be taken in accordance with the Charter of the United Nations and applicable international law.[75]

The obligation of corporations to respect the right to water means that corporations are obliged to refrain from interfering with the enjoyment of the fundamental human rights of the others. In other words, it is an obligation to do no harm to the enjoyment of water resources of others. These rules derive from the ancient Roman law principle *sic utere tuo ut alterum non laedes*.[76] The obligation to protect the right to water includes the obligations of corporations to protect the individual's enjoyment of right to water and to support the protection of water by employing its expertise and resources to protect the fundamental human rights of individuals and local communities.

A corporation may become the primary holder of an obligation to fulfil the right to water foremost in states, where there is no efficient governmental control or authority. Another situation may occur when corporations operate in the territory where the state is unable to fulfil the rights of the people living there. However, states are and should be primarily responsible for their obligation to fulfil people's rights. It is true, though, that a corporation may have a secondary responsibility towards society that reinforces its obligation to respect and protect fundamental human rights. The size and availability of resources of a corporation will play a large role in meeting its obligations.[77] While the resources available for fulfilling fundamental human rights obligations may not be as plentiful in small corporations as in large, corporations may adopt such policies to the maximum

---

[75] General Comment 15 on the Right to Water, UN Doc. E/12/2002/11, 20 January 2003.

[76] Act in a way that does not do harm to others.

[77] Jägers, *Corporate Human Rights Obligations*, p. 85.

of their available resources.[78] Assuming that corporations have some obligations to ensure the right to food, the following tri-partite obligations of corporations to 'respect, protect and fulfil' the right to water can be identified:

Obligations to respect: corporations are to **refrain from**:

- taking measures that negatively affect the right to water
- damaging the environment and health of communities
- the production and marketing of products that are detrimental to the availability and accessibility of clean and safe water
- direct involvement in any violation of the right to water in relation to its employees, other individuals, and the wider community
- complicity in violations of the right to water
- supporting corrupt regimes and giving bribes in exchange for access to water services and other natural resources, goods, and services.

Obligations to protect: corporations are to **adopt regulations and other measures in order to**:

Internal obligations:

- prevent violations of the right to water internally in their own activities
- adopt, disseminate, and implement international human rights law standards in their internal business policies and codes of conducts, and to adopt internal guidelines in weak governance zones, emphasizing the need to respect the right to water
- introduce 'human rights impacts assessments as part of investment and procurement decisions, including selection of suppliers and contractors'[79]
- institute effective monitoring to ensure that the aforementioned policies are being followed, and to initiate disciplinary proceedings when they are violated.[80]

---

[78] In line with the state obligation under Article 2(1) ICESCR, to realize the rights in the ICESCR 'to the maximum of their available resources'.

[79] GRI (Global Reporting Initiative) Guidelines (G2), HR 2, available at http://www.unic.or.jp/globalcomp/pdf/glo_compro_an6.pdf. See also: http://www.globalreporting.org/ReportingFramework/.

[80] GRI (Global Reporting Initiative) Guidelines (G2), HR 1, available at http://www.unic.or.jp/globalcomp/pdf/glo_compro_an6.pdf. See also: http://www.globalreporting.org/ReportingFramework/.

- to protect individuals from abusive conduct by third parties and to adopt internal procedures whereby victims can submit complaints of allegations of violations of the right to water.

External obligations:

- introduce policies and procedures to evaluate and address compliance with the right to water within the supply chain and with contractors
- prevent violations of the right to water in their supply chains and in business relationships with contractors, subcontractors and business partners, implying the following obligations of corporations:
  - to apply human rights law and the framework of the right to water in their contracts, and in relation to others dealing with contractors, subcontractors, and any other business partners
  - to condemn public and private human rights violations of the right to water by all parties in the respective country, and possibly to address the inappropriate use of facilities by government forces; to establish procedures to ensure that the activities of the corporations, their company members, and their subcontractors do not result in, benefit from, or contribute to human rights abuses.

*Obligations to fulfil: corporations are to **take active measures to ensure the availability of:***
Internal obligations:

- to create a safe working environment not endangering the right to water
- to adopt a human rights policy and strategy, and internal codes of conduct that address human rights challenges and include measures to prevent and to respond to human rights violations of the right to water.

External obligations: where government services are not available (for example, in remote areas):

- to cooperate in creating an environment where human rights, including the right to water, are understood and respected, and not to operate or reconsider operating in countries where there is a 'high level of human rights violations or where legislation, governmental practice or other constraints make it imperative to address specific abuses and devise ways of promoting respect for human rights'[81]

- to introduce the necessary reforms to existing corporate structures or business policies, partly by the adoption of internal supervisory mechanisms and control
- to promote and protect fundamental human rights, including the framework of the right to water, in the wider local community
- to adopt a proactive strategy for the protection of water in the area in which they operate
- if necessary, to provide water services for the family of the workers and/or the public as a whole in the area in which they operate.

CONCLUSION

We have asserted that corporations bear a certain responsibility for the realization of economic, social, and cultural rights, which can be derived from international as well as from national (constitutional) law. We have argued that this responsibility can potentially be based on all the economic, social, and cultural rights that are set forth in the international human rights treaties and in national (constitutional) law. We maintain that this responsibility is different and separate from the responsibility of governments and should never undermine the primary governmental responsibility under these rights.

It has not been possible to give a complete overview of all the potential obligations of corporations under economic, social, and cultural rights. In this chapter we have given some examples of corporate obligations that are inherent in the rights to health and water. We have attempted to make it clear that corporations play an important role in the realization of economic, social, and cultural rights. We have also tried to demonstrate that violations of these rights by corporations can be quite serious and need to be addressed.

It has been made clear that corporations have an obligation to respect, protect, and fulfil the rights to health and water deriving primarily from

---

[81] 'Amnesty International Human Rights Principles for Companies: An Introduction', available at http://www1.umn.edu/humanrts/links/aihrprinc.html.

national legal orders. It has been submitted that the concept of corporate responsibility primarily derives legal authority from national legal orders as one of the sources of law. It does not undermine the proposition that the concept can also derive authority from other sources. The state is the primary source of legal authority for fundamental human rights obligations and the responsibility of corporations follows from the embryonic stage of development of binding international principles for the corporation and their fundamental human rights obligations. Corporations are under obligations to comply with those norms.

Even though legislation on corporate responsibility for the rights to health and water already exists in many countries at the national level, and sometimes even at the regional level, disparities in definition and scope, and a piecemeal approach in implementation come in the way of effective investigation and enforcement. As we have suggested, national legal orders regulate corporate responsibility for human rights in a number of laws, which makes it difficult to have a clear and transparent landscape of obligations of corporations in a particular legal order. This problem, though, can be met by introducing a uniform national law that would clearly identify the obligations and responsibility of corporations in relation to fundamental human rights.

We suggest that further obligations of corporations need to be defined along the lines of the distinction between obligations to 'respect, protect, and to fulfil', which can be seen as an elaboration of the 'obligation to respect' as defined by John Ruggie. This identification can offer governments, civil society organizations, corporations, and judicial and quasi-judicial bodies a framework for addressing the responsibilities of corporations. As such, we argue that corporations have both 'negative' obligations to refrain from doing harm as well as 'positive' obligations to, for example, actively protect the environment or to provide certain services where governments are falling short. We are aware that such positive obligations are difficult to define and that the question as to whether a positive obligation exists will depend on the setting in which the corporation operates, for example, whether there is a vulnerable ecosystem or whether it operates in a remote area. But, in the final analysis, we argue that, based on economic, social, and cultural rights, 'doing no harm' goes beyond merely avoiding workplace accidents and environmental damage. This is because corporations have become simply too powerful to refrain from taking on a larger responsibility.

The international community can and should ensure that individuals subjected to violations of their fundamental human rights by or involving corporations and their officers do not continue to suffer because of absence of legal remedies. Yet, that is exactly the problem encountered by most victims of corporate conduct. Unless something changes, there will continue to be victims of alleged human rights violations by or involving corporations in Africa, Asia, East Europe and Latin America. Reform is possible, but it remains to be seen whether the international community has the will to undertake it. Admittedly, the aims and proposals listed in this chapter are ambitious and, some might say, unrealistic, but they should be considered reasonable and achievable.

BIBLIOGRAPHY

Books

Černič, Letnar J. (2010), *Human Rights Law and Business*, Groningen: Europa Law Publishing.

Clapham, A. (2006), *Human Rights Obligations of Non-State Actors*, Oxford: Oxford University Press.

Coomans, Fons (2006), *Justiciability of Economic, Social and Cultural Rights*, Antwerp/Oxford: Intersentia.

Horn, Frank (ed) (1999), *Economic, Social and Cultural Rights of the Ogoni*. Finland: University of Lapland.

Jägers, Nicola (2001), *Corporate Responsibility for Human Rights Violations*, Antwerp/Oxford: Intersentia/HART.

Salomon, Margot, Arne Tostensen, and Wouter Vandenhole (eds) (2007), *Human Rights, Development and New Duty-Bearers*, Antwerp/ Oxford: Intersentia/HART.

Shue, H. (1980), *Basic Rights, Subsistence, Affluence and U.S. Foreign Policy*, New Jersey: Princeton.

Toebes, Brigit (1999), *The Right to Health as a Human Right in International Law*, Antwerp/Groningen/Oxford: Intersentia/Hart.

Wright, Michael and Lehr, Amy (2006), *Business Recognition of Human Rights*, Harvard University: Center for Business & Government, Kennedy School of Government.

Articles in Books and Journals, and Theses

Baker, M.B., 'Promises and Platitudes: Toward a New 21st Century Paradigm for Corporate Codes of Conduct?' *Connecticut Journal of International Law*, 23, 2007, pp. 123–63.

Coomans, Fons, 'The Ogoni Case before the African Commission on Human and Peoples' Rights', *International and Comparative Law Quarterly*, 52, July 2003, pp. 749–60, available at http://www.righttoenvironment.org/ip/uploads/downloads/OgoniCaseProf.Coomans.pdf (accessed August 2009).

Eide Asbjørn, 'Economic, Social and Cultural Rights as Human Rights', in *Economic, Social and Cultural Rights* (2nd edn), A. Eide, Catarina Krause, and Allan Rosas (eds) (2001), Dordrecht/Boston/London: Martinus Nijhoff Publishers, pp. 9–28.

Eide, Asbjørn and Allan Rosas, 'Economic, Social and Cultural Rights: A Universal Challenge', in *Economic, Social and Cultural Rights* (2nd edn), A. Eide, Catarina Krause, and Allan Rosas (eds) (2001), Dordrecht/Boston/London: Martinus Nijhoff Publishers, pp. 3–8.

Hardberger, A., 'Life, Liberty, and the Pursuit of Water: Evaluating Water as a Human Right and the Duties and Obligations it Creates', *Northwestern University Journal of International Human Rights*, 4, 2005, p. 331.

Muchlinski, P. T., 'Human Rights and Multinationals—Is There a Problem?', *International Affairs*, 77, 2001, pp. 31–47.

Murphy S. D., 'Taking Multinational Corporate Codes of Conduct to the Next Level', *Columbia Journal of Transnational Law*, 43(2), 2005, pp. 389–433.

Ssenyonjo, Manisuli, 'Non-State Actors and Economic, Social and Cultural Rights', in *Economic, Social and Cultural Rights in Action,* Mashood A. Baderin and Robert McCorquodale (eds) (2007), pp. 109–38, Oxford: Oxford University Press.

Toebes, Brigit, 'Taking a Human Rights Approach to Health Care Commercialisation', in *Health Capital and Sustainable Socioeconomic Development*, Patricia A. Cholewka and Mitra M. Motlagh (eds) (2008). Boca Raton/London/New York: Taylor and Francis Group, pp. 442–54.

Toebes, Brigit, 'Human Rights and Health Sector Corruption', in *Global Health and Human Rights: Legal and Philosophical Perspectives,* J. Harrington and Maria Stuttaford (eds) (2009) Routledge.

Van Hoof, G. J. H., 'The Legal Nature of Economic, Social and Cultural Rights: a Rebuttal of Some Traditional Views', in *The Right to Food*, P. Alston and K. Tomaševski (eds) (1984). Utrecht: SIM, pp. 97–111.

Weissbrodt, D. and M. Kruger, 'Current Developments: Norms on the Responsibilities of Transnational Corporations and Other Business Enterprises with Regard to Human Rights', *American Journal of International Law*, 97, 2003, pp. 913–21.

UN Documents

Amao Olufemi, 'Protect, Respect and Remedy: A Framework for Business and Human Rights', Review of the Report of John Ruggie to the United Nations Human Rights Council, HRC/8/5, 7 April 2008, available at http://www.papers.ssrn.com/sol3/papers.cfm?abstract_id=1131682, p. 5.

Brussels Convention Relating to Civil Liability in the Field of Maritime Carriage of Nuclear Material, 17 December 1971, 974 UNTS.

COE Convention on Civil Liability for Damage Resulting from Activities Dangerous to the Environment, 21 June 1993, available at http://conventions.coe.int/treaty/en/treaties/html/150.htm (accessed 20 February 2009).

Committee on Economic, Social and Cultural Rights, 'The Right to the Highest Attainable Standard of Health', available at http://www2.ohchr.org/english/bodies/cescr/ (accessed 20 February 2009).

Convention on the Elimination of All Forms of Discrimination against Women, 1969, G.A. res. 34/180, 34 UN GAOR Supp. (no. 46).

Convention on the Elimination of All Forms of Discrimination against Women, 1979, 1249 UNTS 13.

Convention on the Rights of the Child, 1989, 28I.L.M. 1456.

Council of Europe Convention on Civil Liability for Damage Resulting from Activities Dangerous to the Environment, 21 June 1993.

General Comment No. 14, UN Doc. E/C12/200/4, 11 August 2000, available at www.unhchr.ch.

General Comment 15 on the Right to Water, UN Doc. E/12/2002/11, 20 January 2003, available online at www.unhchr.ch.

European Convention on Human Rights, 1950, ETS no. 5.

European Social Charter of the Council of Europe, 1961, ETS no. 35.

International Covenant on Civil and Political Rights (ICCPR), including Optional Protocol, 1966/1976, 999 UNTS 171.

International Covenant on Economic, Social and Cultural Rights (ICESCR), 1966/1976, 999 UNTS 195.

International Convention on Civil Liability for Oil Pollution Damage (CLC), 29 November 1969.

International Labour Organization Governing Body, 'Overview of Global Developments and Office Activities Concerning Codes of Conduct, Social Labelling and Other Private Sector Initiatives Addressing Labour Issues', Working Party on the Social Dimensions of the Liberalization of International Trade, Executive Summary, GB 273/WP/SDL/1, 273rd session Geneva, November 1998.

OECD Convention on Combating Bribery of Foreign Public Officials in International Business Transactions, 18 December 1997, S. Treaty Doc. 105–43 (1998), 37 ILM.

OECD Directorate for Financial, Fiscal and Enterprise Affairs, 'Codes of Corporate Conduct: Expanded Review of their Contents', May 2001. Working Papers on International Investment, Number 2001/6, May 2011.

Paris Convention on the Third Party Liability in the Field of Nuclear Energy, 1960, 956 UNTS 251.

Report of the United Nations High Commissioner for Human Rights on the Scope and Content of the Relevant Human Rights Obligations Related to Equitable Access to Safe Drinking Water and Sanitation under International Human Rights Instruments, 16 August 2007, available at http://daccessdds.un.org/doc/UNDOC/GEN/G07/136/55/PDF/G0713655.pdf?OpenElement, para. 47.

Report of the Special Rapporteur on the Right to the Highest Attainable Standard of Health, Paul Hunt, Mission to the World Trade Organization, 1 March 2004, UN Doc. E/CN.4/2004/49/Add.1.

Report of the Special Rapporteur on the Right to the Highest Attainable Standard of Health, Paul Hunt, 'The Human Rights Responsibilities of Pharmaceutical Companies in Relation to Access to Medicines', 11 August 2008, UN Doc. A/63/263.

Right to Health Unit of the Essex University Human Rights Centre, Human Rights Guidelines for Pharmaceutical Companies, available online at http://www2. essex.ac.uk/human_rights_centre/rth/projects.shtm (accessed August 2009).

Special Representative on Business and Human Rights (John Ruggie), Interim Report of the Special Representative of the Secretary-General on the Issue of Human Rights of Transnational Corporations and Other Business Enterprises, para. 24–27, 22 February 2006, UN Doc. E/CN.4/2006/97.

UN Global Compact, available at http://www.unglobalcompact.org/Participants AndStakeholders/index.html.

UN High Commissioner for Human Rights, Summary Report on Geneva Consultation, 'Corporate Responsibility to Respect Human Rights', Geneva, 4–5 December 2007, available online at http://www.reports-and-materials.org/ Ruggie-Geneva-4-5-Dec-2007.pdf (accessed 15 January 2011).

UN Human Rights Council, 'Promotion and Protection of All Human Rights, Civil, Political, Economic, Social and Cultural Rights, Including the Right to Development: Protect, Respect and Remedy: A Framework for Business and Human Rights', UN Doc. A/HRC/8/5, 7 April 2008, available at http://www. reports-and-materials.org/Ruggie-report-7-Apr-2008.pdf.

UN Doc. A/HRC/8/5, 7 April 2008, para. 6.

UN Doc. A/HRC/11/13.

UN World Conference on Human Rights: Vienna Declaration and Programme of Action, UN Doc. A/CONF.157/23.

Http://www.globalreporting.org/ReportingFramework/ (accessed 20 February 2009).

Legal Case

Bhopal Gas Disaster Case, *Charan Lal Sahu* v. *Union of India*, 1990 (1) SCC, p. 613.

Corporate Codes of Conduct

British Petroleum, 'Human Rights: A Guidance Note', 2005.

Chevron Corporation, 'Human Rights Statement', available at http://www.chevron. com/globalissues/humanrights/ (accessed 20 February 2009).

'Compare World's Largest Corporations (Global 500)', *Fortune*, 21 July 2008, at p.165, available at http://money.cnn.com/magazines/fortune/global500/2008/ full_list>.

Conoco–Philips Corporation, 'Human Rights Position', available at, http://www. conocophillips.com/social/values_policies/humanrights/index.htm (accessed 20 February 2009).

Daimler–Chrysler, available at http://www.daimler.com/dccom/0-5-880434-1-881989-1-0-0-0-0-0-8-876574-0-0-0-0-0-0-1.html (accessed 20 February 2009).

Equal Opportunity Practices (accessed 20 February 2009).

Exxon Mobil, available at http://www.exxonmobil.com/Corporate/community_local_rights.aspx (accessed 20 February 2009).

General Motors, available at http://www.gm.com/corporate/responsibility/reports/00/vision/social/human.html (accessed 20 February 2009).

Total Corporation, 'Code of Conduct', p. 10.

Wal-Mart, 'Requirements for Suppliers', available at http://walmartstores.com/Suppliers/248.aspx.

Official Documents/Reports

'Amnesty International Human Rights Principles for Companies: An Introduction', available at http://www1.umn.edu/humanrts/links/aihrprinc.html.

FIAN International, 'Identifying and Addressing Violations of Human Right to Water—Applying the Human Rights Approach', available at http://www.menschen-recht-wasser.de/downloads/violations_human-rights-water.pdf.

FIAN International, 'Investigating Some Alleged Violations of the Human Right to Water in India', Report of the International Fact-Finding Mission to India, January 2004, available at http://www.menschen-recht-wasser.de/downloads/report_komplett.pdf.

Food and Water Watch, available at http://www.foodandwaterwatch.org/water/world-water/right.

GRI (Global Reporting Initiative) Guidelines (G2), HR 1, available at, http://www.unic.or.jp/globalcomp/pdf/glo_compro_an6.pdf.

Institute for Business and Human Rights, 'Business, Human Rights & Right to Water: Challenges, Dilemmas, Opportunities', Roundtable Consultative Report, January 2009, available at http://www.institutehrb.org/Downloads/Draft%20Report%20-%20Business,%20Human%20Rights%20and%20Water.pdf.

Inter-American Commission on Human Rights (IACHR), 'Report on the Situation of Human Rights in Ecuador', Doc. 10 rev 1, 24 April 1997, pp. 106–07.

Kamminga, M.T., 'Corporate Obligations under International Law', Paper presented at the 71st Conference of the International Law Association, Plenary Session on Corporate Social Responsibility and International Law, Berlin, 17 August 2004.

Knox, J. H., 'Concept Paper on Facilitating Specification of the Duty to Protect, prepared for UN SRSG on Business and Human Rights', Wake Forest University, 14 December 2007.

Right to Health Unit of the Essex University Human Rights Centre, 'Human Rights Guidelines for Pharmaceutical Companies', available at http://www2.essex.ac.uk/human_rights_centre/rth/projects.shtm (accessed August 2009).

Shell, 'Business and Human Rights: A Management Primer', available at http://www-static.shell.com/static/responsible_energy/downloads/management_primers/business_and_human_rights_primer.pdf.

The Right to Water, 'Legal Redress: The Right to Water under the Right to Life: India', available online at http://www.righttowater.org.uk/code/legal_3.asp.

Unitarian Universalist Service Committee, A Bibliograhy of Primary and Secondary Sources of Law on the Human Right to Water, 2008.

United States Federal Alien Torts Claims Act, 1789, 28 U.S.C. § 1350.

'World Development Indicators: Gross Domestic Product', 2007, available online at http://siteresources.worldbank.org/DATASTATISTICS/Resources/GDP.pdf (accessed 15 January 2009).

2

Globalization, Climate Change, and Indigenous Peoples in the Arctic
An Interface between Free Trade and the Right to Culture

Kamrul Hossain

INTRODUCTION

It is always tricky to make a choice between economic development and the protection of socio-cultural values and environment. Globalization leads to economic development by integrating regional economies, societies, and cultures through a global network of trade and communication. Trade liberalization through multilateral trading agreements and the free-trade policy imposed by the World Trade Organization (WTO) accelerate globalization. While globalization contributes to gradual economic development, it has to be adapted to specific regions in order to mitigate any adverse consequences. A short-term economic development may cause an adverse impact in the long run. Any development, therefore, will have to be cost-effective so that long-term catastrophe can be avoided. The environmental consequences of globalization, which we will consider in this chapter from the Arctic perspective, cannot simply be ignored. Today it is more than ever apparent that global environmental changes are mostly caused by large-scale globalization. The environmental agenda throughout the last decade focused on the necessity of the integration of economic development and environment. The idea that emerged from this notion of integration was termed as 'sustainable development', a concept that has been addressed as a fundamental principle in international environmental laws. International environmental laws are embodied in various multilateral environmental agreements (MEAs) and regional agreements, while trade laws, which contribute to globalization, are embodied in the structures of the WTO and regional trade agreements. It is, therefore, obvious that these two bodies of laws will interact. The negotiations on the relationship between MEAs and WTO rules were mandated in the Doha Declaration in paragraph 31(i).[1] The discussions on the relationship between MEAs and WTO rules are complex, and to a large extent are centred on the issue of the legitimacy of the WTO authority to decide on the restrictions to be placed on environmental grounds. It is not, however, within the scope of this chapter to discuss the relationship between MEAs and WTO rules or the effectiveness of MEAs within the structure of free trade regime under the WTO. The point, however, is that globalization resulting from free trade has something to do with the protection of the environment, especially the environment that is vulnerable because of rapid climate change.

The focus of this chapter is on the Arctic region—a region that suffers hugely from environmental changes due to global climate change. Environmental preservation in the Arctic has a significant link to certain socio-cultural rights associated with its indigenous peoples. These rights are fundamental for the survival of the indigenous communities of the Arctic. The chapter looks into the environmental changes in the Arctic occurring due to the large-scale globalization accelerated by climate change. These changes are contributing to an alteration of the entire ecosystem. The alteration of the ecosystem then adversely affects the indigenous communities in the Arctic. Their identity, culture, language, and overall survival are under serious threat. At the same time, the chapter examines how, with reference to the EU import ban on seal products, the indigenous communities in the Arctic are being deprived of the benefits of globalization that are due to them. As a result, they suffer from a denial of the fundamental human rights guaranteed to them under international laws. The chapter, while addressing the basic issues of the indigenous peoples of the Arctic, shows how they are affected by globalization from

---

[1] See Ministerial Declaration, Doha WTO Ministerial 2001, adopted on 14 November 2001, available at http://www.wto.org/english/thewto_e/minist_e/min01_e/mindecl_e.htm (accessed 17 April 2010).

the viewpoint of both internal (environmental change) and external (free-trade regime) factors. The chapter also shows how indigenous peoples' fundamental human rights are guaranteed by international law, in particular by the International Covenant on Civil and Political Rights (ICCPR). The chapter then examines whether globalization resulting out of the free-trade regime contradicts the human rights guaranteed to the indigenous peoples in the Arctic, especially regarding their right to culture, which is the core of their identity.

THE ARCTIC AND ITS INDIGENOUS PEOPLES

The area of the Arctic region is about 14.5 million square kilometre. It includes the ice-covered Arctic Ocean and the surrounding land covering all of Greenland and Spitsbergen, and the northern parts of Alaska, Canada, Norway, and Russia.[2] In addition, the northern parts of Finland and Sweden in the north of Arctic Circle belong to the Arctic region.[3] Some of the land parts of the Arctic, such as Greenland, are covered with ice sheets whereas others, such as Alaska, have lush tundra. These areas have large mammals, such as caribou, bear, wolf, and fox, and many varieties of plants. In summer, migratory birds and other wildlife come to the Arctic to raise their young.[4] The Arctic is inhabited by significant numbers of indigenous and coastal communities. There are over 40 ethnic groups. These groups have inhabited the region for thousands of years.[5] Out of the total population of 4 million people, 10 per cent are indigenous peoples.[6] They

[2] See 'Polar Discovery', available at http://polardiscovery.whoi.edu/arctic/geography.html (accessed 9 April 2010).

[3] There is no generally accepted definition of the Arctic. The Arctic Monitoring and Assessment Programme (AMAP)—a working group of the Arctic Council—defined the Arctic marine area as north of the Arctic Circle (66°32"N), north of 62°N in Asia, and 60°N in North America, including the northern parts of Finland and Sweden. See 'Introduction to the Background Papers', *Arctic Transform,* available at http://arctic-transform.org/download/Intro.pdf (accessed 9 April 2010).

[4] See 'Polar Discovery', *supra* n.2.

[5] See 'Arctic Indigenous peoples', http://www.arcticcentre.org/?Deptid=24486 (accessed 7 April 2010).

[6] See M.L. Parry *et al.* (eds), *Climate Change 2007: Impacts, Adaptation and Vulnerability,* Contribution of Working Group II to the Fourth Assessment Report of the Intergovernmental Panel on Climate Change (Cambridge University Press, 2007), p. 657.

include the Inupiat and Yup'ik Eskimos, Alutiiq and Athabascans in Alaska; the Kalaallit and Inughuit in Greenland; the Sami in northern Fennoscandia; and the so-called Northern Minorities in Russia, who include the Chukchi, Evens, Evenks, Nenets, Mivkhi, Sami, Sakhas, and Khants.[7] Each of these groups has its own culture, language, history, and traditional ways of livelihood. The traditional activities of the Arctic indigenous peoples include reindeer herding, subsistence hunting, sheep farming, fishing, and so on.[8]

Despite the variations in the means of livelihood and in the practise of culture and language, all the groups have something in common. Most of the indigenous communities have already undergone substantial changes, or 'modernity', due to globalization, including the Western way of life, state policies, and introduction of mixed economy. Today the activities of the Arctic indigenous peoples include, among others, commercial salmon canning, timber production, and oil-related businesses. Many indigenous groups, nevertheless, still mostly rely on the natural resources of the traditional lands on which they live. Their connection to the traditional activities embraces their economic and cultural survival. Nevertheless, technology, industrial development, immigration, and tourism are causing large-scale social change and adversely affecting the Arctic environment. As a result, for the indigenous peoples, the survival of their traditional culture and livelihood, and indeed identity, has become a big challenge.[9]

GLOBALIZATION IN THE ARCTIC ACCELERATED BY CLIMATE CHANGE

It is obvious that globalization results in increasing industrialization and other anthropogenic activities, leading to economic development that causes increased emission of greenhouse gases. The emission of

---

[7] M. Nuttal, *Protecting the Arctic Indigenous Peoples and Cultural Survival* (Harwood: Routledge, 2002), p. 2.

[8] Ibid., p. 2.

[9] See for detailed discussions, Kamrul Hossain, 'The Human Rights Committee on Traditional Cultural Rights: the Case of the Arctic Indigenous Peoples' in *Global and Local Encounters Norms, Identities and Representations in Formation*, Renvall Institute Publication 25, Tuija Veintie and Pirjo Kristiina Virtanen (eds) (University of Helsinki, 2009), pp. 29–30. See also Nuttal, *Protecting the Arctic Indigenous Peoples*, p. 2.

greenhouse gases contributes to global warming. Due to global warming, the overall climate of the world is changing rapidly. In the Arctic, the general warming is likely to be faster, with temperature increases likely to range between 2°C and 9°C by 2100.[10] During the winter, the warming could be three to four times greater than global averages.[11] The results will be visible in the Arctic with higher temperatures, rise in sea level, melting of sea ice and glaciers, increased precipitation in some areas and drought in others.[12] There will be large-scale impacts on the unique Arctic environment. Arctic ecosystems support species well adapted to the extreme conditions, such as short growing seasons, low light availability and cold temperatures.[13] In the marine area of the Arctic, sea ice is the dominant feature.[14] The survival of certain marine animals, such as polar bears, is dependent on the existence of ice. Although the absence of sea ice is causing a reduction in Arctic marine species, it is important to note that some species, especially commercial fish (for example, cod and herring in the North Atlantic and walleye and pollock in the Bering Sea), are expected to benefit from the larger expanse of open water leading to increased productivity.[15]

The rapid melting of sea ice, as a consequence of the warming of the Arctic, is, on the one hand creating new opportunities and, on the other hand, posing new challenges to the Arctic environment. The opportunities are the increased economic activities, whereas the challenges are mostly about preserving the unique nature of the Arctic environment. The opening up of two major sea routes for a longer period of time will increase shipping and navigation.[16] In addition, the regional waters

---

[10] See Timo Koivurova et al., 'Background Paper Indigenous Peoples in the Arctic', *Arctic Transform* 5 (2008), http://arctic-transform.org/download/Intro.pdf (accessed 6 April 2010).

[11] Jennifer McIver, 'The Arctic', in *Indigenous Peoples, the Environment and Law*, Lawrence Watters (ed.) (Carolina Academic Press, 2004), p. 160.

[12] See James J. McKarthy et al. (eds), *Climate Change 2001: Impacts, Adaptation and Vulnerability*, Contribution of Working Group II to the Third Assessment Report of the Intergovernmental Panel on Climate Change (Cambridge University Press, 2001), p. 26.

[13] See *Arctic Climate Impact Assessment* (Cambridge University Press, 2005), p. 481.

[14] See 'Introduction to the Background Papers', *Arctic Transform*, p. 4.

[15] See Parry et al., *Climate Change 2007*, p. 669.

[16] The Arctic Climate Impact Assessment (ACIA) Report 2004 identified ten major findings as consequences of the rapid climate change in the Arctic. One of the findings (number six) states that the reduced sea ice is very likely to increase

surrounding the Arctic countries will also be used for shipping. Due to these facts there will be a rise in commercial activities. Transportation routes will also be established on the land area to carry goods from the sea ports. The Arctic seabed is considered to be the next big reservoir of the world's undiscovered oil and gas resources. It can thus be foreseen that seabed activities will increase. An increase in the onshore and off-shore mining and mineral activities will take place. Tourism industry will flourish. Consequently, there will be a gradual rise in industrial and other commercial activities, as well as societal changes resulting from large-scale infrastructural developments.[17]

The increase in the commercial activities will have negative consequences on the Arctic environment. Increased shipping and navigation will hinder the movement of migratory marine mammals and, at the same time, there will be an increase in the risk of oil spills.[18] Mineral and mining activities as a whole will contribute to the emission of greenhouse gases into the atmosphere, which will further accelerate climate change, causing an even faster melting of the Arctic sea ice. Seabed activities will rise, and will likely generate pollution caused by oil spills occurring during, for example, hydrocarbon exploitation and transportation. As clean-up operations, especially in the areas of sea ice, will be extremely difficult and expensive, a single large oil spill in the wrong place and at the wrong time of the year would have very serious, population-wide impacts on seabirds, fish, and marine mammals.[19] Pollution as a whole will cause the extinction of

---

marine transport and access to resources. See Susan Hasso, *ACIA: Impacts of a Warming Arctic* (Cambridge: Cambridge University Press, 2004), pp. 10–11, 82–85.

[17] According to the Arctic Human Development Report, it is unlikely that Arctic societies and cultures can remain resilient in the face of all the biophysical and societal changes. The Arctic societies face an unusual combination of biophysical and socio-economic stresses, many of which can be linked to oil and gas development. See Oran R. Young and Niels Einarsson, 'A Human Development Agenda for the Arctic: Major Findings and Emerging Issues', in *Arctic Human Development Report* (Akureyri: Stefansson Arctic Institute, 2004), p. 230. See also Oluf Langhelle *et al.*, 'Framing Oil and Gas in the Arctic from a Sustainable Development Perspective', in *Arctic Oil and Gas Sustainability at risk*, Aslaug Mikkelsen and Oluf Langhelle, (eds) (Routledge, 2008), p. 32.

[18] *Arctic Climate Impact Assessment*, 2005, pp. 84–85.

[19] Samantha Smith, 'Environmental Impacts of Offshore Oil and Gas Development in the Arctic', WWF International Arctic Programme, available at http://old.

endemic species and will alter the biosystem irreversibly, resulting in far-reaching consequences for the ecosystem at large. Industrial and other commercial activities as well as infrastructural development will have negative environmental impacts in the whole region.[20] Consequently, the coastal communities in the Arctic, whose livelihoods depend upon the unique nature of the Arctic environment, will be affected greatly. The indigenous communities will likely lose their livelihoods and culture, since their 'traditional lifestyle and cultural heritage depend upon the preservation of the Arctic environment.'[21] The Arctic Climate Impact Assessment (ACIA) report—a scientific report of over thousand pages describing the impacts of climate change in the Arctic—states that indigenous peoples are exceptionally vulnerable to the climate change.[22] The following sections show how indigenous peoples in the Arctic are affected through the changes born out of climate change.

Societal Change

Indigenous peoples in the Arctic live as a community. They are closely connected to each other just as their livelihood and culture are deeply connected to the land on which they live. Hunting, gathering, trapping, and reindeer and caribou herding have been the traditional activities. As climate change creates opportunities for rapid globalization, social changes occur through capital flows, human migration, and gradual industrialization. Consequently, new lifestyles, educational systems, technology, food, and diseases are introduced. In addition, modern transportation, infrastructural change, and state policies have increasingly affected all features of the

---

pame.is/sidur/uploads/offshoreoilsndgasWWF.pdf (accessed 23 October 2009).

[20] See Brent Carpenter, 'Warm is the New Cold: Global Warming, Oil, UNCLOS Article 76, and How an Arctic Treaty Might Stop a New Cold War', *Environmental Law Review*, 39, 2009, p. 239.

[21] The Arctic region is inhabited by more than thirty indigenous peoples. See Nele Matz-Lück, 'Planting the Flag in Arctic Waters: Russia's Claim to the North Pole,' *Göttingen J. of Int'l Law* 1 (2009) 2:255.

[22] See *Arctic Climate Impact Assessment*, 2005, pp. 651, 685, 1014. See also Parry et al., *Climate Change 2007*, p. 672.

indigenous peoples' lifestyles.[23] The break up of interpersonal ties leads to more and more nuclear families.[24]

The traditional knowledge, which gives members of the indigenous communities the understanding of their environment and binds them strongly with nature, has now become inadequate as changes are occurring so fast. Many people feel alienated from the land of their ancestors.[25] The introduction of mixed culture, gradual loss of traditional activities,[26] and the introduction of modern school system—which has resulted in the younger generations to slowly lose their languages—contribute to large scale societal change. The greatest challenges for many indigenous communities, thus, include: relocation, urbanization, as well as the northward advancement of agriculture.[27] The ultimate effect of the societal change is the emergence of various social problems, such as impoverishment, depression, alcoholism, drug addiction, permanent unemployment syndromes, and rising suicide rates.[28]

Economic Disparities

Climate change and globalization have introduced a mixed economy within the indigenous community in the Arctic. Cash flow from the south has gradually replaced traditional harvesting. International trade, investment, tourism, and other commercial activities are creating new opportunities, the benefits of which can be enjoyed by the indigenous communities. Agricultural growth, increase in fisheries, and resource extraction (offshore and onshore) will probably create more jobs and promote greater

---

[23] See *supra* n. 17, p. 49. See also Nuttal, *Protecting the Arctic Indigenous Peoples and Cultural Survival*, p. 53–54.

[24] See Koivurova *et al.*, 'Background Paper Indigenous Peoples in the Arctic', p. 16.

[25] See *Arctic Climate Impact Assessment*, 2005, pp. 670, 675. See also Parry *et al.*, *Climate Change 2007*, p. 668.

[26] Due to rapid climate change, traditional cultural festivals of the indigenous communities, which need certain climatic conditions to be observed, now need to be re-timed or are not being celebrated, resulting in a loss of traditional culture. See Koivurova *et al.*, 'Background Paper Indigenous Peoples in the Arctic', p. 17.

[27] See *supra* n. 17, pp. 62–63. See also Nuttal, *Protecting the Arctic Indigenous Peoples and Cultural Survival*, pp. 4–5, 11–13.

[28] See *supra* n. 17, p. 17.

investments in infrastructure.[29] It is also likely that the development of tourism will create more job opportunities for the locals. With the socio-cultural changes, modern schooling systems are being introduced, which enable the younger members of the community to access the job opportunities, especially as they speak non-indigenous language/s.[30] Despite these opportunities, indigenous peoples in the Arctic face high rates of unemployment and poverty. Globalization has caused high living costs. In addition, climate change is causing the thawing of permafrost, resulting in higher maintenance costs; the devastation of roads is causing many remote coastal communities to be cut off from the main population centres, resulting in disruption of intercommunity trade. However, with the melting of sea ice, marine transportation has become more accessible, and for longer periods of time,[31] which will eventually open up new routes. But the traditional hunting ground of ice-dependent marine species, such as the polar bear, has been affected as hunters need to travel longer distances than before. Traditional hunting rooted in the culture of the indigenous communities provides traditional foodstuff that cannot be replaced by imported food because of nutrition and costs.[32] The gap between rising costs of living and decreasing possibilities to acquire financial resources may mean for many people impoverishment and may threaten their food security,[33] despite the possibility of alternative sources of subsistence from the increased production in agriculture and fisheries. The traditional subsistence activities bring economic benefit from the production of different kinds of goods from, for example, skins of the hunted animals, such as clothing, handicrafts, souvenirs, and other accessories, which the indigenous peoples export. However, both production and export are being affected on account of the overall changes in the Arctic, and therefore, indigenous communities suffer an economic loss.

---

[29] Ibid., p. 16.

[30] Ibid., p. 10.

[31] See *Arctic Climate Impact Assessment*, 2005, pp. 668–70.

[32] See for example, Finn Lynge, 'Indigenous Peoples between Human Rights and Environmental Protection—An Arctic Perspective', *Nordic Journal of International Law*, 64, 1995, p. 491.

[33] See *Arctic Climate Impact Assessment*, 2005, p. 657.

Infrastructural Development

With the increase in capital flow, industrial activities in the Arctic are gradually growing, resulting in drastic infrastructural changes. Building of roads, construction activities, and transportation are adversely affecting the region. Due to high noise levels, wildlife relocation is taking place. Reindeer and caribou herding activities are being affected, which will eventually cause suffering to the indigenous communities. Coastal erosion, together with rising sea levels, is resulting in the disruption of inter-community communication. Moreover, sewage systems, airstrips, power lines, and roads built on permafrost are already being endangered.[34] The maintenance and repair of any damage to the infrastructure are highly expensive. The indigenous communities do not have the financial resources available to maintain and repair any such damage.[35] Permafrost thawing, coastal erosion, lower lake water levels and changing river run-off—especially potential decreases in summer months—are threatening to jeopardize fresh water supply, due to damage to water containers and lake drainage in coastal areas. As a result hydropower generation, oil pipelines and permafrost-based waste containers may be affected. It is then probable that contamination and pollution will grow.[36] However, temperature rise will lower the costs of heating and insulation throughout the Arctic from which the indigenous communities will benefit.[37]

Livelihood and Cultural Changes

Changes in societal structure, economy, and infrastructure in the Arctic significantly impact the lives and livelihood of its indigenous communities. As discussed previously, hunting, trapping, and gathering are significant aspects of the indigenous culture in the Arctic. Traditionally indigenous peoples in the north are also engaged in reindeer or caribou herding. Their livelihood and culture are rooted in these activities. Polar bears, seals, and some fish stocks depend on

---

[34] See Koivurova *et al.*, 'Background Paper Indigenous Peoples in the Arctic', p. 14.
[35] See *Arctic Climate Impact Assessment*, 2005, pp. 660, 670, 1004.
[36] Ibid., p. 1011, 1013, 2005. See also Parry *et al.*, *Climate Change 2007*, pp. 665, 672; Koivurova *et al.*, 'Background Paper Indigenous Peoples in the Arctic', p. 15.
[37] See *Arctic Climate Impact Assessment*, 2005, p. 1004.

ice cover.[38] Due to the melting of sea ice, the population of the ice-dependent mammals might not only decline in numbers but also move to other locations.[39] For hunters, reaching harvesting areas located offshore would become impossible.[40] Moreover, the construction of new infrastructure both onshore and offshore (such as the construction of oil installations and transportation routes) is causing the relocation of wildlife habitats. Hunters are, therefore, forced to move to new locations for hunting. The other issue is the inappropriateness of traditional knowledge, which has become less accurate because of the environmental change. This is making hunting more expensive and is worsening the harvesting outcome. As there are frequent storms and other natural disasters, hunters face frequent accidents, and they need to be prepared for many new situations.[41] Especially in cases where traditional subsistence is primarily based on one species, for example, the ringed seal for some Inuit communities,[42] the threat to basic food supply is very real. However, some indigenous communities stand to benefit from the newly gained access to large fish stocks.[43]

Summing Up

In the Arctic, globalization and climate change are interrelated, in that globalization is taking place more dramatically with greater climate change. The ultimate victims of this dilemma are the indigenous peoples whose livelihood depends on the preservation of specific geographic and environmental conditions, and who maintain a traditional way of lives for their subsistence. The impact of globalization on the Arctic indigenous peoples is, therefore, significant. As already discussed, although some positive impacts in general can be seen, indigenous peoples are mostly vulnerable to globalization as they gradually lose their traditional ways of life, which is deeply rooted in their culture. In other words, globalization seriously threatens their identity as distinct groups of peoples.

[38] Especially ringed seal, arctic fox, and polar bear, ibid., p. 660.
[39] Ibid., pp. 75, 660.
[40] Ibid., p. 662.
[41] Ibid., p. 670.
[42] See Koivurova *et al.*, 'Background Paper Indigenous Peoples in the Arctic', p. 13.
[43] See *Arctic Climate Impact Assessment*, 2005, pp. 659, 669.

THE OTHER SIDE OF THE COIN: ECONOMIC LOSS DUE TO RESTRICTION ON FREE TRADE

Free trade is institutionally formalized through the strong body of the WTO.[44] The WTO supervises the implementation of international rules on trade liberalization, and also serves as a negotiating forum for further liberalization. The mandate of the organization also includes areas such as liberalization of trade in services as well as protection of intellectual property rights. The main idea in any case is the promotion of free trade. States should produce the goods they are best at and export them. At the same time concurrent trade barriers should be removed in order to enhance economic efficiency, with all states providing to the others the things that they are best at producing.[45] The greater economic efficiency then is expected to alleviate poverty and enhance the ability of states to implement human rights, such as the right to an adequate standard of living, the right to an adequate standard of healthcare, and so on.[46] This conclusion is, however, contested with respect to the Arctic indigenous peoples, given the aforementioned facts. This section focuses on the other side of the coin—the adverse affects arising out of restrictions on globalization (free trade). The discussions here are based on the impacts on the indigenous peoples of trade restrictions with reference to the European Union (EU) ban on trade of seal skin products within the common market.

EU Ban on Trade in Seal Products

On 16 September 2009, the EU adopted a regulation banning the trade in seal products in the internal market.[47] The regulation applies to seal products produced in the EU and to imported products.

---

[44] WTO was created in 1994 after the conclusion of the Uruguay round of negotiations under the General Agreement on Tariffs and Trade (GATT) by the Marrakesh Agreement. See Marrakesh Agreement Establishing the World Trade Organization (15 April 1994), 1867 UNTS 3.

[45] See Sarah Joseph, 'Human Rights and the WTO: Issues for the Pacific', *Victoria University of Wellington Law Review*, 40, 2009, pp. 351–52.

[46] See ibid., p. 352.

[47] The EU Regulation (EC) no. 1007/2009 of the European parliament and of the Council, L 286/36, 16 September 2009, available at http://ec.europa.eu/food/animal/welfare/trade_seals_products.pdf (accessed 6 April 2010).

The regulation is the follow-up measure resulting from the previous concerns over seal hunting, and the use and import of certain seal products that are hunted by a cruel method not consistent with the EU animal welfare policy.[48] The basic aim of the regulation is to ensure that the EU rules concerning seal products or trade in seal products are harmonized. At the same time it seeks to ensure that animal welfare concerns are fully met.[49] The overall goal is to put a complete ban on the trade in seal and seal products in the EU market, provided that a narrow margin of exception is allowed. The EU aims to prevent the sale of products that come from seals—everything from seal pelts to Omega -3 capsules made from seal oil.[50]

The EU ban attracted strong reactions from some of the countries engaged in the export of seal products. Canada was the first country to strongly oppose the regulation. Canada threatened to challenge the EU decision in the WTO dispute settlement body. On 2 November 2009, Canada formally requested consultation with the EU through the WTO. Canada claimed that the EU regulation violates various international trade agreements, including the agreement on Technical Barriers to Trade (TBT), the General Agreement on Tariffs and Trade (GATT) and the Agriculture Agreement.[51] The member states of the North Atlantic Marine Mammal Commission (NAMCO) in a statement issued on 10 September 2009, just before the regulation was adopted, criticized the EU ban on seal products—the ban that was previously adopted by the EU council on 27 July 2009—and upheld

---

[48] See, for example, the EU Directive 83/129/EEC of 18 March 1983, OJ L 91, 9.4.1983, at 30, where import into member states for commercial purposes of skins of harp seal pups and hooded seal pups and products derived therefrom was prohibited. There was, however, an exception that the products resulting from traditional hunt by the Inuit is allowed. This was then followed in 1991 by the Council Regulation (EEC) No 3254/91, which called for a ban on imports of skins and some manufactured products of certain species trapped in countries allowing the use of trapping methods that did not meet 'international humane trapping standards'.

[49] See Joseph, 'Human Rights and the WTO: Issues for the Pacific', preambular part, para. 10.

[50] See ibid., operative part, para. 3.

[51] See Matthew Hamilton-Smith, 'Competing Interests: Canada and Inuit Oppose EU Ban on Seal Products', available at http://thebucampus.ca/2010/01/competing-interests-canada-and-inuit-oppose-eu-ban-on-seal-products/ (accessed 15 April 2010).

that the decision seriously disrupted the international cooperation on responsible management and sustainable use of renewable natural resources in general. The statement stressed that the ban on the import of seal products into the European Community market was in direct contradiction to these fundamental considerations. The ban did not provide a tool to ensure the conservation of seal stocks; nor did it recognize the important work that had been undertaken by the North Atlantic sealing communities to monitor and improve compliance with the strict standards of animal welfare that are required in the methods used to harvest seals.[52]

Before the regulation was adopted, the Norwegian foreign minister Jonas Gahr Store noted that the EU ban would restrict the freedom of his country to manage its marine resources. Norwegian sealing takes a sustainable and modern approach to harvesting marine resources. Norway believed that the EU would take due account of the scientific basis of Norwegian sealing. The ban was a serious challenge for Norway, which is an important partner of the EU.[53] Norway has also threatened a WTO suit as confirmed by its foreign minister who stated that the government has decided to initiate consultations under the WTO dispute Settlement Understanding to inquire into the legality of the ban.[54]

WTO Regulations on Free Trade

The question is whether a ban on the import of seal products by the EU is inconsistent with the WTO rules. The basic idea of the WTO is trade liberalization by removing unnecessary restrictions in trade. However, there are some exceptions: for example, a restriction can be imposed when it is necessary, but such a restriction should be based on the principle of non-discrimination. The key provisions

---

[52] Statement issued at the 18th Annual Meeting of the North Atlantic Marine Mammal Commission, Tromso, Norway, 10 September 2009, available at http://www.nammco.no/webcronize/images/Nammco/935.pdf (accessed 4 April 2010).

[53] See 'Norway Critical to the EU's Proposed Ban on Trade in Seal Products', available at http://www.eu-norway.org/news/Norway_EU_seal/ (accessed 13 April 2010).

[54] See 'Norway Threatens WTO Suit if EU Bans Seal Imports', available at http://ictsd.org/i/news/bridgesweekly/45449/ (accessed 13 April 2010).

with respect to the EU ban are found in GATT Articles I:1 and III:4, which provide for the principles of 'most favored nation treatment' and 'national treatment' respectively. In addition, Article 2.1 of the TBT agreement is also applicable as it provides for these two principles. Therefore, in this case, whether or not the EU ban discriminates against (or among) foreign products is an important question. As the regulation does not discriminate between 'foreign' or 'imported' products, but rather applies to all seal products regardless of their country of origin, there seems to be apparently no violation of the WTO rules concerning the policy of non-discrimination. The practical consequences of the ban, however, will fall upon the foreign entities, in particular those of Canada and Norway since the import of the seal products from these two countries is significant. It may also be pointed out that the EU has not put a ban on bullfighting or other arguably similar cruel or inhumane practices involving livestock or other animals. As a result, one may argue, the EU has discriminated by not adopting a broad animal welfare regulation. The current regulation focuses only on the narrow sub-category of seal and seal products, which is[55]. Therefore, the EU compliance with the policy of non-discrimination is questionable.

The other overarching issue is the necessity of the ban imposed by the EU. The GATT rules provide for exceptions to trade restriction: for example, its Article XX(a) provides for measures necessary to protect public morals and Article XX (b) provides for measures necessary to protect human, animal, or plant life or health, which may be applicable in the case of the EU ban. However, the EU's arguments on public morals and animal health may be judged by weighing the measure's contribution to animal welfare and its negative impact on trade. The relevant question then might be whether the EU could have adopted alternative measures that could have served its policy goal towards animal welfare and at the same time that might not have impaired free trade.[56] One other argument against the EU ban

---

[55] See for detailed discussions, Simon Lester, 'The WTO Seal Products Dispute: A Preview of the Key Legal Issues', American Society of International Law, *Insights Issue*, 14(2), 2010, available at http://www.asil.org/files/insight100113pdf.pdf (accessed 11 April 2010).

[56] For example, instead of placing the ban, the EU could label seal products to inform consumers about the harms to seals, thus allowing the consumers to make an informed purchasing decision. See ibid.

might be whether an importing WTO member can justify the import ban in response to events occurring outside its own territory. If the WTO were to accept the argument based on EU consumers' moral concerns about seal harvesting practices abroad, then there is room for counteractions from the other WTO members. Their law could then punish imports from countries that do not legally guarantee labour rights based on moral concerns.[57] In addition, Article 2.2 of the TBT agreement is also relevant as far as 'necessity' is concerned. This article provides that the technical regulation shall not be more trade-restrictive than 'necessary' to fulfil the legitimate objective. The trade-restrictive measures on the ground of the protection of animal and environment are included as valid to prove 'necessity' under the TBT Agreement. However, proof as such will have to be grounded on available scientific and technical information. Thus, again, it is questionable whether 'necessity' on the grounds of animal health and environment is strong enough to justify the EU restriction on trade in seal products.[58]

Effect of Ban on the Arctic Indigenous Peoples

The EU ban clearly mentions that the placing on the market of seal products shall be allowed where the products result from hunts traditionally conducted by the Inuit and other indigenous communities and contributes to their subsistence.[59] Apparently, indigenous peoples should not be the aggrieved party in the EU ban on import of seal products. In reality, however, the case is not as clear as it seems. As the indigenous community will eventually be seriously affected by the regulation, they have critically responded to the regulation. The response came from the organizations representing the Inuit people of Canada and Greenland, the Inuit Tapiriit Kanatami (ITK) and the Inuit Circumpolar Council (ICC). The Inuit people have united with these organizations in a lawsuit filed against the EU in the European General Court to overturn the EU legislation.[60] Both Canadian and

---

[57] Ibid.
[58] Ibid.
[59] See Article 3 of the EU Regulation Joseph, 'Human Rights and the WTO: Issues for the Pacific'.
[60] See Joseph, 'Human Rights and the WTO: Issues for the Pacific', operative part, para. 3.

Greenlandic Inuits are taking part in the proceedings.[61] Inuits have been hunting seals for food, clothing, and trade for many generations. They claim that there is no valid conservation or 'humane' harvesting argument to justify the EU ban, despite the fact that the EU ban provides exemptions for seal products resulting from hunts traditionally conducted by the Inuit and other indigenous communities and contributing to their subsistence.[62] According to the Inuit, the exemptions are unclear, flawed, and unfair; and the exemptions will eventually cause economic damage to the Inuit peoples as no distinction can be made between Inuit hunts and other commercial hunts.[63] On the other hand, no indigenous participation was ensured in the making of the decision that directly affects them; and, sadly, the regulation does not reflect the reality of the Inuit commercial harvest, which is both humane and necessary for the survival of the Inuit.[64]

On 13 September 2007, in its Sixty-first Session, the General Assembly of the United Nations overwhelmingly adopted the declaration on the rights of indigenous peoples.[65] The declaration, in addition to the basic human rights, sets out a number of religious, traditional, spiritual, and linguistic rights that are unique to indigenous peoples as distinct from other peoples. However, the declaration does not have any binding force under international law, and, thus, can only be treated as a 'soft law' instrument, which recognizes the rights that the indigenous peoples are entitled to have. Legal protection of human rights is ensured in a number of

---

[61] See 'Inuit Sue European Union (EU) to Overturn Seal Product Import Ban, Defending Inuit Rights and Upholding the Rule of Law', available at http://www.itk.ca/media-centre/media-releases/inuit-sue-european-union-eu-over-turn-seal-product-import-ban-defending-i (accessed 18 April 2010).

[62] Article 3 of the EU Regulation 16 September 2009. See Joseph, 'Human Rights and the WTO: Issues for the Pacific'.

[63] See Joseph, 'Human Rights and the WTO: Issues for the Pacific', operative part, para. 3

[64] Ibid.

[65] The Declaration on Rights of Indigenous Peoples has been termed as 'major steps forward towards human rights for all' by the president of the General Assembly session. The declaration was adopted by a vote of 143 in favour to four against (Australia, Canada, New Zealand, and the USA), with eleven abstentions. See Sixty-first General Assembly Plenary, 107th & 108th meetings (AM & PM), GA/10612, 13 September 2007.

international and regional treaties. The indigenous peoples, as with the other citizens in a state, enjoy civil, political, economic, social, and cultural rights guaranteed in the two international covenants adopted in 1966, the International Covenant on Civil and Political Rights (ICCPR) and the International Covenant on Economic, Social, and Cultural Rights (ICESCR). The covenants have not provided special rights to be accorded to the indigenous peoples. Yet, the ICCPR provided a minority protection article to guarantee the religious, linguistic, and cultural rights of the minorities living in a state.[66] The term 'minority' is not defined in the treaty itself, nor is it defined anywhere in international law. Indigenous peoples mostly comprise small minorities in most of the countries, except in a few countries where they form the majority. Therefore, the 'minority protection' article is applicable to indigenous peoples when they form a minority in a country. The article guarantees their right to practise culture, language, and religion. In addition, it is also argued that indigenous peoples are treated as 'peoples' within the meaning of Article 1 of the ICCPR, and, thus, are entitled also to right to self-determination at least in the sense of resource management implied in Article 1(2) of the covenant. This observation has been confirmed in the interpretation accepted by the Human Rights Committee (HRC)—the body entrusted to monitor the treaty obligation under the covenant. The protection of right to culture under Article 27 and the right to self-determination within the meaning of Article 1(2) when read together strengthens the human rights arguments of indigenous peoples as special and unique as compared to any other minority within a sovereign state. But before discussing how the right to culture of indigenous peoples is protected by international law, it is important to discuss first who indigenous peoples are.

DEFINING INDIGENOUS PEOPLES

The term 'indigenous peoples' is not defined in any international instrument, not even in the Declaration on the Rights of the Indigenous Peoples. The term, however, can be found in the debates of the 1989

---

[66] See Article 27 of the International Covenant on Civil and Political Rights (ICCPR), available at http://www2.ohchr.org/english/law/ccpr.htm (accessed 9 April 2010).

International Labour Organization (ILO) Convention concerning Indigenous and Tribal Peoples in Independent Countries, which entered into force on 5 September 1991.[67] No definition was nonetheless invoked in the convention. It is important also to note that the proposed Organization of American States (OAS)'s declaration on the rights of indigenous peoples, in its Article I(1) provides that the declaration applies to 'indigenous peoples' as well as peoples whose social, cultural, and economic conditions distinguish them from other sections of the national community, and whose status is regulated wholly or partly by their own customs or traditions or by special laws or regulations.[68]

However, the clearest idea of 'indigenous peoples' has been put forward by Jose R. Martinez Cobo, the special rapporteur of the Sub-Commission on Prevention of Discrimination and Protection of Minorities, thus:

> Indigenous communities, peoples and nationals are those which, having a historical continuity with pre-invasion and pre-colonial societies that developed on their territories, consider themselves distinct from other sectors of the societies now prevailing on those territories, or parts of them. They form at present non-dominant sectors of society and are determined to preserve, develop and transmit to future generations their ancestral territories, and their ethnic identity, as the basis of their

[67] Article 1 of the ILO Convention (ILO Convention no. 169) states:
1. This Convention applies to: a) Tribal peoples in independent countries whose social, cultural and economic conditions distinguish them from other sections of the national community, and whose status is regulated wholly or partially by their own customs or traditions or by special laws or regulations; b) Peoples in independent countries who are regarded as indigenous on account of their descent from the populations which inhabited the country, or a geographical region to which the country belongs, at the time of conquest or colonisation or the establishment of present State boundaries and who, irrespective of their legal status, retain some or all of their own social, economic, cultural and political institutions. 2. Self-identification as indigenous or tribal shall be regarded as a fundamental criterion for determining the groups to which the provisions of this Convention apply. See Convention (no. 169) concerning Indigenous and Tribal Peoples in Independent Countries (1989).
available at http://www.unhchr.ch/html/menu3/b/62.htm (accessed 24 January 2010).

[68] See Proposed American Declaration on the Rights of the Indigenous Peoples, Approved on 26 February 1997, available at http://www.cidh.oas.org/Indigenous.htm (accessed 14 April 2010).

continued existence as peoples, in accordance with their own cultural patterns, social institutions and legal system.[69]

In addition, two other definitions are of importance. Special rapporteur Francesco Capotorti suggested the following: 'A group, numerically inferior to the rest of the population of a State, in a non-dominant position, whose members—being nationals of the State—possess ethnic, religious or linguistic characteristics differing from those of the rest of the population and show, if only implicitly, a sense of solidarity, directed towards preserving their culture, traditions, religion or language.'[70] Another definition is provided by Jules Deschenes, special rapporteur to the Commission on Human Rights (Resolution 1984/62):

> A group of citizens of a State, constituting a numerical minority and in a non-dominant position in that State, endowed with ethnic, religious or linguistic characteristics which differ from those of the majority of the population, having a sense of solidarity with one other, motivated, if

[69] See 'The Concept of Indigenous Peoples', A background paper prepared by the Secretariat of the Permanent Forum on Indigenous Issues, 2004, UN PFII/2004WS.1/3, available at http://www.un.org/esa/socdev/unpfii/documents/PFII%202004%20WS.1%203%20Definition.doc (accessed 2 December 2009). See also, 'Study of the Problem of Discrimination against Indigenous populations', Sub-Commission on the Promotion and Protection of Human Rights, UN Doc. E/CN.4/Sub.2/1986/7/Add.4, para. 379. The Cobo definition further continues to mean historical continuity as consisting of the presence of one or more of the following factors: *a*) occupation of ancestral lands, or at least of part of them; *b*) common ancestry with the original occupants of these lands; *c*) culture in general, or in specific manifestations (such as religion, living under a tribal system, membership of an indigenous community, dress, means of livelihood, lifestyle, etc.); *d*) language (whether used as the only language, as mother tongue, as the habitual means of communication at home or in the family, or as the main, preferred, habitual, general, or normal language); *e*) residence on certain parts of the country, or in certain regions of the world; *f*) other relevant factors. On an individual basis, an indigenous person is one who belongs to these indigenous populations through self-identification as indigenous (group consciousness) and is recognized and accepted by these populations as one of its members (acceptance by the group). This preserves for these communities the sovereign right and power to decide who belongs to them, without external interference.

[70] See 'Study on the Rights of Persons belonging to Ethnic, Religious and Linguistic Minorities', Sub-Commission on the Promotion and Protection of human Right, UN Doc. E/CN.4/ Sub.2/384/Rev.1 (1979).

only implicitly, by a collective will to survive and whose aim is to achieve equality with the majority in fact and in law ...[71]

From these discussions an understanding can be derived as to who indigenous peoples are although they are not clearly defined.

Despite the lack of formal definition there has been a steady evolution in the normative development towards a greater recognition of the rights of indigenous peoples, starting with the adoption of the Declaration on the Rights of the Indigenous Peoples. Today it is possible to clearly identify indigenous peoples, even in the absence of any formal definition.

Right to Culture under Article 27

The ICCPR was adopted in 1966. The international political movement to improve the standards of protection for the world's indigenous peoples was not yet up by then. Consequently, there was no reference to 'indigenous peoples' in the ICCPR. Yet, the ICCPR adopted Article 27, which is applicable also to indigenous peoples as already mentioned. The article reads as follows: 'In those States in which ethnic, religious or linguistic minorities exist, persons belonging to such minorities shall not be denied the right, in community with the other members of their group, to enjoy their own culture, to profess and practise their own religion, or to use their own language.'

Culture manifests, among the other things, a different identity and dignity through traditional practices, which indigenous peoples, among the other minorities, possess strongly.[72] In the first stage of

[71] See 'Proposal Concerning a Definition of the Term 'Minority'', Sub-Commission on the Promotion and Protection of human Right', UN Doc. E/CN4./Sub.2/985/31 (1985). For a general treatment, see Eyassu Gayim, 'The Concept of Minority in International Law: A Critical Study of the Vital Elements', *Juridica Lapponica*, 27, Arctic Centre, 2001, p. 14.

[72] Indigenous peoples are also in many instances classified as both minority and indigenous at the same time, although indigenous rights as developed by the inter-governmental organization is far more extensive, stronger and detailed than minority rights. See Rergus MacKay, 'The Rights of Indigenous Peoples in International Law', (Berkeley, 1998), available at http://www.omced.org/cases/case_McKay.pdf (accessed 17 March 2010). See also Bruce Robbins and Elsa Stamatopoulou, 'Reflections on Culture and Cultural Rights', *The South Atlantic*

evolvement of indigenous peoples' rights under the covenant, their rights were specified by the HRC as part of protecting minority culture where they form the minority. Clearly, the HRC viewed that traditional livelihoods were at the heart of protecting the culture of indigenous peoples. This view was earlier adopted by the HRC in 1988 in the *Kitok* case, where the HRC upheld the rights of persons, in community with others, to engage in economic and social activities that are part of the culture of the community to which they belong.[73]

The right to enjoy one's culture within the meaning of Article 27 of the ICCPR has further been clarified by the General Comment,

---

Quarterly, 2(3), 2004, p. 430, where the authors state that indigenous peoples are claiming, among others, the protection for their tangible and intangible cultural heritage and traditional knowledge—for example, the assertion of intellectual property rights to dances, songs, stories, and so on as their cultural rights. Under this heading the indigenous peoples are claiming intellectual property rights over knowledge of any kind that concerns them, knowledge that over the decades has been commercially exploited and occasionally even patented by the private sector.

73 See *Kitok* v. *sweden*, (Communication no. 197/1985), Official Records of the Human Rights Committee 1987/1988, vol. II, 442–45 (New York, United Nations), para. 9.2: 'The regulation of an economic activity is normally a matter for the State alone. However, where that activity is an essential element in the culture of an ethnic community, its application to an individual may fall under Article 27.' See also the *Lubicon Lake Band* case decided in 1990, where the committee found a violation of Article 27 by Canada because it had permitted various economic activities endangering the traditional hunting and fishing by the band. See the case of Bernard Ominayak, *Chief of the Lubicon Lake Band* v. *Canada* (Communication 167/1984). The band invoked Article 1 of the ICCPR that their right under the said article was violated by the state party, but the Human Rights Committee viewed that it was not possible to examine self-determination under Article 1. However, the committee agreed to examine the communication based on Article 27. The wording of Article 1 of the Optional Protocol makes it clear that it is only individuals who can resort to this procedure. Article 1 reads:
    A State Party to the Covenant that becomes a Party to the present Protocol recognizes the competence of the Committee to receive and consider communications from individuals subject to its jurisdiction who claim to be victims of a violation by that State Party of any of the rights set forth in the Covenant. No communication shall be received by the Committee if it concerns a State Party to the Covenant which is not a Party to the present Protocol.
(Optional Protocol to the International Covenant on Civil and Political Rights, entry into force on 23 March 1976). As of 9 June 2004, there were 104 parties to the protocol. Available at http://www.unhchr.ch/html/menu3/b/a_opt.htm (accessed 23 April 2010).

which is meant to systematize the committee's interpretation of specific provisions or aspects of the covenant, adopted by the HRC on Article 27 in 1994. The HRC observed that culture manifests itself in many forms, including a particular way of life associated with the use of land resources, especially in the case of indigenous peoples. That right may include such traditional activities as fishing or hunting, and the right to live in reserves protected by law. The enjoyment of these rights may require positive legal measures of protection and measures to ensure the effective participation of members of minority communities in decisions that affect them.[74] Article 27 places restrictions on the state in the use of traditional land on which indigenous peoples live and with which their traditional livelihoods are associated. The restrictions may be found in two of the communications before the HRC, where Finland was accused by the Sami people to have interfered with reindeer herding. The committee, in the first *Länsman* case decided in 1994, developed a two-part test, the first aspect being procedural (consultation) and the second material (economic sustainability).[75] According to the first part of the test, indigenous peoples need to be meaningfully consulted before the state may permit interference with their traditional livelihood. Second, Article 27 prohibits states not to endanger the practising of traditional livelihood to the extent

---

[74] General Comment no. 23 (50th Session, 1994) by the HRC, UN Doc. HRI/ GEN/1/Rev.3, para. 7. See also the following paragraphs:

3.2. The enjoyment of the rights to which article 27 relates does not prejudice the sovereignty and territorial integrity of a State party. At the same time, one or other aspect of the rights of individuals protected under that article—for example, to enjoy a particular culture—may consist in a way of life which is closely associated with territory and use of its resources. This may particularly be true of members of indigenous communities constituting a minority.

6.1. Although Article 27 is expressed in negative terms, that article, nevertheless, does recognize the existence of a 'right' and requires that it shall not be denied. Consequently, a State party is under an obligation to ensure that the existence and the exercise of this right are protected against their denial or violation. Positive measures of protection are, therefore, required not only against the acts of the State party itself, whether through its legislative, judicial or administrative authorities, but also against the acts of other persons within the State party.

[75] *I. Länsman et al.* v. *Finland* (Communication no. 511/1992), UN Doc. CCPR/ C/57/1, pp. 74–85.

that it would lose its capacity to sustain the members of the community.[76] In the second *Länsman* case decided in 1996, the HRC underlined that when assessing what amounts to a denial of culture, states need to take into account the cumulative effect of activities interfering with the livelihood when assessing whether Article 27 may be breached.[77] The committee also made it clear that the economic well-being of the majority is not a legitimate justification for interfering with the culture of minorities (margin of appreciation) but that it is the sustainability of the indigenous livelihood that is protected by Article 27.

The HRC also took a clear stance on what livelihoods count as part of the culture of indigenous peoples and, thus, protected by Article 27. The HRC stated that the right to enjoy one's culture cannot be determined *in abstracto* but has to be placed in context. The committee observed that Article 27 does not only protect *traditional* means of livelihood of national minorities, as indicated in the state party's submission. The method of traditional practices may have developed over the years, which may now include modern technology. The HRC confirmed that such use of modern technology does not prevent the indigenous peoples from invoking Article 27.[78] Hence, modern ways of practising traditional livelihoods are also protected by Article 27. This view was further made clear by the *Apirana Mahuika* case decided in 2000, where the committee regarded commercial and non-commercial fishing by Maoris—even Maoris' becoming major shareholders in a modern fishing company—as protected by Article 27.[79]

Subsistence Rights under Article 1(2)

Indigenous peoples often argue for their status as 'peoples', and thereby demand the right to self-determination as fundamental. This

[76] Ibid., para. 9.5–9.8.

[77] *J. Länsman et al.* v. *Finland* (Communication no. 671/1995), UN Doc. CCPR/C/58/D/671/1995, para. 10.7. This kind of approach was adopted already in the *Lubicon Lake Band* case by the committee.

[78] See *I. Länsman et al.* v. *Finland* (Communication no. 511/1992), UN Doc. CCPR/C/57/1, 74–85, para. 9.3.

[79] *Apirana Mahuika et al.* v. *New Zealand* (Communication no. 547/1993), UN Doc. A/56/40 (Vol. II): 11–29, para. 9.4.

issue has generated a great deal of debate both in terms of meaning and scope. There is a huge amount of literature on this issue. The question of whether the indigenous peoples form 'peoples' who can claim the right to self-determination under Article 1 of the covenant, although important, is not, however, relevant in the context of this chapter. Suffice it to say that the HRC in its interpretation of Article 1 of the covenant advocates the idea that indigenous peoples are 'peoples' in the sense of resource management of the traditional land on which they live. This accords them the right of internal self-governance as 'peoples',[80] since '[i]n no case may a people be deprived of its own means of subsistence' by virtue of Article 1(2) of the covenant. The idea was reiterated in the Declaration on Rights of Indigenous Peoples. The declaration has accepted the view of internal self-governance with respect to indigenous peoples' traditional and cultural belongings,[81] so that they can maintain and develop their political, economic, and social systems or institutions in order to enjoy their own means of subsistence and development.[82] Also, the right to practise and revitalize their cultural traditions and customs,

[80] Today, it is well established that a people can exercise their self-determination through political participation both as groups and/or individual, for instance, by gaining membership in the state delegation to international treaty participation, if the matters are of interest to the people. See also General Recommendation XXIII of the Committee on Elimination of Racial Discrimination (CERD), (51st Session, 1997) UN Doc. A/52/18, Annex. V, where the committee called on the governments to recognize and protect the rights of indigenous peoples to own, develop, control and use their common lands, territories and resources. The committee also stressed that members of indigenous peoples have equal rights in respect of effective participation in public life and that no decisions directly relating to their rights and interests are taken without their informed consent.

[81] Article 3 of the declaration states that indigenous peoples have right to self-determination, but up to the extent to which they freely determine their political status and freely pursue their economic, social and cultural development. Also in Article 4, the declaration cautiously proclaims that the exercise of self-determination is limited to autonomy or self-government in matters relating to their internal and local affairs, as well as ways and means for financing their autonomous function. See Joseph, 'Human Rights and the WTO: Issues for the Pacific', operative part, para. 3.

[82] See Article 20 (1) of the declaration. See also Article 26, which proclaims that indigenous peoples have the right to own, use, develop, and control the lands, territories, and resources that they possess by reason of traditional ownership or other traditional occupation or use and those otherwise acquired. See ibid.

which includes the right to maintain, protect, and develop the past, present, and future manifestations of their cultures, has been clearly stated in the declaration.[83]

However, it is important to address the protection of traditional cultural rights of indigenous peoples under international law. While reading together the right to enjoy one's culture as a minority under Article 27, and the right to self-governance of the resources belong to 'peoples' under Article 1(2) of the ICCPR, a cultural manifestation of self-determination can be found, which includes a particular way of life associated with the indigenous peoples. This view has also been acknowledged by national governments. For example, Canada acknowledges indigenous peoples' inherent rights to govern themselves in relation to matters that are internal to their communities and integral to their unique cultures, identities, traditions, languages, and institutions, with respect to their special relationship to their land and resources.[84] The concept of such rights is found in both customary and treaty laws, as is suggested from the foregoing discussions. The indigenous peoples are, therefore, protected by law to enjoy the right to natural and cultural resources through traditional activities, and to maintain the traditional way of life including traditional commercial activities. As far as, Article 1 of the ICCPR is concerned, indigenous peoples' effective participation has to be ensured in any decision-making that affects them.[85]

EU Ban Contests Human Rights Aspect of Indigenous Peoples

The EU may have a strong argument that the import ban would not affect seal products from traditional hunts conducted by the indigenous peoples. The regulation clearly articulated this exception applicable to the Inuit and other indigenous peoples. Therefore, the EU, while putting a ban on seal products, has not violated the WTO

---

[83] See Article 11 of the declaration, ibid.

[84] See 'The Government of Canada's Approach to Implementation of the Inherent Right and the Negotiation of Aboriginal Self-Government', available at http://www.ainc-inac.gc.ca/pr/pub/sg/plcy_e.html (accessed 7 November 2008).

[85] See UN Human Rights Committee, General Comment no. 23 on ICCPR Article 27, para. 7.

rules, as the ban has not discriminated between home products and foreign products. Nor has it violated the obligation arising out of international law with respect to the human rights of indigenous peoples. Although this seem to be sufficient grounds to justify the EU action, one may find a loophole, especially where the exception regarding hunts by indigenous peoples is concerned. The EU, whether acted in accordance with the WTO rules or not is yet to see what opinion the Dispute Settlement Panel may come up with.

The exception, however, is unclear since it is difficult to distinguish between seal products obtained from the indigenous peoples and seal products obtained from other commercial suppliers. The regulation provides that the exception would be for hunts that are 'traditionally conducted'—a term that has not been defined in the legislation. Consequently, there is no clear understanding of the methods to be used for hunts that may be regarded as 'traditional', despite the fact that the HRC has concluded any modern usage by the indigenous peoples to be 'traditional' within the meaning of Article 27 of the covenant. Neither has the EU consulted with the indigenous peoples before implementing the ban that significantly affects their subsistence right. By not consulting with the indigenous peoples the EU has undermined the spirit of Article 1(2) of the ICCPR. It is also important to note that the hunting of seals and commercializing of the by-products derived from the hunts are part of the culture traditionally practised by the Inuit and other indigenous peoples in Canada, Greenland, and Norway. Their culture is being undermined as there is a general restriction on marketing seal products in the EU market, causing them economic loss and eventually threatening their subsistence rights.[86]

An import control, however, may be necessary to introduce a better wildlife harvest system. But that has to come through scientific assessment so that the livelihood of indigenous peoples is not threatened.[87] There were no such scientific assessments available before the EU to demonstrate that seals are an endangered species, and that their conservation is important. Moreover, the application of WTO rules relating to animal welfare is uncertain because there has

---

[86] See *Arctic Climate Impact Assessment*, 2005, p. 490.
[87] Ibid., p. 491.

never been a GATT panel to date on any animal welfare issue.[88] The ban, therefore, is contradictory, not only because it challenges the subsistence rights and the right to enjoy the culture guaranteed to the indigenous peoples by virtue of Article 27 and Article 1(2) of the ICCPR, but also because it undermines the normative force enshrined in Principles 12 and 22 of the Rio Declaration,[89] which includes a non-discrimination policy and a consensus-based decision-making in the restriction on trade as well as a recognition of the role of indigenous peoples in environmental management and their effective participation in decision-making.

CONCLUSION

The Arctic indigenous peoples form significant actors in the region. Climate change and its impacts on the region are so drastic that the overall changes are occurring faster in the Arctic than in any other region. The changes are creating opportunities for rapid globalization, which is severely affecting its indigenous population. The survival of the indigenous peoples in the Arctic mostly depends on the unique character of its ecosystem. However, as discussed, the changes in the ecosystem and globalization resulting from such changes are adversely impacting the indigenous peoples of the region. On one

---

[88] See 'Seals and trade rules: can they live together?', available at http://www.rspca.org.uk/ImageLocator/LocateAsset?asset=document&assetId=1232712338227&mode=prd (accessed 8 April 2010).

[89] According to Principle 12 of the Rio Declaration, States should cooperate to promote a supportive and open international economic system that would lead to economic growth and sustainable development in all countries, to better address the problems of environmental degradation. Trade policy measures for environmental purposes should not constitute a means of arbitrary or unjustifiable discrimination or a disguised restriction on international trade. Unilateral actions to deal with environmental challenges outside the jurisdiction of the importing country should be avoided. Environmental measures addressing transboundary or global environmental problems should, as far as possible, be based on an international consensus. Principle 22 suggests that indigenous people and their communities and other local communities have a vital role in environmental management and development because of their knowledge and traditional practices. States should recognize and duly support their identity, culture and interests and enable their effective participation in the achievement of sustainable development. See the Rio Declaration. http://www.unep.org/Documents.Multilingual/Default.asp?DocumentID=78&ArticleID=1163 (accessed 26 April 2010).

hand globalization is adversely affecting their traditional livelihood and culture; and on the other hand they are being deprived of the benefits of globalization that are due to them. They are being marginalized from both sides, and are ultimately suffering from the infringement of the rights guaranteed under international law, in particular under Articles 27 and 1(2) of the ICCPR.

BIBLIOGRAPHY

Books

Anaya, S.J., (1996), *Indigenous Peoples in International Law*, New York and Oxford: Oxford University Press.

Arctic Climate Impact Assessment (2004), *Impacts of a Warming Arctic*, Cambridge: Cambridge University Press.

———— (2005), Cambridge/New York: Cambridge University Press.

Behrendt, L., (1995), *Aboriginal Dispute Resolution: A Step Towards Self-Determination and Community Autonomy*. Sydney: Federation Press.

Davis, S.H.(ed.) (1993), *Indigenous Views of Land and the Environment*, World Bank Discussion Papers 188, Washington DC: The World Bank.

McKarthy, James J., *et al.* (eds) (2001), *Climate Change 2001: Impacts, Adaptation and Vulnerability*, Contribution of Working Group II to the Third Assessment Report of the Intergovernmental Panel on Climate Change, Cambridge: Cambridge University Press.

Nuttal, M., (2002), *Protecting the Arctic Indigenous Peoples and Cultural Survival*, Harwood: Routledge.

Parry, M.L., *et al.*, (eds) (2007), *Climate Change 2007: Impacts, Adaptation and Vulnerability*, Contribution of Working Group II to the Fourth Assessment Report of the Intergovernmental Panel on Climate Change, Cambridge: Cambridge University Press.

Articles in Books and Journals

Carpenter, Brent, 'Warm is the New Cold: Global Warming, Oil, UNCLOS Article 76, and How an Arctic Treaty Might Stop a New Cold War', *Environmental Law Review*, 39, 2009, pp. 215–52.

Gayim, Eyassu, 'The Concept of Minority in International Law: A Critical Study of the Vital Elements', *Juridica Lapponica*, Arctic Centre, 27, 2001.

Hamilton-Smith, Matthew, 'Competing Interests: Canada and Inuit Oppose EU Ban on Seal Products', January 2010, available at http://thebucampus.ca/2010/01/competing-interests-canada-and-inuit-oppose-eu-ban-on-seal-products/ (accessed 15 April 2010).

Heinämäki, L., 'Indigenous Peoples' Right to Traditional Way of Life in Human Rights Law', in *Reforming Mining Law in a Changing World with Special Reference to Finland*, T. Koivurova and A. Stepien (eds) (2008), pp. 41–90, 34, *Juridica Lapponica*.

Henriksen, J. B., 'Oil and Gas Operation in Indigenous Peoples' Lands and Territories in the Arctic: A Human Rights Perspective', *Journal of Indigenous Peoples Rights*, 4, 2006. http://www.galdu.org/govat/doc/oilengelsk2.pdf (accessed 27 April 2010).

Hossain, Kamrul, 'The Human Rights Committee on Traditional Cultural Rights: the Case of the Arctic Indigenous Peoples', in *Global and Local Encounters Norms, Identities and Representations in Formation*, Tuija Veintie and Pirjo Kristiina Virtanen (eds) (2009), pp. 29–42, University of Helsinki: Renvall Institute Publication.

Joseph, Sarah, 'Human Rights and the WTO: Issues for the Pacific', *Victoria University of Wellington Law Review*, 40, 2009, pp. 351–67.

Koivurova, Timo, *et al.*, 'Background Paper Indigenous Peoples in the Arctic', *Arctic Transform*, 2008. http://arctic-transform.org/download/Intro.pdf (accessed 6 April 2010).

Langhelle, Oluf, *et al.*, 'Framing Oil and Gas in the Arctic from a Sustainable Development Perspective', in *Arctic Oil and Gas Sustainability at Risk,* Aslaug Mikkelsen and Oluf Langhelle (eds) (2008), pp. 15–43, London: Routledge.

Lester, Simon, 'The WTO Seal Products Dispute: A Preview of the Key Legal Issues', American Society of International Law, *Insights Issue* 14(2), 2010, http://www.asil.org/files/insight100113pdf.pdf (accessed 11 April 2010).

Lynge, Finn, 'Indigenous Peoples between Human Rights and Environmental Protection—An Arctic Perspective', *Nordic Journal of International Law*, 64, 1995, pp. 489–94.

Matz-Lück, Nele, 'Planting the Flag in Arctic Waters: Russia's Claim to the North Pole', *Göttingen Journal of International Law*, 2 (1), 2009, pp. 235–55.

McIver, Jennifer, 'The Arctic', in *Indigenous Peoples, the Environment and Law*, edited by Lawrence Watters (ed.) (2004), pp. 159–70, Durham, N.C.: Carolina Academic Press.

Robbins, Bruce and Stamatopoulou Eka, 'Reflections on Culture and Cultural Rights', *The South Atlantic Quarterly*, 2 (3), (2004), pp. 419–34.

Scheinin, M., 'The Right to Enjoy a Distinct Culture: Indigenous and Competing Uses of Land', in *The Jurisprudence of Human Rights Law: A Comparative Interpretive Approach,* S. Theodore Orlin and M. Scheinin (eds) (2000), pp. 159–222, Turku/Abo: Åbo Akademi University.

Smith, Samantha, 'Environmental Impacts of Offshore Oil and Gas Development in the Arctic', *WWF International Arctic Programme*, available at http://old.pame.is/sidur/uploads/offshoreoilsndgasWWF.pdf (accessed 23 October 2009).

Ulfstein, G., 'Indigenous Peoples' Right to Land', 8 *Max Planck Yearbook of United Nations Law*, 1, 2004, pp. 1–47.

Young, Oran R. and Einarsson, Niels, 'A Human Development Agenda for the Arctic: Major Findings and Emerging Issues', in *Arctic Human Development Report*, pp. 229–42, Akureyri: Stefansson Arctic Institute, 2004.

Official Documents and Reports

Convention (no. 169) concerning Indigenous and Tribal Peoples in Independent Countries (1989), available at http://www.unhchr.ch/html/menu3/b/62.htm (accessed 24 January 2010).

Declaration on Rights of Indigenous Peoples, Sixty-first General Assembly Plenary, 107th & 108th Meetings (AM & PM), GA/10612, 13 September 2007.

EU Regulation (EC) no. 1007/2009 of the European Parliament and of the Council, L 286/36, 16 September 2009, available at http://ec.europa.eu/food/animal/welfare/trade_seals_products.pdf (accessed 6 April 2010).

EU Directive 83/129/EEC of 18 March 1983, OJ L 91, 9 April1983.

General Recommendation XXIII of the Committee on Elimination of Racial Discrimination (CERD), (Fifty-first Session, 1997) UN Doc. A/52/18, Annex. V.

International Covenant on Civil and Political Rights (ICCPR), available at http://www2.ohchr.org/english/law/ccpr.htm (accessed 09 April 2010).

MacKay, F., (1998), *The Rights of Indigenous Peoples in International Law*, Berkeley, CA, 1998, available at http://www.omced.org/cases/case_McKay.pdf (accessed 21 April 2010).

Marrakesh Agreement Establishing the World Trade Organization, 15 April 1994, 1867 UNTS 3.

Ministerial Declaration, Doha WTO Ministerial 2001, adopted on 14 November 2001, available at http://www.wto.org/english/thewto_e/minist_e/min01_e/mindecl_e.htm (accessed 17 April 2010).

Optional Protocol to the International Covenant on Civil and Political Rights, entry into force on 23 March 1976, available at http://www.unhchr.ch/html/menu3/b/a_opt.htm (accessed 23 April 2010).

Proposed American Declaration on the Rights of the Indigenous Peoples, Approved on 26 February 1997, available at http://www.cidh.oas.org/Indigenous.htm (accessed 14 April 2010).

Proposal Concerning a Definition of the Term 'Minority', Sub-Commission on the Promotion and Protection of human Right, UN Doc. E/CN4./Sub.2/985/31 (1985).

Rio Declaration 1992, available at http://www.unep.org/Documents.Multilingual/Default.asp?DocumentID=78&ArticleID=1163 (accessed 26 April 2010).

Scheinin, M., (2004), 'Indigenous Peoples' Land Rights Under the International Covenant on Civil and Political Rights', Norwegian Centre for Human Rights, available at http://www.galdu.org/govat/doc/ind_peoples_land_rights.pdf (accessed 22 April 2010).

'Study of the Problem of Discrimination against Indigenous Populations, Sub-Commission on the Promotion and Protection of Human Rights', UN Doc. E/CN.4/Sub.2/1986/7/Add.4.

'Study on the Rights of Persons belonging to Ethnic, Religious and Linguistic Minorities', Sub-Commission on the Promotion and Protection of Human Right, UN Doc. E/CN.4/ Sub.2/384/Rev.1 (1979).

'Statement issued at the 18th Annual Meeting of the North Atlantic Marine Mammal Commission', Tromso, 10 September 2009, available at http://www.nammco.no/webcronize/images/Nammco/935.pdf (accessed 4 April 2010).

Online Documents

'Arctic Indigenous Peoples', available at http://www.arcticcentre.org/?Deptid=24486 (accessed 7 April 2010).

'The Concept of Indigenous Peoples', Background Paper prepared by the Secretariat of the Permanent Forum on Indigenous Issues (2004), UN PFII/2004WS.1/3, available at http://www.un.org/esa/socdev/unpfii/documents/PFII%202004%20WS.1%203%20Definition.doc (accessed 2 December 2009).

'The Government of Canada's Approach to Implementation of the Inherent Right and the Negotiation of Aboriginal Self-Government', available at http://www.ainc-inac.gc.ca/pr/pub/sg/plcy_e.html (accessed 7 November 2008).

'Introduction to the Background Papers', *Arctic Transform*, available at http://arctic-transform.org/download/Intro.pdf (accessed 9 April 2010).

'Inuit Sue European Union (EU) to Overturn Seal Product Import Ban, Defending Inuit Rights and Upholding the Rule of Law', available at http://www.itk.ca/media-centre/media-releases/inuit-sue-european-union-eu-overturn-seal-product-import-ban-defending-i (accessed 18 April 2010).

'Norway Critical to the EU's Proposed Ban on Trade in Seal Products', available at http://www.eu-norway.org/news/Norway_EU_seal/ (accessed 13 April 2010).

'Norway Threatens WTO Suit if EU Bans Seal Imports', available at http://ictsd.org/i/news/bridgesweekly/45449/ (accessed 13 April 2010).

'Polar Discovery', available at http://polardiscovery.whoi.edu/arctic/geography.html (accessed 9 April 2010).

'Seals and Trade Rules: Can They Live Together?', available at http://www.rspca.org.uk/ImageLocator/LocateAsset?asset=document&assetId=1232712338227&mode=prd (accessed 8 April 2010).

Communications to the HRC

Apirana Mahuika et al. v. *New Zealand* (Communication no. 547/1993).

Ilmari Lansman et al. v. *Finland*, HRC Communication no 511/1992, available at http://www.bayefsky.com/pdf/116_finland511.pdf (accessed 17 April 2010).

Ivan Kitok v. *Sweden*, Communication no. 197/1985, CCPR/C/33/D/197/1985 (1988), available at http://www1.umn.edu/humanrts/undocs/197-1985.html (accessed 17 April 2010).

Jouni E. Lansman et al. v. *Finland*, HRC Communication no. 671/1995, available at http://www1.umn.edu/humanrts/undocs/html/VWS67158.htm (accessed 17 April 2010).

Lubicon Lake Band v. *Canada*, Communication no. 167/1984 (26 March 1990), UN Doc. Supp. no. 40 (A/45/40) (1990), available at http://www1.umn.edu/humanrts/undocs/session45/167-1984.htm (accessed 17 April 2010).

General Comments of the HRC

General Comment no. 23 (50th Session, 1994) by the HRC, UN Doc. HRI/GEN/1/Rev.3, Human Rights Committee, General Comment 23, Article 27 (Fiftieth session, 1994), Compilation of General Comments and General Recommendations Adopted by Human Rights Treaty Bodies, U.N. Doc. HRI/GEN/1/Rev.1 at 38 (1994), available at http://www1.umn.edu/humanrts/gencomm/hrcom23.htm (accessed 17 April 2010).

General Comment no. 12 (1984) of the Human Rights Committee. Human Rights Committee, General Comment 12, Article 1 (Twenty-first session, 1984), Compilation of General Comments and General Recommendations Adopted by Human Rights Treaty Bodies, UN Doc. HRI/GEN/1/Rev.1 at 12 (1994), available at http://www1.umn.edu/humanrts/gencomm/hrcom12.htm (accessed 17 April 2010).

3

Freedom of Religion in a Globalized World
The European Experience
Edel Hughes

INTRODUCTION

Religious freedom and the toleration of religious diversity have, since the Peace of Westphalia, been considered fundamental tenets of international law.[1] In Europe this is tempered by the fact that it is a region that is also a historically secular one. Since the age of the Enlightenment, religion has, on the whole, been confined to the private sphere[2] and countries such as France and Turkey maintain a

---

[1] The Peace of Westphalia of 1648 ended the Thirty Years War, marking an end to religious warfare and a move towards religious toleration. See generally Derek Croxton and Anuschka Tischer, *The Peace of Westphalia: A Historical Dictionary* (Westport, CT/London: Greenwood Pub. Group, 2001).

[2] On the distinction between the public and private spheres in the context of religion, see Jose Casanova, *Public Religions in the Modern World* (Chicago: The University of Chicago Press, 1994), chapter 2, p. 40. He notes:

> Of all dichotomous pairs of relational terms few are as ambiguous, multivocal, and open to discursive contestation as the private/public distinction. Yet the private/public distinction is crucial to all conceptions of the modern social order and religion itself is intrinsically connected with the modern historical differentiation of private and public spheres. As inaccurate as it may be as an empirical statement, to say that 'religion is a private affair' is nonetheless constitutive of Western modernity in a dual sense. First it points to the fact that religious freedom, in the sense of freedom of conscience, is chronologically 'the first freedom' as well as the precondition of all modern freedoms. Insofar as freedom of conscience is intrinsically related to 'the right to privacy'—to the

strict policy of secularism or laicism. However, in a region that has long associated secularism with 'progress', it is increasingly becoming apparent that Europe is no longer in an age of progressive secularism but rather is included in an era of global 'desecularization,' as sociologists of religion have defined it.[3]

The principal mechanism for the protection of freedom of religion in Europe stems from Article 9 of the European Convention on Human Rights (ECHR). This rather robust provision not only protects the right to freedom of thought, conscience, and religion but also ostensibly provides strong safeguards against interference with the manifestation of religious beliefs (while allowing for certain limitations as imposed by domestic authorities). Nonetheless, this chapter asserts that the supervisory body of the European Convention on Human Rights, the European Court of Human Rights, has failed to adequately protect this right, particularly in cases where the manifestation of the religious belief concerned is Islam. This chapter begins with a brief outline of the current state of religion in Europe and provides an overview of the Article 9 jurisprudence. It will then turn to the question of Islam and the European Court of Human Rights and assess the court's attitude thereto.

RELIGION IN EUROPE: A RESURGENT FORCE?

Although Europe is frequently lauded as a secular region, religion has not always been confined to the private sphere and it is certainly the case that religion maintains a public function in numerous European countries. The constitutions of some European countries are particularly revealing in this regard. The drafting of the *Bunreacht na héireann* (Constitution of Ireland) in 1937, for example, was greatly influenced by Catholic teaching and in fact retained a reference to the 'special position of the Holy Catholic Apostolic and Roman Church as the guardian of the Faith professed by the great majority of the citizens' in

---

modern institutionalization of a private sphere free from governmental intrusion as well as free from ecclesiastical control—and inasmuch as 'the right to privacy' serves as the very foundation of modern liberalism and of modern individualism, then indeed the privatization of religion is essential to modernity.

[3] See, for example, Peter L. Berger (ed.), *The Desecularization of the World: Resurgent Religion and World Politics* (Washington: Ethics and Public Policy Center & Eerdmans Publishing Co., 1999).

Article 44(2) until this section was deleted from the constitution by virtue of the Fifth Amendment of the Constitution Act, 1972. The preamble to the Irish Constitution acknowledges 'all our obligations to our Divine Lord, Jesus Christ, Who sustained our fathers through centuries of trial'. Similarly, the Constitution of Poland, adopted by the National Assembly on 2 April 1997, refers in its preamble to a 'responsibility before God'. Even in countries that are more outwardly secular, where religion has been relegated to the private sphere, its influence can still be seen. As McCrea has suggested, 'many such denominations, most notably the Catholic Church, continue to intervene in political matters and to influence legislation in areas such as the family, abortion and homosexual equality ...'[4]

Recent data from the *European Values Study* also suggests that Europe may not be as secular as we would perhaps have thought. Approximately half of Europeans pray or meditate at least once a week and three out of four Europeans say they are 'religious persons'.[5] While the study reports a gap between the more secular north-western European countries and the more traditional south-western European region, even in Holland, a country renowned for its liberal tradition, one in four people say that they attend church.[6] Coupled with these statistics is the fact that for a purportedly secular region, there are at present a number of debates in Europe with explicitly religious overtones. Issues such as the headscarf dispute in France and the potential accession of Turkey, a majority Muslim country, to the EU means that religious questions are increasingly coming to the fore in Europe. Thus, whilst the process of privatizing religion and confining it to the sphere of civil society may be said to have begun as early as the Protestant Reformations of the sixteenth century,[7] there is evidence to suggest that we are currently in a period of global desecularization, from which Europe is not immune.

---

[4] Ronan McCrea, 'Limitations on Religion in a Liberal Democratic Polity: Christianity and Islam in the Public Order of the European Union', London School of Economics Law, Society and Economy Working Papers, 18, 2007), p. 2.

[5] Results of study available at http://www.europeanvaluesstudy.eu/evs/research/themes/religion/ (accessed 2 October 2009).

[6] Ibid.

[7] Daniel H. Nexon, 'Religion, European Identity, and Political Contention in Historical Perspective', in Timothy Byrnes and Peter Katzenstein (eds), *Religion in an Expanding Europe* (Cambridge: Cambridge University Press, 2006), p. 261.

Despite clear signs that Europe is not as secular as some would proclaim, it is evident that tensions arise when the manifestation of religious belief is not confined to the private sphere. Both domestic case law and that of the ECHR is instructive in this regard. In Germany, for example, the *Teacher Headscarf* case[8] before the German Constitutional Court and in the UK, *R. (on the application of Begum [by her litigation friend, Rahman])* v. *Headteacher and Governors of Denbigh High School*[9] have highlighted this tension. Briefly, the facts of the *Teacher Headscarf* case concerned Fereshta Ludin, a German national of Afghan origin who, on completion of her teacher-training (*Referendariat*) applied for employment in the Civil Service.[10] The state of Baden-Württemberg's Board of Education (*Oberschulamt Stuttgart*), rejected her application on the grounds of a lack of 'personal aptitude' or 'fitness' to carry out the job, which specifically related to her refusal to remove the headscarf whilst teaching. This was due to the fact that the headscarf, the *Oberschulamt* claimed, was not only a religious symbol but also a political manifestation that was incompatible with the principle of state neutrality because of its 'signalling effect' (*Signalwirkung*) and the separation of church and state as provided for in the German Basic Law (*Grundgesetz*).[11] Young children, it was argued, are easily influenced and could be negatively affected by the presence of a headscarf-wearing teacher. Furthermore, forcing impressionable young students to confront Islam would also undermine the objective of integration, notably of Muslim girls.[12]

---

8 BVerfG, 2B v. R 1436/02 of 24 September 2003, available at http://www.bundesverfassungsgericht.de/en/decisions/re20030924_2bvr143602en.html.

9 [2006] UKHL 15.

10 For discussion of case, see Christine Langenfeld and Sarah Mohsen, 'Germany: The Teacher Head Scarf Case', *International Journal of Constitutional Law*, 3(1), 2005, pp. 86–94.

11 The concept of a State Church in Germany was rejected through the incorporation into the *Weimarer Reichsverfassung* (Weimar Reich Constitution) of 11 August 1919 of Article 137 (1), which states 'Es besteht keine Staatskirche' ('There is no State Church'). Article 137 is added as an appendix to the Basic Law (*Grundgesetz*). See Christine R. Barker, 'Church and State Relationships in German "Public Benefit" Law', *The International Journal of Not-for-Profit Law*, 3(2), 2000, available at http://www.icnl.org/KNOWLEDGE/ijnl/vol3iss2/art_1.htm (accessed 3 October 2009).

12 BVerfG, 2B v. R 1436/02 of 24 September 2003, para. 2. See Cindy Skach, 'Religious Freedom—State Neutrality—Public Order—Role of International

Ms Ludin unsuccesfully appealed the decision of the *Oberschulamt* at all three levels of administrative courts in Germany; the Administrative Court (*Verwaltunggsgericht*) of Stuttgart, the Administrative Court (*Verwaltungsgerichtshof*) of Baden-Württemberg, and the Federal Administrative Court (*Bundesverwaltungsgericht*). The Federal Adminsitrative Court denied Ms Ludin's appeal in upholding the Board of Educations's denial of employment to her and also ruled that teachers in public schools must refrain from openly displaying religious symbols in class. The court noted that public school teachers are representatives of the state and must serve as role models for students. The Islamic headscarf was a religious symbol, not simply a cultural tradition; thus, it was asserted that the conflict between the religious freedom of the teacher and the fundamental rights of students and parents could only be adequately resolved by a prohibition of the headscarf.[13]

Having exhausted all lines of appeal before the administrative court system, Ms Ludin lodged a constitutional complaint to the German Constitutional Court (*Bundesverfassungsgericht*). Claiming that she wore the headscarf as a personal symbol rather than a political provocation, Ms Ludin alleged violations of her rights under Articles 1(1) (human dignity), 2(1) (personal freedom), 3(1) (equality before the law), (3) (non-discrimination), 4(1) (freedom of conscience), (2) (right to practise religion), 33(2) (equal citizenship), and (3) (equal access to public office) of the German Basic Law.[14] At the

---

Standards in Interpreting and Implementing Constitutionally Guaranteed Rights [decisions]', *American Journal of International Law*, 100, 2006, pp. 186–96.

13 Decision of 4 July 2002, BverwGE 116, 359. See Christine Langenfeld and Sarah Mohsen, 'Germany: The Teacher Head Scarf Case', *International Journal of Constitutional Law*, 3(1), 2005, p. 87.

14 The relevant articles provide: Article 1(1): 'Human dignity shall be inviolable. To respect and protect it shall be the duty of all state authority.' Article 2(1): 'Every person shall have the right to free development of his personality insofar as he does not violate the rights of others or offend against the constitutional order or the moral law.' Article 3(1): 'All persons shall be equal before the law.' Article 3(3): 'No person shall be favoured or disfavoured because of sex, parentage, race, language, homeland and origin, faith, or religious or political opinions. No person shall be disfavoured because of disability.' Article 4(1): 'Freedom of faith and of conscience, and freedom to profess a religious or philosophical creed, shall be inviolable.' Article 4(2): 'The undisturbed practice of religion shall be guaranteed.' Article 33(2): 'Every German shall be equally eligible for any public office

Constitutional Court, the applicant claimed that her right to act in accordance with her beliefs should be protected; that the Islamic headscarf in itself should not be equated with Islamic fundamentalism; and that the alleged 'signalling effect' of the headscarf was less significant than had been stated by the Board of Education.[15] The Baden-Württemberg Board of Education asserted that regardless of Ms Ludin's motive for wearing the headscarf, the state's principal source of concern was the symbolic meaning and 'signalling effect' of the Islamic scarf itself.[16] The principle of state neutrality as well as increased immigration in Germany obliged the state to be vigilant with respect to all religious matters, and particularly with respect to school children, who, it was claimed, learn through imitation and are at a critical stage of development when entering primary and secondary schools.[17]

On 24 September 2003, by a margin of five to three, the Constitutional Court held that the school board's rejection of Ms Ludin's application was a violation of the Constitution.[18] Crucially though, the court declined to state that the headscarf is not a 'danger', a refusal which Gerstenberg notes, 'has enormous legal and political consequences' and essentially makes the headscarf subject to state regulation. The majority opinion of the court rejected the decision of the school board *solely* on the ground that Baden-Württemberg had no legislation in place at the time that explicitly authorized the board to ban the headscarf because of the danger it represented.[19] It would thus appear that it was the manner in which the decision was reached, rather than the decision itself, which the court found unconstitutional. It has also been asserted that the minority opinion of the court was

---

according to his aptitude, qualifications, and professional achievements.' Article 33(3): 'Neither the enjoyment of civil and political rights, nor eligibility for public office, nor rights acquired in the public service shall be dependent upon religious affiliation. No one may be disadvantaged by reason of adherence or non-adherence to a particular religious denomination or philosophical creed.'

[15] See Skach, 'Religious Freedom—State Neutrality—Public Order', p. 189.

[16] Ibid.

[17] Ibid.

[18] BVerfG, 2BvR 1436/02 of 24 September 2003, available at http://www.bundes-verfassungsgericht.de/en/decisions/re20030924_2bvr143602en.html

[19] Oliver Gerstenberg, 'Germany: Freedom of Conscience in Public Schools', *International Journal of Constitutional Law*, 3(1), 2005, p. 96.

... even more troubling; it said that the school board's decision was the only correct response to Ms. Ludin's claim. According to the dissent, her claim did not even present an issue of freedom of conscience, which would apply at the personal level but not in the 'inner sphere of the state' that the claimant sought to enter—a sphere where private rights are 'functionally limited'. Accordingly the school board did not overstep the bounds of its administrative discretion but, rather, used that discretion in the only way possible. The head scarf, on which Ludin 'uncompromisingly' insisted, would provoke conflict, according to the dissent, and, in particular, ran counter to the state's commitment to gender equality.[20]

The manner in which the German Constitutional Court reached its decision in the case, while ultimately meaning success for the applicant, does not, however, promote confidence in the protection of manifestation of religious belief in Germany. Similarly, in the English case of *R. (on the application of Begum (by her litigation friend, Rahman) v. Headteacher and Governors of Denbigh High School*, the question at issue was whether the applicant's manifestation of her religious belief, by wearing a jilbab to school, which the school uniform policy did not permit, should be protected under Article 9 of the European Convention on Human Rights.[21] The facts of this case have been well documented elsewhere[22] but ultimately Ms Begum's application under Article 9 failed, with the English House of Lords noting with approval the view of the European Court as outlined in *Kalaç v. Turkey*[23] that Article 9 'does not protect every act motivated or inspired by a religion or belief. Moreover, in exercising his freedom to manifest his religion, an individual may need to take his specific situation into account'.[24]

In its consideration of the interference with Ms Begum's rights under Article 9, the court pointed to the efforts of the school in question in formulating its policy on the school uniform, which included

---

[20] Ibid.
[21] The UK incorporated the European Convention on Human Rights into domestic law by virtue of the Human Rights Act 1998. This means that the convention can be directly relied upon in the British domestic courts.
[22] See, for example, Mohammad Mazher Idriss, '*R. (Begum) v. Headteacher and Governors of Denbigh High School*: A Case Note', *Judicial Review*, 10, 2005, pp. 296–302 and 'The Defeat of Shabina Begum in the House of Lords', *Liverpool Law Review*, 27, 2006, pp. 417–36.
[23] Application no. 61/1996/680/870, judgment of 1 July 1997.
[24] Application no. 61/1996/680/870, judgment of 1 July 1997, para. 27.

a working party to consult with imams of the three local mosques and different sections of the school community.[25] This point appeared to be the issue on which the case turned before the House of Lords. As Idriss notes, '[b]ecause great care was taken by the school to create an inclusive uniform policy, their Lordships ruled that the school was fully justified in acting as it did'.[26] This arguably suggests that as long as the lowest common denominator of religious belief is catered for, then schools, or whatever the state institution in question may be, will be considered as fulfilling their duty to uphold freedom of religion.

If a common thread can be drawn from these two illustrative cases, it is that some European countries appear to be invoking illiberal policies in order to maintain the strictly secular status quo. This occurs against the backdrop of clear bans on the public manifestation of religion such as that imposed in France, which was 'intended to send a powerful message to Islamists'.[27] Nonetheless, it is hardly surprising, given the rulings of European Court of Human Rights in cases concerning public manifestation of religious belief.

OVERVIEW OF ARTICLE 9 JURISPRUDENCE

As noted in the Introduction, freedom of religion in Europe is protected by Article 9 of the European Convention on Human Rights. Entitled 'Freedom of Thought, Conscience and Religion', it states:

> 1. Everyone has the right to freedom of thought, conscience and religion; this right includes freedom to change his religion or belief and freedom, either

---

[25] R. (on the application of Begum (by her litigation friend, Rahman)) v. Headteacher and Governors of Denbigh High School, 2006, UKHL 15, para. 7.

[26] Idriss, 'The Defeat of Shabina Begum', p. 426. See also Manisuli Ssenyonjo, 'The Islamic Veil and Freedom of Religion, the Rights to Education and Work: a Survey of Recent International and National Cases', Chinese Journal of International Law, 6(3), 2007, p. 680, noting that '[d]eferring to the school authorities granted to the school an almost unlimited "margin of discretion" thereby enabling the court to avoid the "difficult" jilbab question and its failure to recognize the rights of the most marginalized individuals within minority groups—in this case being the rights of a female Muslim pupil wearing a jilbab at school.'

[27] John R. Bowen, Why the French Don't Like Headscarves: Islam, the State, and Public Space (Princeton and Oxford: Princeton University Press, 2006), p. 243.

alone or in community with others and in public or private, to manifest his religion or belief, in worship, teaching, practice and observance.

Freedom to manifest one's religion or beliefs shall be subject only to such limitations as are prescribed by law and are necessary in a democratic society in the interests of public safety, for the protection of public order, health or morals, or for the protection of the rights and freedoms of others.

It is clear from the wording of paragraph two of the article that the right in question is not an absolute one but rather one that can be subjected to limitations that are 'prescribed by law' and 'necessary in a democratic society' for one of the listed aims. It is also evident from the manner in which Article 9 has been interpreted that the court adopts a deferential attitude towards domestic authorities in the determination of the parameters of this right. This is highlighted by the fact that it was not until 1993, some 35 years after the court commenced operating, that a violation of Article 9 of the convention was found.[28] As commentators have noted, this undoubtedly suggests that '[t]he sensitivity of religious issues has long chilled any ardour that the European Court of Human Rights might have had to address cases involving Article 9'.[29]

In its assessment of cases involving Article 9 of the convention, the European Court considers whether limitations or restrictions on the right exceeded the state's margin of appreciation, which, as the court has stated on numerous occasions, is not unlimited but rather is accompanied by European supervision. It does this by examining whether the interference was prescribed by law; whether it pursued a legitimate aim under Article 9(2); and whether the measures taken were necessary in a democratic society. In the *Kokkinakis* case, the court stressed the importance of the rights protected by Article 9:

As enshrined in Article 9 (art. 9), freedom of thought, conscience and religion is one of the foundations of a 'democratic society' within the meaning of the Convention. It is, in its religious dimension, one of the most vital elements that go to make up the identity of believers and their conception of life, but it is also a precious asset for atheists, agnostics, sceptics and the unconcerned. The pluralism indissociable

---

[28] *Kokkinakis* v. *Greece*, judgment of 23 May 1993, 17 EHRR 397.

[29] Mark W. Janis, Richard S. Kay and Anthony W. Bradley, *European Human Rights Law: Text and Materials*, 3rd edn (Oxford: Oxford University Press, 2008), p. 323.

from a democratic society, which has been dearly won over the centuries, depends on it.[30]

The court in determining the scope of Article 9 has not confined its application to traditional established religions but has used it to offer protection to newer, less mainstream religious organizations also, such as the Church of Scientology (in *Church of Scientology Moscow* v. *Russia*[31]) and Jehovah's Witnesses (in *Manoussakis* v. *Greece*[32]). Additionally, the term 'beliefs' in the text of Article 9 has been afforded broad interpretation, with opposition to abortion (*Knudsen* v. *Norway*[33]), veganism, and pacifism all being held to come within the ambit of Article 9 (in *H.* v. *UK*[34] and *Arrowsmith* v. *UK*[35] respectively). Indeed, as Harris *et al.* have noted, rulings suggest that even political ideals as controversial as fascism, communism, and neo-Nazi principles could amount to 'beliefs' for the purposes of Article 9.[36] The purpose of applying such a broad interpretation of Article 9 is to avoid 'any determination of what is meant by the term 'religion'. This approach is understandable, because any definition of 'religion' would need to be flexible enough to satisfy a broad cross-section of world faiths, as well as sufficiently precise for practical application in specific cases. Such a balance would be practically impossible to strike …[37]

Nonetheless, not all 'beliefs' are afforded protection under Article 9. In *Pretty* v. *UK*[38], the court noted that 'not all opinions or convictions constitute beliefs in the sense protected by Article 9 § 1 of the convention' while 'the term "practice" as employed in Article 9 § 1 does not cover each act which is motivated or influenced by a religion or belief …'[39] The practice of the court in extending the

---

[30] *Kokkinakis* v. *Greece*, judgment of 23 May 1993, 17 EHRR 397, para. 31.

[31] Application no. 18147/02, judgment of 5 April 2007.

[32] Application no. 59/1995/565/651, judgment of 26 September 1996.

[33] Application no. 11045/84, admissibility decision of 8 March 1985.

[34] Application no. 18197/91, decision of 1993.

[35] Application no. 7050/75, admissibility decision of 16 May 1977.

[36] David J. Harris, Michael O'Boyle, Ed P. Bates, and Carla M Buckley, *Harris, O'Boyle & Warbrick Law of the European Convention on Human Rights*, 2nd edn (Oxford: Oxford University Press, 2009).

[37] Ibid., p. 426.

[38] Application no. 2346/02, judgment of 29 April 2002.

[39] *Pretty* v. *UK*, Application no. 2346/02, judgment of 29 April 2002, § 82.

protection of Article 9 to a broad group of beliefs and organizations is undoubtedly laudable. This protection is not, however, as apparent when it comes to the court's assessment of manifestation of religious belief, although it is more likely to extend protection to manifestations of religious belief that are carried out in private.[40] As such, this highlights the court's distinction between the 'internal' and 'external' aspects of the protection afforded in Article 9. The 'internal' aspect consists of the freedom to believe, including the freedom to choose beliefs and to change religion/beliefs and is given absolute protection, whereas the 'external' dimension of the article encompasses the freedom to act according to the religion/belief and 'is by its very nature *relative*'.[41] As Martìnez-Torrón has outlined: 'Article 9(2) clearly states that the limitations specified therein may be applied only to the '[f]reedom to manifest one's religion or beliefs'. Freedom to believe, on the contrary, may not be restricted, probably not even in the exceptional circumstances that, according to Article 15, permit the states to derogate some of their obligations under the ECHR.'[42]

Overall, whilst the increasing willingness of the court to engage with Article 9 is to be welcomed, problems undoubtedly remain. Ovey and White assert that while most commentators would agree with the court's view that governments should work to promote pluralism and tolerance in situations of religious tension and therefore be allowed a wide margin of appreciation to place restrictions on the freedom to manifest religion or belief,

> ... it is the more mundane cases—the teacher who wishes to wear the Islamic headscarf to school, the children whose Jehovah's Witness parents do not wish them to attend a militaristic parade —that the Court has demonstrated a certain lack of empathy for the believer, and has appeared only to pay lip-service to the commitment to religious freedom proclaimed in such judgments as *Kokkinakis v. Greece*.[43]

---

40 See Kathleen Cavanaugh, 'Islam and the European Project', (2007) *Muslim World Journal of Human Rights*, 4(1), p. 12.

41 Javier Martìnez-Torrón, 'Limitations on Religious Freedom in the Case Law of the European Court of Human Rights', *Emory International Law Review*, 19, 2005, p. 590.

42 Ibid.

43 Clare Ovey and Robin C. A. White, *The European Convention on Human Rights*, 4th edn (Oxford: Oxford University Press, 2006), p. 316.

EUROPEAN COURT OF HUMAN RIGHTS AND THE QUESTION OF ISLAM

The protection afforded by Article 9 is clearly limited by the scope of its application and the fact that states are afforded a wide margin of appreciation in its interpretation, provided they comply with the principle of state neutrality, has been confirmed by the Court in numerous cases.[44] The Islamic headscarf (or hijab) is perhaps the most readily identifiable visual symbol of religion in the public sphere and the European Court has been called on to adjudicate in issues concerning the headscarf in a number of cases. Prior to the seminal case of *Leyla Şahin* v. *Turkey*,[45] the Strasburg machinery had considered the headscarf in the admissibility decisions in *Karaduman* v. *Turkey*[46] and *Dahlab* v. *Switzerland*,[47] both of which were declared inadmissible. The first substantive evaluation of the headscarf as a manifestation of religious belief did not, therefore, come until the *Şahin* case and in which the court appeared to broaden its consideration of the reasons for which an arguably illiberal secularist agenda may be pursued by contracting states. While the facts of the case have been outlined at length elsewhere,[48] the *Şahin* decision undoubtedly sees the court move to rather paternalistic territory in which the headscarf is proffered as a powerful symbol, which women may feel obliged to wear. Although this aspect of the judgment is couched in the language of gender equality, the decision of the court

---

[44] See, for example, *Hasan and Chaush* v. *Bulgaria*, Application no. 30985/96, judgment of 26 October 2006, para. 63, confirming the seriousness with which the court treats attempts by the state to interfere in the running of mainstream religious organizations, noting 'the believer's right to freedom of religion encompasses the expectation that the community will be allowed to function peacefully free from arbitrary state intervention ...' See also *Holy Synod of the Bulgarian Orthodox Church (Metropolitan Inokentiy) and Others* v. *Bulgaria*, Application nos 412/03 and 35677/04, judgment of 22 January 2009.

[45] Application no. 44774/98, judgment of 10 November 2005.

[46] Application no. 16278/90, admissibility decision of 3 May 1993.

[47] Application no. 42393/98, admissibility decision of 15 February 2001.

[48] See Benjamin D. Bleiberg, 'Unveiling the Real Issue: Evaluating the European Court of Human Rights' Decision to Enforce the Turkish Headscarf Ban in *Leyla Şahin* v. *Turkey*', (2005–2006) *Cornell Law Review*, 91, 2005–2006, pp. 129–70 and Anastasia Vakulenko, '"Islamic Headscarves" and the European Convention on Human Rights: An Intersectional Perspective', *Social & Legal Studies*, 16(2), 2007, pp. 183–199.

undoubtedly gives credence to the increasing tendency of states to ban religious symbols in the public sphere, thereby encroaching on religious freedoms. Whilst this is a regrettable trend, perhaps of greater concern is the assessment of Islam given by the court in the case of *Refah Partisi (The Welfare Party) and Others* v. *Turkey*[49]. The applicants in the case alleged that the dissolution of *Refah Partisi*, overseen by the Turkish Constitutional Court, and the order preventing its leaders, including Necmettin Erbakan, Şevket Kazan, and Ahmet Tekdal, from holding similar office in any other political party had infringed their right to freedom of association established in Article 11 of the ECHR.[50]

In its examination of the *Refah* case the court first assessed whether or not there was an interference with the rights of Refah Partisi under Article 11 of the convention. It concluded that there was, in fact, an interference with the applicants' right to freedom of association.[51] The court then looked at whether this interference could be justified by looking in turn at whether it was 'prescribed by law', whether it served a 'legitimate aim', and whether the interference was 'necessary in a democratic society'.[52] In its assessment of the first element—whether the interference was 'prescribed by law'—the court noted that Article 69 of the Turkish Constitution gave the Constitutional Court sole discretion in the issue of dissolution of political parties and the measures imposed by the Constitutional Court were based on Sections

---

[49] Application no. 41340/98 & 41342-4/98, judgment of 13 February 2003. The case was taken by four applicants; Refah Partisi, Necmettin Erbakan, the chairman of Refah Partisi, Şevket Kazan, a vice chairman of Refah and Ahmet Tekdal, also a vice chairman of Refah.

[50] *Refah Partisi and Others* v. *Turkey,* Application ns. 41340/98 & 41342–44/98, judgment of 13 February 2003, para. 49. Article 11 of the convention provides: 1. Everyone has the right to freedom of peaceful assembly and to freedom of association with others, including the right to form and to join trade unions for the protection of his interests. 2. No restrictions shall be placed on the exercise of these rights other than such as are prescribed by law and are necessary in a democratic society in the interests of national security or public safety, for the prevention of disorder or crime, for the protection of health or morals or for the protection of the rights and freedoms of others. This article shall not prevent the imposition of lawful restrictions on the exercise of these rights by members of the armed forces, of the police or of the administration of the State.

[51] Ibid., para. 50.

[52] Ibid., para. 51.

101 and 107 of Law no. 2820 on the Regulation of Political Parties, as well as Articles 68, 69, and 84 of the Constitution of Turkey.[53] The provisions in question were accessible to the applicants and given the status of Refah as a large political party with legal advisors familiar with constitutional law and the rules applicable to political parties, the applicants were reasonably able to foresee that they ran the risk of dissolution of the party if they or the party's members engaged in anti-secular activities.[54] The interference was therefore prescribed by law.

Regarding whether the interference served a legitimate aim, the Turkish government asserted that it pursued several, namely the protection of public safety, national security, the rights and freedoms of others, and the prevention of crime.[55] The applicants argued, however, that the real reason for Refah's dissolution was that its economic policy, which included reducing the national debt to zero, would threaten the interests of major businesses and the military.[56] With a 'notably brief analysis',[57] the European Court concluded that the applicants had not presented sufficient evidence to suggest that Refah had been dissolved for reasons other than those cited by the Constitutional Court and, having taken into account 'the importance of the principle of secularism for the democratic system in Turkey', agreed with the position advanced by the government and concluded that Refah's dissolution pursued several of the legitimate aims listed in Article 11.[58]

Having regard to whether the interference was 'necessary in a democratic society', the applicants submitted a number of arguments. In the first instance, they argued that the speeches advancing political Islam had been made several years prior to the institution of dissolution proceedings and therefore Refah could not be said to constitute a threat to secularism and democracy in Turkey at the

---

[53] Ibid., paras 56, 59.
[54] Ibid., para. 62, 63.
[55] Ibid., para. 65.
[56] Ibid., para. 66.
[57] David Schilling, 'European Islamaphobia and Turkey—*Refah Partisi (The Welfare Party)* v. *Turkey*', *Loyola Los Angeles International & Comparative Law Review*, 26, 2003–04, p. 510.
[58] *Refah Partisi and Others* v. *Turkey*, application no. 41340/98 & 41342–44/98, judgment of 13 February 2003, para. 67. The aims included protection of national security and public safety, prevention of disorder or crime and protection of the rights and freedoms of others.

time of the proceedings.[59] In its thirteen-year existence it had taken on many responsibilities of the local and Central Governments and, accordingly in coming to its decision, the court should assess all of the factors that had led to the decision to dissolve the party and all of the party's activities since it had come into existence.[60] The applicants also pointed to the fact that during the year in which it was in power (from June 1996 to July 1997), it made no attempt to introduce legislation that would facilitate a regime based on Islamic law.[61] Furthermore, Refah had expelled the members who had made the inflammatory statements and Erbakan's comments, when read in context, contained no apologia for violence; nor did Refah's constitution or programme make any reference to either sharia or Islam.[62] The sanctioning of the dissolution of Refah, the imposition of restrictions on the political activities of its members, and the financial losses the party would suffer as a result would, the applicants argued, constitute an interference which was disproportionate to the legitimate aims pursued.[63]

The Turkish government refuted the applicants' arguments by alleging that had Refah been the sole party in power in the government, it 'would have been quite capable of implementing its policy and thus putting an end to democracy'.[64] A number of other arguments were advanced, including the assertion that certain aspects of the party's activities and speeches indicated that the party would in fact seek to introduce sharia if it held power; would introduce a plurality of legal systems based on religious affiliation; and would 'do away with' the principle of secularism altogether.[65] Also, the government alleged that some members of *Refah* advocated the use of violence in order to resist certain government policies or to gain power, constituting incitement to a popular uprising.[66]

The court reaffirmed that the freedom of thought, conscience, and religion, protected by Article 9 of the convention, is one of the

---

[59] Ibid., para. 68.
[60] Ibid., para. 69.
[61] Ibid., para. 71.
[62] Ibid., para. 71, 73.
[63] Ibid., para. 77.
[64] Ibid., para. 78.
[65] Ibid., paras 81, 83.
[66] Ibid., para. 84.

foundations of a 'democratic society' within the meaning of the convention.[67] Nevertheless, it noted that the principle of secularism is
'one of the fundamental principles of the State which are in harmony
with the rule of law and respect for human rights and democracy'[68]
and justified the dissolution of Refah as being within the power of
preventive intervention on the part of the state and as being consistent
with a state's positive obligations under Article 1 of the convention to
secure the rights and freedoms of persons within their jurisdiction.[69]
Furthermore, the dissolution of Refah was deemed to have met the
'pressing social need' of averting the danger to democracy, which *Refah*
allegedly held, and accordingly the decision to dissolve the party was
a proportionate response to the legitimate aim of upholding democracy and the principles of secularism.[70] In agreeing with the decision
of the Turkish Constitutional Court, the ECHR, Koğacioğlu contends, followed 'the logic of collapsing unity, democracy and progress'
employed by the domestic Court, which had indicated that Refah
was a 'political representation of the general Islamist threat':[71]

> The root of the Islamist threat was in its being backward-looking,
> threatening to steer Turkey away from the road of progress. According
> to the Court, the major threat Refah represented was to the laicism
> principle of the constitution. At the hands of the Court, laicism became
> not merely the tenet of separation of religious and governmental spheres,
> or even of state control over religion, but also a crucial embodiment of
> the idea of progress. In turn, laicism functioned as a means of enhancing
> national unity.[72]

A number of concerns can be raised about the European Court's
reasoning in the *Refah* case. Among these are the fact the court paid
no attention to the constitution of Refah Partisi, which made no
reference to either sharia or Islamic law forming the basis of the
Turkish system; and also the contention that even if the proposals of
Refah were inconsistent with the principle of secularism set out in

---

[67] *Refah Partisi and Others* v. *Turkey*, application no. 41340/98 & 41342-4/98,
judgment of 13 February 2003, para. 90.

[68] Ibid., para. 93.

[69] Ibid., para. 103.

[70] Ibid., paras 132, 135.

[71] Dicle Koğacioğlu, 'Progress, Unity, and Democracy: Dissolving Political Parties
in Turkey', *Law & Society Review*, 38(3), p. 454.

[72] Ibid., p. 455.

the Turkish Constitution, the European Court should refrain from being 'the judge of secularism' and concentrate instead on ensuring the freedom to associate and publicly debate ideas, as provided for in Article 11.[73] Schilling further asserts that the court added two additional obstacles to its consideration of Refah's arguments that were not present in previous dissolution cases, namely, the likelihood that Refah would have been successful in its attempts to impose its own programme were it to achieve an overall majority as opposed to functioning within a coalition government and the assumption that Refah's leaders knew the risk associated with their conduct.[74] The court also took it upon itself to pronounce on the suitability of sharia as a legal system, which it found to be incompatible with the fundamental principles of democracy as set forth in the convention:

> Like the Constitutional Court, the Court considers that sharia, which faithfully reflects the dogmas and divine rules laid down by religion, is stable and invariable. Principles such as pluralism in the political sphere or the constant evolution of public freedoms have no place in it. The Court notes that, when read together, the offending statements, which contain explicit references to the introduction of sharia, are difficult to reconcile with the fundamental principles of democracy, as conceived in the Convention taken as a whole. It is difficult to declare one's respect for democracy and human rights while at the same time supporting a regime based on sharia, which clearly diverges from Convention values, particularly with regard to its criminal law and criminal procedure, its rules on the legal status of women and the way it intervenes in all spheres of private and public life in accordance with religious precepts ... In the Court's view, a political party whose actions seem to be aimed at introducing sharia in a State party to the Convention can hardly be regarded as an association complying with the democratic ideal that underlies the whole of the Convention.[75]

Boyle has noted in this regard that the

> ... stridency of the European Court's assessment of Islamic law and shariah is regrettable. In effect the Court seems to say that shariah, *tout court*, is incompatible with universal rights, or at least European ideas

---

[73] Schilling, 'European Islamaphobia and Turkey', pp. 511–12.

[74] Ibid., p. 513.

[75] *Refah Partisi and Others* v. *Turkey*, application no. 41340/98 & 41342–44/98, judgment of 13 February 2003, para. 123.

of democracy and rights ... the judgment represents an unsympathetic dismissal of what is a central element of a 1400-year-old civilization, comprising today the cultures of in excess of a billion people, and the religion of at least 100 million Muslims in the Council of Europe countries. The Court makes no effort, in its thinking or language, to separate the vast majority of Muslim people and their religious practices from extremists.[76]

CONCLUSION

Thus, despite the importance the court purports to attach to democracy, the decision in the *Refah* case to uphold the dissolution of an elected party in government that, it is suggested, 'did not challenge democracy as such, but rather sought to question an ideology imbued in the institutions of the State and enforced by the Turkish military'[77] arguably serves not only to undermine democracy itself, but also the court in its assessment of a religion with over 100 million followers within its jurisdiction. The foregoing cursory examination of case laws emanating from both domestic courts and the ECHR would suggest that the protection of the manifestation of religious beliefs in Europe is not as strong as might be expected. This is despite the fact that Europe, although largely a secular region, has not been immune to the global resurgence in religion over the past decade. Whether Europe's adjudicatory bodies evolve to reflect this reality remains to be seen.

BIBLIOGRAPHY

Books

Berger, Peter L. (ed.) (1999), *The Desecularization of the World: Resurgent Religion and World Politics*, Washington: Ethics and Public Policy Center & Eerdmans Publishing Co.

Bowen, John R., (2006), *Why the French Don't Like Headscarves: Islam, the State, and Public Space*, Princeton and Oxford: Princeton University Press.

[76] Kevin Boyle, 'Human Rights, Religion and Democracy: The Refah Party Case', *Essex Human Rights Review*, 1(1), 2004, p. 12.

[77] Ibid.

Byrnes, Timothy A. and Peter Katzenstein (eds) (2006), *Religion in an Expanding Europe*, Cambridge: Cambridge University Press.

Casanova, Jose, (1994), *Public Religions in the Modern World*, Chicago: University of Chicago Press.

Croxton, Derek and Anuschka Tischer, (2001), *The Peace of Westphalia: A Historical Dictionary*, Westport, CT/London: Greenwood Pub. Group.

Ovey, Clare and C.A. Robin White (2006), *The European Convention on Human Rights* (4th edn), Oxford: Oxford University Press.

Articles in Books and Journals

Barker, Christine R. 'Church and State Relationships in German "Public Benefit" Law', *The International Journal of Not-for-Profit Law*, 3(2), 2000.

Bleiberg, Benjamin D., 'Unveiling the Real Issue: Evaluating the European Court of Human Rights' Decision to Enforce the Turkish Headscarf Ban in *Leyla Şahin* v. *Turkey*', Cornell Law Review, 91 (2005–2006), pp. 129–70.

Boyle, Kevin, 'Human Rights, Religion and Democracy: The Refah Party Case', *Essex Human Rights Review*, 1(1), 2004, pp. 1–16.

Cavanaugh, Kathleen, 'Islam and the European Project', *Muslim World Journal of Human Rights*, 4(1), 2007, pp. 1–20.

Gerstenberg, Oliver, 'Germany: Freedom of Conscience in Public Schools', *International Journal of Constitutional Law*, 3(1), 2005, pp. 94–106.

Harris, David J., Michael O'Boyle, Ed P. Bates, and Carla M. Buckley, (2009), *Harris, O'Boyle & Warbrick Law of the European Convention on Human Rights* (2nd edn), Oxford: Oxford University Press.

Idriss, Mohammad Mazher, '*R (Begum)* v. *Headteacher and Governors of Denbigh High School*: A Case Note', *Judicial Review*, 10 (2005), pp. 296–302.

Idriss, Mohammad Mazher, 'The Defeat of Shabina Begum in the House of Lords', *Liverpool Law Review*, 27 (2006), pp. 417–36.

Janis, Mark W., Richard S. Kay and Anthony W. Bradley, (2008), *European Human Rights Law: Text and Materials* (3rd edn), Oxford: Oxford University Press.

Koğacioğlu, Dicle, 'Progress, Unity, and Democracy: Dissolving Political Parties in Turkey', *Law & Society Review*, 38(3), 2004, pp. 433–62.

Langenfeld, Christine and Sarah Mohsen, 'Germany: The Teacher Head Scarf Case', *International Journal of Constitutional Law*, 3(1), 2005, pp. 86–94.

Martìnez-Torrón, Javier, 'Limitations on Religious Freedom in the Case Law of the European Court of Human Rights', *Emory International Law Review*, 19, 2005, pp. 587–636.

McCrea, Ronan, 'Limitations on Religion in a Liberal Democratic Polity: Christianity and Islam in the Public Order of the European Union', London School of Economics Law, Society and Economy Working Papers (18/2007).

Schilling, David, 'European Islamaphobia and Turkey—*Refah Partisi* (*The Welfare Party*) v. *Turkey*', *Loyola Los Angeles International & Comparative Law Review*, 26, 2003–2004, pp. 501–15.

Skach, Cindy, 'Religious Freedom—State Neutrality—Public Order—Role of International Standards in Interpreting and Implementing Constitutionally Guaranteed Rights [Decisions]', *American Journal of International Law*, 100, 2006, pp. 186–96.

Ssenyonjo, Manisuli, 'The Islamic Veil and Freedom of Religion, the Rights to Education and Work: a Survey of Recent International and National Cases', *Chinese Journal of International Law*, 6(3), 2007, pp. 653–710.

Vakulenko, Anastasia, '"Islamic Headscarves" and the European Convention on Human Rights: An Intersectional Perspective', *Social & Legal Studies*, 16(2), 2007, pp. 183–99.Freedom of Religion in a Globalized World

4

Globalization, Terrorism, and Human Rights
The Mouse that Roared
Edwin Tanner

INTRODUCTION

Since the terrible attacks of 11 September 2001, the governments of the 'Coalition of the Willing' have told their citizens that global terrorism is new and represents a major security threat to all liberal democracies. Indeed, following the Bali bombing in Indonesia, the Australian government issued its citizens with kits in preparation for further attacks. They were told to 'be alert but not alarmed'. As the years have passed, little attempt has been made to reconsider and reprioritize security threats. Conducting the 'war on terrorism', and capturing, detaining and interrogating 'suspected terrorists', whether they are global, local, rural or urban, have become ends in themselves. This has resulted in serious violations of human rights for citizens, suspected terrorists, and the civilian populations of Afghanistan and Iraq. Many critics of these wars, and the 'war on terrorism' in general, have been asking how best to recast foreign policy so that the protection of human rights is regarded as central and indispensable.

It comes as some surprise then, that nearly eight years after the September 11 attacks, the Australian government is about to expunge the phrase 'war on terrorism' from its official lexicon. In announcing this change, the attorney general, Robert McClelland, stated:

'Experience has shown that the language used to describe terrorism can be counter-productive .... Certain words have the potential to glorify terrorism and terrorists, while others can cause anxiety among Australians and create divisions within and between them.'[1] For that reason, the attorney general[2] suggested that words or phrases like 'jihad', 'Islamic extremists', 'the war on terror', 'the global war on terror', or, more simply, 'the war on terrorism', are to be eschewed. The attorney general stated: 'We need to use language that does not inadvertently glorify terrorism, but rather describes it in terms of base criminal behaviour of the most reprehensible kind.'

Several issues arise from these statements. They include: Have the forces of globalization changed the nature of terrorism? Is there a specific type of terrorism that can be attributable to those forces? Has the so-called war on terror since September 11, resulted in an increase or diminution of human rights? What can be done to reinstate human rights as a central issue guiding foreign policy? Before these questions can be answered, it is necessary to illuminate the term 'globalization' and provide a timeline for the development of human rights.

ILLUMINATING THE TERM 'GLOBALIZATION'

Confusion has been produced by the term 'globalization'. There are those who regard it as generating a narrow nationalism. To others it means an increase in the cultural imperialism of the great powers, in particular the USA. To those who believe in free trade it means that world markets would be liberated, with the result that those in power will have less ability to impose their will on the less able. To some supporters of local economies, it has led to a fear of world control by corporate capitalism.[3]

Donald Horne[4] has argued that the problem with the term 'globalization' is that it is sometimes regarded as synonymous with the term 'free market'. The free market has been regarded as invulnerable and, therefore, not requiring regulation. Indeed, regulation has been

---

[1] Reported by Stephanie Peatling in 'Canberra Declares War on the Language of Terrorism', *The Age*, 7 July 2009, News Section, p. 3.

[2] Ibid.

[3] Barack Obama, *The Audacity of Hope* (Melbourne: The Text Publishing Company, 2006–09), p. 305.

[4] Donald Horne, *Looking for Leadership: Australia in the Howard Years* (Ringwood Victoria: Viking Penguin Books Australia Ltd, 2001), p. 39.

seen as intervention that is highly undesirable. By definition, the free market has become sacrosanct, and profit-making an end in itself.

Unfettered free-market capitalism has led to the current international financial worldwide crisis. To avoid their liquidation, corporations have been supported by huge government handouts; banks have been nationalized; individuals have lost their jobs and life savings, and the potential of a worldwide depression, not recession, has occurred. If that is what unfettered free-market capitalism can lead to, then unfettered globalization can lead to environmental catastrophe, the weakening of employment rights, and excessive tax evasion.[5]

For the purposes of this chapter, the meaning of the term 'globalization' has been confined to the process which makes use of technology to facilitate communications and transportation. As a result, freer movement within nations and across their borders becomes possible for people, goods, money, technology, ideas, and cultures.[6]

HUMAN RIGHTS AFTER THE SECOND WORLD WAR

Before the Second World War, the treatment of citizens was the concern of their respective governments. It was not the business of other governments or the international community. The Holocaust changed this attitude because it impacted on the conscience of people worldwide. This resulted in the USA demanding, despite Winston Churchill's objections, that Nazi leaders be shown due process and tried in a formal court setting. The result was the creation of the new crime, 'crimes against humanity'. This crime involved serious offences against civilian populations. These offences could be characterized by the effect they had on the whole of humanity and not just on the people who were directly affected by them. A concomitant was that persons who committed such crimes were liable to the jurisdiction of courts in any country and not just those where the crimes were committed or the victims found. Effectively, this extended the idea of universal criminal jurisdiction that had, until then, applied only to the crime of piracy. Universal jurisdiction was included in

---

[5] Ibid., p. 39.
[6] David Kilcullen, *The Accidental Gorilla* (Carlton/Victoria: Scribe Publications, 2009), p. 8.

the Geneva Conventions of 1949. In 1973, it was given to all the national courts for the crime of apartheid. In the Torture Convention of 1984, apartheid was included as a 'crime against humanity'.[7]

To combat terrorism, universal jurisdiction was conferred on all courts by a series of international conventions entered into in the 1970s. The 1948 Genocide Convention had not provided for universal jurisdiction. Rather, that convention assumed that genocide would be dealt with by an independent international criminal court. Initially, such an independent international criminal court was not established. Nevertheless, customary international law came to recognize universal jurisdiction for the crime of genocide.

With the end of the Cold War, the USA became the dominant world power. It was in a position to facilitate and encourage the restructuring of the United Nations as an institution charged with the promotion of international justice. However, following September 11, the USA failed to take a humanitarian leadership role, and it significantly contributed to an international climate of fear. By talking about the war against terrorism or the war on terror, it elevated terrorism to the status of the pre-eminent security threat and contributed significantly to a serious erosion of human rights. As part of the strategy for this 'war', it refused to recognize the International Criminal Court (ICC). It did this because it feared that members of the US military might be charged with war crimes. The USA also played a negative role, until recently, in its opposition to the Kyoto Protocol on Global Warming, and the Protocol to the Torture Convention that sought to make goals subject to international inspection.

In the last ten years or so, several nations, especially those of Western Europe, have conferred universal jurisdiction on their domestic courts for genocide and other serious war crimes. This trend culminated in the Rome Statute, which created the ICC. The Rome Statute came into force in 2002, some 60 days after it had been ratified by 60 nations. The ICC provided a system for the adjudication of violations of humanitarian law. It has jurisdiction over genocide, war crimes, and crimes against humanity. Its jurisdiction arises when national court systems have not dealt with these crimes adequately.

---

[7] Richard Goldstone, 'The Tension between Combating Terrorism and Protecting Civil Liberties', in *Human Rights in the 'War on Terror'*, Richard A. Wilson (ed.) (New York: Cambridge University Press, 2005), p. 158.

The ICC attributes criminal responsibility both to individuals who are responsible for planning military action that violates international humanitarian law, and to those who carry it out. It specifically extends criminal liability to heads of state, government leaders, government officials, and military personnel.[8] As part of its involvement in the creation and implementation of the ICC, Australia has introduced into its own domestic law a series of offences that closely reflect the offences over which the ICC has jurisdiction.[9]

As discussions were being undertaken for the creation and implementation of the ICC, the United Nations Security Council established individual criminal tribunals for Yugoslavia and Rwanda. It gave these tribunals jurisdiction to hear cases where the offences could be characterized as international crimes attracting universal jurisdiction. Pinochet provides an example. In 1998, the Spanish courts sought to extradite Pinochet from Great Britain for the offences of directing the Chilean army, the police, and the secret service to torture his political opponents. What is most significant about this case is that the British House of Lords decided that torture did not fall within the official duties of a head of state. As a result, it waived the centuries-old doctrine of 'sovereign immunity'. The fact that Pinochet did not appear before the Spanish courts in no way detracts from the significance of the decision of the Law Lords.[10] Another example is the trial of former Liberian president, Charles Taylor. Ideally his trial should have taken place locally. However, for security reasons, he is currently appearing before the UN-backed Special Court for Sierra Leone, at The Hague. He faces eleven charges. They include murder, rape, conscription of child soldiers, enslavement, and pillage. In short, he has been charged with 'crimes against humanity'.

HUMAN RIGHTS FOLLOWING SEPTEMBER 11

Anyone who had watched the destruction of the Twin Towers could only have been transfixed and shocked. In the years to come, the

---

[8] Geoffrey Robertson, *Crimes against Humanity: The Struggle for Global Justice* (Melbourne: Penguin Books, 1999/2008), p. 463.

[9] Julian Burnside, *Watching Brief* (Melbourne: Scribe Publishing, 2007), p. 79.

[10] For a discussion the Pinochet cases see Robertson, *Crimes against Humanity*, pp. 332–71.

response of the USA and the Coalition of the Willing may be seen as the defining characteristic of the twenty-first century.

Immediately following the attack, George W. Bush declared a 'war on terror' and told members of the international community that unless they supported his administration in its response to the September 11 attacks, they were against it. To declare a war on a process —because terror is a process—is questionable, at the very least. It is also questionable because a war of this nature is timeless and non-specific and does not fit within the traditional definition of 'war'. Is it a war against national or international terrorist groups?

The USA attempted to get the Taliban to hand over Osama bin Laden and his al-Qaeda leadership group, then in Afghanistan. When it failed, it invaded that country in late 2001. This leads to the conclusion that at least, in the beginning, it was a war against a global or international terrorist group, namely al-Qaeda. The difficulty with this thesis is that subsequent events showed that the 'war' was extended to national terrorist groups as well.

Soon after the September 11 attacks, the US Congress passed the Patriot Act, 2001. This act granted unprecedented powers to homeland security agencies to invade the privacy of individual citizens on scant circumstantial evidence and with few accountability mechanisms.[11] Similar legislation was passed by other countries, including the UK, India, and Australia.

In the UK, legislation already existed for dealing with the terrorist activities of the Irish Republican Army. However, following September 11, new legislation was enacted. Perhaps its most controversial provision provided for internment without trial of any person who was a 'suspected international terrorist'. Internment could occur if the home secretary, firstly, reasonably believed that the presence of such a person in the UK represented a risk to national security, and, secondly, that such a person was a suspected terrorist. Should the suspected terrorist not be a citizen of the UK then that person could be detained for an unspecified period without charge or trial. No appeal lay within the existing court hierarchy. However, an appeal

---

[11] See for example, N. Henoff, *The War on the Bill of Rights and the Gathering of Resistance* (New York: Steven Stories Press, 2003) and C. Brown (ed.), *Lost Liberties: Ashcroft and the Assault on Personal Freedom*, (New York: New Press, 2003).

did lie with a government appointed commission. This represented a violation of the human rights provisions of the European Convention on Human Rights.[12]

In India, similar legislation was passed. This legislation resulted in a substantial invasion of privacy. It permitted the detention of suspected terrorists without trial for periods of up to ninety days. When the Manmohan Singh government initially came to power, it allowed this legislation to lapse because of strong opposition from the National Human Rights Commission and NGOs. This ensured that Ajmal Kasab, the only Lashkar-e-Taiba participant in the 2008 Mumbai attacks to be captured alive, was tried according to the rule of law rather than by a US-style military commission. The lapsing of the legislation also had far-reaching consequences for progressive improvements to India's relationships with Pakistan and with the USA. It signalled that India, the world's largest democracy, did not require Anti-terrorism legislation to deal with such reprehensible criminal behaviour. There is little doubt that President Barack Obama respected the decision to let the Anti-terrorism legislation lapse. This is illustrated by the November 2010 meetings between President Obama and Prime Minister Manmohan Singh, who announced that their countries 'have formed a partnership for the twenty first Century founded on shared interests, including education, counter-terrorism and nuclear non-proliferation'. In addition, President Obama stated a willingness to support India's bid to become a permanent member of the United Nations Security Council.[13]

The Australian government passed legislation that vastly increased the powers of the Australian Security Intelligence Organization (ASIO), the Federal Police, and the Australian Protective Services. This legislation gave these bodies the power to investigate and prosecute suspected terrorists. To their existing powers were added more extensive powers to conduct surveillance, and to search, seize, and detain suspected terrorists. The attorney general was granted power to declare particular organizations as 'terrorist organizations'. A new

---

[12] Goldstone, *Crimes against Humanity*, p. 165.

[13] Julianna Goldman and Hans Nichols, 'Obama, Singh Talks to Shape "Indispensable Partnership"', available at http://www.bloomberg.com.news/ 2010-11-07/obama-singh-talks-in-delhi-to-shape-century-s-indispensable-partnership-.html.

part was also added to the Australian Criminal Code, 1995 (Cth). This part created new terrorism offences and established a regime of control and preventative detention orders.[14]

It is clear from the US, British, Indian and Australian terrorism legislation that it was not confined to terrorism carried out by international terrorist groups like al-Qaeda, but included 'terrorism' instigated by national guerrilla movements. The conflation of the two was bound to cause policy difficulties. The motivation for national guerrilla movements is distinct from that carried out by international terrorist groups. For example, the motivation of those involved in the liberation movement in Chechnya is confined to national liberation. The motivation of al-Qaeda, as will be seen, was international in focus. The Western powers lumped the two together. This resulted in, for example, the Russian government, after September 11, being able to use brutal tactics to put down the insurgency in Chechnya without much criticism from Western powers. Before September 11, it had been the subject of growing international criticism. On 16 July 2009, Natalya Estemerova, a human rights advocate, was murdered in Chechnya. She was, perhaps, the last vocal human rights advocate for that country.

In Australia, the security threat from alleged terrorist groups was used to frame the Pacific Solution. Also called the Border Security Solution, it enabled the Australian government to largely ignore the Refugee Convention and turn genuine refugees into 'illegal', 'queue-jumping' immigrants who were subject to mandatory detention, sometimes for years, and in one case potentially for life. This was particularly the case for those people who arrived on Australia's shores in boats. These people were singled out for special attention following the Tampa incident. They were scapegoated so that the Australian government could maximize its ability to be re-elected.

Under the auspices of the war on terror, the CIA was able to establish clandestine prisons that criss-crossed Europe and in which suspected terrorists were tortured. These included a prison in Syria's Palestine Branch Interrogation Centre, where inmates were detained for months in cells as small as coffins, and secret CIA prisons in Afghanistan in which prisoners were bombarded by continuous loud rock music,

---

[14] George Syrota, 'The Definition of "Terrorist Act" in Part 5.3 of the Commonwealth Criminal Code', *University of Western Australia Law Review*, 33, 2007, p. 309.

deprived of sleep, and water-boarded. These prisoners were subjected to what is called 'extraordinary rendition'—a terrifying world of endless interrogations and frequent transfers by plane from one prison to another, all without charge. Stephen Grey traced the international movement of the CIA planes involved in the 'extraordinary rendition program'.[15] His view of Guantanamo Bay was expressed as follows:

> The international disdain did not come from the creation of the prison itself, but from the manifestly hypocritical rules that governed its operation. There has always been torture, but the Bush Administration added a new twist—torture committed by those who were loudly condemning it at the same time. The prison base evolved into an icon of US hypocrisy, established in the name of democracy and the rule of law to preserve 'our values' against the onslaught of Islamic fundamentalism.[16]

Alfred McCoy[17] read the reports and looked at the photographs provided by soldiers who were charged with torturing prisoners at Abu Ghraib. He could see that the techniques had emanated from the CIA. He wrote: 'At the deepest level, the abuse at Abu Ghraib, Guantanamo and Kabul are manifestations of a long history of a distinctive type of US covert-warfare doctrine developed since World War II, in which psychological torture has emerged as a central, if clandestine, facet of American foreign policy.'[18]

The sinister 2002 Department of State 'Torture Memo', set the limit to psychological torture. This limit was 'significant harm of significant duration, lasting months or even years'. The same memo defined the threshold for physical torture as the use of any technique that 'caused or could be associated with serious injury so severe that death, organ failure, or permanent damage resulting in a loss of significant body function'.[19]

Christopher Hitchens decided to find out for himself what was involved in water-boarding. He found people trained in water-boarding and got them to subject him to it. He lasted only a few seconds

[15] Stephen Grey, *Ghost Plane: The Untold Story of the CIA's Torture Program* (Carlton: Scribe Publishing, 2007).

[16] Ibid., p. 271.

[17] Alfred McCoy, *A Question of Torture* (New York: Metropolitan Book/Henry Holt and Company LLC, 2006).

[18] Ibid., p. 7.

[19] Leigh Sales, *Detainee 002: The Case of David Hicks* (Melbourne: Melbourne University Press, 2007), p. 128.

before his 'torturers' realized he was in real trouble. He decided that water-boarding was nothing less than drowning and that drowning could quickly lead to asphyxiation and death. He concluded that had his 'torturers' not stopped he would have died.[20]

There is a growing number of harrowing accounts from former CIA prisoners like Moazzam Begg.[21] Begg was a UK citizen who was abducted, without justification, from his home in Pakistan, where he had relocated his family. He was one of nine UK citizens who were imprisoned as 'enemy combatants'. All were eventually released without charge. Hooded and shackled, Begg was taken first to the US detention centre at Kandahar, then to the Bagram Air Force Base, and finally to Guantanamo Bay. In all, he spent more than three years in prison, much of it in solitary confinement. He was subjected to over three hundred interrogations, as well as death threats and torture. Under torture he finally admitted to terrorist activity that, if his interrogators had had the wit to check, they would have known that he could not have committed. Begg wrote:

> They allowed me to make some selected alterations, but kept in the most blatant untruths, like being a front-line fighter for al-Qa'idah, and, money I had sent to the Kashmiris in 1994 being used in the September 11th attacks. I felt surprisingly calm. I was imagining the damage this statement could do to them in court; it would expose much of their tactics too. However, I didn't know what the parameters of the law were any more: everyone had said that after 9/11, new laws had taken effect in the US, and that was frightening. How could American laws apply, in retrospect, to a British citizen, who had never travelled west of Dublin, for crimes that never existed in the first place?[22]

In addition, there are the accounts of lawyers who had been appointed to represent those confined to Guantanamo Bay. Clive Stafford Smith, a lawyer, provided a detailed account of some fifteen visits to Guantanamo Bay.[23] He noted, in particular, the difficulty

---

[20] Christopher Hitchens was interviewed by Philip Adams on his programme 'Late Night Live', Ratio National, Australian Broadcasting Commission, Australia, 2008.

[21] Moazzam Begg, *Enemy Combatant: A British Muslim's Journey to Guantanamo and Back* (London: Free Press and imprint of Smon & Shuster UK Ltd, 2006), p. 211.

[22] Ibid.

[23] Clive Stafford Smith, *Bad Men: Guantanamo Bay and the Secret Prisons* (London: Weidenfeld & Nicholson).

facing any lawyer or journalist attempting to represent prisoners or report on what was happening in the prison. He stated:

> After censorship and the threats, there were the lies, damned lies and semantics. The [US] Administration indulged in a remarkable gerrymandering of the [English] language to facilitate 'the mission'. This allowed the Pentagon PR officers to look the public in the eye and dissemble. For example, 'enhanced interrogation techniques' were reasonable steps taken to extract critically important information. Not the same thing as torture at all. Did 'mild non-injurious physical contact' mean a beating? No sir! 'Exploiting individual phobias?' An approved interrogation method. No need to explain the dogs.[24]

Stafford Smith also reported on the suicide attempts made by prisoners at Guantanamo Bay. By September 2003, the official estimate was 22. After 2003, the Pentagon reported a radical reduction in the attempted suicide rate. It cut it effectively to zero. It did this by changing 'attempted suicide' to 'manipulative self-injurious incident'.[25] In other words, it was no longer 'attempted suicide' and did not have be reported as such.

In Guantanamo Bay with Moazzam Begg was Australian David Hicks. The Australian government abandoned Hicks. Appointed to legally represent Hicks was a remarkable US military officer, Major Mori. Mori maintained that all the Australian government had to do was to ask for Hicks to be repatriated and this would have occurred. Julian Burnside QC noted: 'The Australian [Liberal Coalition] government has never said publicly that we have asked the Americans to return Hicks. We may confidently assume that we have not asked.'[26]

Despite Hicks having pleaded guilty before a Guantanamo Bay Military Commission, there is little doubt that, had he been willing to remain longer in prison, he would have been released without conviction. Hicks was finally charged with providing material support to terrorists. The charge hinged on his knowledge in 1999. If he had known in that year that the US government had named al-Qaeda as a 'foreign terrorist organisation' pursuant to Section 219 of the Immigration and Nationality Act, then a finding of guilt was justified. This was because Hicks had trained with al-Qaeda before

---

[24] Ibid., p. 138.
[25] Ibid., p. 139.
[26] Burnside, *Watching Brief*, p. 165.

September 11 and had travelled to various parts of Afghanistan. He had also fought with the Taliban against the Northern Alliance at the time that the USA was invading Afghanistan. This was the case even if all that Hicks had done after the USA invaded Afghanistan was to guard a Taliban tank. With regard to what Hicks knew in 1999, Julian Burside QC observed: 'I confess, I had missed that one myself. I heard about al-Qaeda just after 9/11, as President Bush allowed bin Laden's relatives safe passage out of America.'[27]

The confining of people in a legal black hole for long periods with limited or no access to lawyers or family members, and with no charges, was anathema to the previous US human rights record. This response could not have been expected. Britain had had to deal with the IRA, Spain with ETA, India with Kashmir, and Israel with suicide bombing and other forms of terrorism. None of them did anything comparable to Guantanamo Bay. It took the US Supreme Court in *Hambdi* v. *Rumsfeld*[28] and *Rumsfeld* v. *Pandilla*[29] to provide some limits to the way the USA could hold 'enemy combatants'.[30]

As information about the methods used in Guantanamo Bay and other secret CIA prisons came to the attention of citizens of Western liberal democracies, the large reservoir of goodwill that had resulted from the September 11 attack began to disappear. The invasion of Iraq by the Coalition of the Willing, despite almost universal opposition by the citizens of these member countries, hastened the disappearance of goodwill to the point where it was a contributing factor to the demise of the Bush and Howard administrations. The Bush administration would have done well to observe a simple truth that has been expressed in the following terms: '[An essential] rule of counter-terrorism is that if you behave decently, you will get better intelligence from your subjects than if you torture people. There are two elements to this: more people will want to help you, and you are more likely to obtain the truth—and know that it is the truth—when you are asking questions.'[31]

---

[27] Ibid., p. 166.
[28] 124 S Ct 2633, 159 L Ws2nd578, 72 NSLW 4607 (2004).
[29] 124 S Ct 2711, 159 L Ed2nd 513, 72 NSLW 4548 (2004).
[30] Arteh Neirer, 'How Not to Promote Democracy and Human Rights', in *Human Rights in the War on Terror,* Wilson (ed.), p. 140.
[31] Smith, *Bad Men: Guantanamo Baykf,* p. 278.

There are a couple of corollaries to this truth. One is that if you behave decently towards prisoners, you can legitimately insist on similar treatment for your own soldiers if they are captured. Another is that if you behave decently and uphold your own standards, there will 'be fewer people who want to kill you'.[32]

HUMAN RIGHTS AND THE INVASION OF IRAQ

In January 2002, President George W. Bush spoke of an 'Axis of Evil'. This axis consisted of Iran, Iraq, and North Korea. In May of the same year, the US State Department added Syria to the list of 'rogue states' that made up the Axis of Evil. It did this because each of these countries was seeking, it argued, to obtain weapons of mass destruction. It seems evident from this change to the foreign policy that Bush, and his neo-conservative advisers, did not want to resolve any foreign policy dilemmas using diplomacy. Rather they wanted to prepare the groundwork for the invasion of Iraq. This occurred in 2003.

Bush, Blair, and Howard told the citizens of their respective countries that the invasion of Iraq by 'pre-emptive strike' was necessary in order to disarm Saddam Hussein of his vast arsenal of weapons of mass destruction. The doctrine of 'pre-emptive self defence' can be summarized as the right to prevent a future attack by another state, even where there is little or no evidence of a planned attack by that state.[33] Not only was the 'pre-emptive' strike doctrine inconsistent with the UN Charter, but it has been characterized as illegal.[34] In retrospect then, what was the reason for Bush's invasion of Iraq? In part, it stems from the adoption by Bush of the views of neo-conservatives, including Michael Ledeen and Eliot A. Cohen outside the government, and John Bolton, Richard Armitage, Donald Rumsfeld, Paul Wolfowiz, and Douglas Feither, inside the government. Some of these men were in positions of power in the Bush administration before September 11. They were able to utilize the September 11 attacks to draw the Bush foreign policy into one of

---

[32] Ibid., p. 279.
[33] Hilary Charlesworth, 'What's Law Got to do with the War' in *Why the War was Wrong*, Raimond Gaita (ed.), (Melbourne: Text Publishing Company, 2003), p. 36.
[34] Ibid., pp. 35–60.

'total war' against its enemies, particularly radical Islam.[35] One of the more radical of the neo-conservatives, Norman Podhoretz, wrote about the change in Bush following September 11, in the following terms:

> One hears that Bush, who entered the White House without a clear sense of what he wanted to do there, now feels that there was a purpose behind his election all along; as a born-again Christian, it is said he believes that he was chosen by God to eradicate the evil of terrorism from the world. I think it is a plausible rumour.[36]

President Bush confirmed this 'plausible rumour' when he orated: 'The liberty we prize is not America's gift to the world, it is God's gift to humanity.'[37] The god must have been *his* Christian god. As a result, Bush felt he could wage war on 'Islamofacism'.[38] It must be realized that a vocal and active part of the Bush constituency was the US radical religious right. This type of religious fundamentalism now pervades the US armed services. Jeff Scarlet[39] gives the example of a US officer who had an Iraqi interpreter paint 'Jesus killed Mohammed' in giant Arabic script on the side of his Bradley fighting vehicle. The officer then drove his vehicle into a built-up area, firing into the buildings. The return fire was met by devastating fire using cannons and missiles.

For decades, the USA had been seen as a beacon for human rights and the 'linchpin of the international system of human rights protection'.[40] The invasion of Iraq proved, beyond doubt, that the Bush administration was not genuinely motivated by a wish to improve human rights. Rather it was motivated by a form of fundamentalism that obscures vision. Indeed, the extent to which Bush's vision was obscured can be seen from a slip he made when initially providing his justification for

---

35   Robert Manne, 'Explaining the Invasion', in *Why the War was Wrong*, Gaita (ed.), pp. 14–15.

36   Ibid., p. 16.

37   Peter Coghlan, 'War and Liberation', in *Why the War was Wrong*, Gaita (ed.), p. 140.

38   David Sanger, *The Inheritance* (Sydney: Bantam Press, 2009), p. xxvi.

39   Jeff Scarlet, 'Jesus Killed Mohammed: The Crusade for a Christian Military', *Harpers Bizarre*, May 2009.

40   Neil Hicks, 'The Impact of Counter Terrorism', in *Human Rights in the 'War on Terror'*, Wilson (ed.), p. 218.

the invasion—that the invasion was a 'crusade'. Wiktor Osiatynbski has observed that fundamentalism involves:

> ... a peculiar attitude that limits rational discussion in public life by demanding adherence to an ultimate and literal truth, as in the case of religious or ideological fundamentalism ... Fundamentalist attitudes threaten human rights because they tend to demand the imposition of a single interpretation of policies and morality and neglect the opponents' right to disagree and act on their beliefs. Moreover, fundamentalism limits the very spirit of open rational debate.[41]

Osiatynbski went on to write that 'human rights is a rational political framework incompatible with fundamentalism of any sort'.[42] It seems that Bush's vision was clouded by poor intelligence, religious fundamentalism, and a questionable ideology. The ideology, emanating from neo-conservatives was that, after September 11, any country that represented a perceived threat to the USA was to be attacked and overpowered. This was particularly the case with countries with Islamic administrations. It is not surprising then that the war against Iraq accelerated the growth of anti-Americanism worldwide. Indeed, 'the war on Iraq [has been] perceived by a growing number of Muslims worldwide as [requiring] a jihad against the West, particularly against the United States and its allies'.[43] President Barack Obama has seen that this is the case and ordered a staged withdrawal of US troops from Iraq. He has also ordered that Guantanamo Bay be closed. He is attempting to get the few remaining prisoners, who can be charged, before a court system that more closely observes due process. The difficulty is that much of the evidence obtained from these prisoners was obtained by coercion or torture and is, therefore, strictly speaking, inadmissible. If President Obama does order the trial of these prisoners without close observance of due process he leaves himself open to being called a human rights denier.

The type of fundamentalism that permits extreme torture of alleged terrorists does not compare with the religious fanaticism of Islamic jihad or Jamal Islamiya or al-Qaeda. These movements require an unquestioning dedication that can lead members to offer themselves as

---

41 Wiktor Osiatynbski, 'Are Human Rights Universal in an Age of Terrorism', in *Human Rights in the 'War on Terror'*, Wilson (ed.), p. 304.

42 Ibid.

43 Ibid., p. 303.

sacrificial suicide bombers. These bombers don't care who they injure or kill. In order to indoctrinate members, the leaders hide behind the Islamic faith. For example, in 1998, Osama bin Laden declared war on the USA. He called all Muslims 'to go forth, sword in hand, to kill all infidels in a "Jihad against Jews and Crusaders" in order to restore the Seventh Century Islamic Caliphate'.[44] Presumably Noordin Mohammed Top, the leader of a Jamal Islamiya splinter group, would have used similar rhetoric to get his followers to commit suicide by bombing of the two Jakarta hotels in July 2009.

The George W. Bush administration wanted to finish the incomplete business started by George Bush Sr. It could easily move from a war against al-Qaeda (a war on all terrorist groups with global reach) to a war against those states that supported terrorist groups. For example, Saddam Hussein had supplied financial support to the families of Palestinian suicide bombers. By some stretch of logic, Iraq as a 'rogue state', was in the firing line. The difficulty with this view is that it was not supported by reliable intelligence. Indeed, some of the intelligence was distorted. Seymour Herch, for example, had discovered that important sources of intelligence about weapons of mass destruction and links between Saddam Hussein and al-Qaeda were not the usual agencies like the CIA and the DIA. Rather, the intelligence came from a small office inside the Pentagon called the Office of Special Plans. This office was established after September 11 by Paul Wolferwitz and Donald Rumsfeld. It was run by a 'neoconservative idealogue and ex-Cold War Warrior, Abram Shulshy'.[45] This office had special access to Iraqi defectors. Robert Manne observed, 'As all students of intelligence understand, information supplied by defectors must be treated with the greatest circumspection'[46] because it is likely to be unreliable.

It is clear now that when the USA (supported by the UK and Australia) declared war on Iraq by 'pre-emptive strike', Saddam Hussein did not represent a military threat to any of them. In Australia, Andrew Wilkie resigned from Australia's senior intelligence

---

[44] Michael Freeman, 'Order, Rights and Threats: Terrorism and Global Justice', in *Human Rights in the 'War on Terror'*, Wilson (ed.), p. 7.

[45] Robert Manne, 'Explaining the Invasion', in *Why the War was Wrong*, Gaita (ed.), p. 31.

[46] Ibid.

agency, the Office of National Assessment (ONA), in protest over the then imminent invasion. He disputed the reliability and quality of the intelligence available to Washington, London, and Canberra. He was the only serving intelligence officer in the USA, the UK and Australia, to do so. He wrote: 'I was always confident in my intelligence assessment that an invasion of Iraq in early 2003 would be unjustified. The country did not pose a serious enough security threat to justify war, too many things could go wrong, and it was plainly stupid to use force while other options remained. I stand by my judgements.'[47]

Following the invasion of Iraq, UN weapons inspectors were unable to find 'weapons of mass destruction'. Once it became clear that they were not likely to find them, the leaders of the Coalition of the Willing dissembled. They started arguing that Saddam Hussein possessed 'weapons of mass destruction programs'. Then they changed the rationale to the desirability of removing a tyrant—one who had ordered the gassing of his own citizens. The outcome, they alleged, would result in democracy for Iraq and an Iraq that would become a model for other totalitarian regimes.

Leaving aside the issue of the legality or illegality[48] of a 'preemptive strike', the civilian death toll, and the fact that the war is ongoing, the fact is that the leaders of the Coalition of the Willing were dishonest with their citizens. As Peter Coghlan observed[49]:

> Of course, neither Bush, nor Blair, nor Howard will resign. They will continue to defend themselves, as John Howard has done here in Australia, by saying that the war was justified even if no weapons of mass destruction are found. And what made it a just war was the liberation of the Iraqi people from a murderous dictatorship. Actually, that is no justification for their failure to provide their parliaments and their publics with an honest and accurate assessment of Iraq's military capabilities. But it is a clever ploy—a triumph of spin over truth.

Coghlan goes to some length to dispose of the humanitarian or liberation argument.[50] What seems clear is that the war on Iraq leaves the leaders of the Coalition of the Willing open to criticism

---

[47] Andrew Wilkie, *Axis of Deceit* (Melbourne: Black Inc. Agenda, 2004), p. 186.
[48] For a discussion of illegality of the war against Iraq see Manne, 'Explaining the Invasion', pp. 8–34.
[49] Coghlan, 'War and Liberation', p. 115.
[50] Ibid., pp. 113–45.

for hypocrisy. Whatever may be said about their motives, their justifications for the invasion of Iraq were either lies or self-serving rationalizations.

GLOBALIZATION AND TERRORISM?

Following September 11, our governments told us that it was al-Qaeda who had perpetrated the attacks and that al-Qaeda was being harboured by the Taliban. Al-Qaeda, so we were told, represents a new type of global terrorism. Formerly, terrorist groups, or local insurgencies, were based on a highly centralized model. They usually operated within countries and not internationally. Their aim was to overthrow the political order within a given territory using a combination of propaganda, subversion, terrorism, and guerrilla warfare. Al-Qaeda, on the other hand, uses a highly decentralized network of cells based in many countries. The command of this structure may be based in Afghanistan or Pakistan, but once recruits are trained and indoctrinated they are moved to decentralized cells that are autonomous and self-directed.

September 11, and subsequent attacks on places such as Madrid, London, and Bali, led our governments to supplement the list of al-Qaeda-like terrorist groups. These included Jamal Islamiya, Lashkar-e-Taiba, and Hizballah. As groups were added, whether local insurgents or international terrorist groups, the rhetoric remained the same. 'We' were fighting a 'global war on terrorism' or a 'war on terror'. Labels such as these do not add to human knowledge. Indeed, if you add to them, 'water-boarding', 'extraordinary rendition', 'secret CIA prisons', 'state sanctioned torture', and policies like the invasion of Iraq, it is no wonder that many formed the view that the USA had walked away from its previous good human rights record. The difficulty is to establish the current security threat level.

David Kilkullen has observed that 'today's threat environment is nothing if not complex, ambiguous, dynamic, and multifaceted, making it impossible to describe in a single model'.[51] He then proceeds to provide four models or frameworks, which, taken together, give a more complete picture of the threats and their characteristics.

---

[51] David Kilcullen, *The Accidental Guerilla* (Melbourne: Scribe Publications, 2009), p. 7.

The four models are[52] the *Globalization Backlash* thesis, the *Gobalized Insurgency* model, the *Islamic Civil War* theory and the *Asymmetric Warfare* model.

The globalization backlash thesis[53] hypothesizes that today's conflicts can be viewed as a series of 'wars of globalization'. Whilst conflicts may differ, the driver is always globalization. Globalization has generated a Western-dominated world culture that is characterized by an interdependent world economy and global business community with empowered political and intellectual elites. The end result has been the generation of global 'haves' and 'have-nots' and a media that makes each aware of the other's status. The globalization process has prompted a political and cultural backlash against Western powers, particularly, but not always, by Muslim countries. This backlash has many concomitants. First, traditional societies have experienced the corrosive effects of globalization on their social, cultural, and religious identities. Second, because globalization is transparent, it gives its opponents access to its tools that include the Internet, cell phones, satellite communications, and electronic funds transfer, and ease of international movement and trade. In addition, globalization has generated the proliferation of highly lethal individual weapons such as assault rifles, portable anti-aircraft missiles, rocket launchers, mines, and very powerful blast munitions such as thermobarics.[54]

The opponents of globalization, whether G8 activists or al-Qaeda operatives, are amongst the most globalized and networked groups on earth. Third, globalization has facilitated group connections across diverse geographical locations. Fourth, the many different types of globalized media, including Facebook, MySpace, YouTube and Twitter, have made it possible for groups to produce, share, and develop multiple sources of information, almost all of which are outside government control. Fifth, given the uneven spread of globalization, the 'have-not' states harbour international terrorist groups. Finally, globalization is inherently a phenomenon over which governments have little control and which networked anti-globalization groups, such as al-Qaeda, have been able to exploit.

[52] Ibid., p. 8.
[53] Ibid., pp. 7–12
[54] Ibid., p. 9.

The globalized insurgency thesis[55] suggests that the war on terror should not be seen as a traditional terrorism problem. Rather it should be seen as a large-scale, transnational globalized insurgency. For local insurgents, the 'given territory' is a particular locality. For al-Qaeda, the 'given territory' is the entire globe and the 'political order' it seeks to overthrow is the political order within the entire Muslim world. As a result, defining groups according to the tactics they use, for example, terrorism, is less strategically useful than defining them according to their strategic approach. Al-Qaeda draws its power from its demographic base—the world's billions of Muslims. It sees itself as a revolutionary party that aims to build mass opposition to Western powers through provocation and spectacular acts of 'resistance'. It works though regional affiliates such as al-Qaeda in Iraq, Jamal Islamiya and al-Qaeda-Maghreb.

The Islamic civil war theory[56] suggests that globalized insurgency and terrorism arise from the civil war within Islam. The resulting turmoil spills over into the international community. In this context, al-Qaeda and its associated terrorist movements are responding to the internal dynamics within the Muslim world. These include a youth bulge, oppressive and corrupt governments, a dysfunctional relationship between the sexes, and a lack of freedom. It is these deficiencies that al-Qaeda is able to exploit. In this context, the West is a convenient target. Al-Qaeda's objective is initially the overthrow and control of the Islamic world, and then the West.

The asymmetric warfare model[57] examines the security environment from a military standpoint. The theory hypothesizes that the underlying strategic logic of terrorism (whether local or international) arises from the mismatch between the military capabilities of the USA and the rest of the world. This, in itself, poses a security dilemma. As a result, regardless of ideology, any rational adversary is likely to try and remove the USA from 'its perch' using a hybrid of unconventional means—subversion, propaganda, drawn-out guerrilla warfare, hit-and-run attacks, popular agitation, or weapons of mass destruction. Indeed, the events since September 11 may have already put an end to US dominance. Al-Qaeda represents the vanguard of this unconventional warfare.

[55] Ibid., pp. 12–16.
[56] Ibid., pp. 16–22.
[57] Ibid., pp. 22–27.

Seen through these four paradigms, Kilkullen suggests[58] that al-Qaeda's organizational strategy is designed to enable it to become the leading player in a loose coalition of international insurgency movements. It does not want to be 'commander-in-chief', rather it wants to be 'inciter-in-chief'. It uses the tools of globalization to coordinate the diverse actors who are separated by geography and time. Its military strategy is aimed at 'bleeding the United States to exhaustion and bankruptcy, forcing [it] to withdraw from the Muslim world'.[59] Simultaneously, al-Qaeda uses the 'provoking and alienating effects of US intervention as a form of provocation to incite a mass uprising within the Muslim world'.[60]

What then should form a new counter-terrorism strategy? Kilkullen suggests that the strategy we have used since September 11 has been the 'zero-risk' response to terrorism. This approach has led us to try and drive down to almost zero the chances of another September 11 attack and has led us to abandon many of our core values, including a reverence for due process and the rule of law. By elevating terrorism to the status of predominant security threat, international terrorists have been able to 'inflict far greater loss, cost, and damage (physical, political, and economic) than the terrorists themselves could ever directly impose'.[61] In other words, we have elevated Osama bin Laden and his core leadership group, lending prestige and credibility to his claims of importance by treating him as worthy of our attention, resources, and blood. We have turned a mouse into an elephant. 'Turning a mouse into an elephant' is reminiscent of the metaphor used in the title of the 1959 film starring Peter Sellers, *The Mouse that Roared*.

The solutions are complex. They involve us developing new paradigms for the solution of twenty-first century security problems. These include changing the language we use as was suggested by Australian attorney general, Robert McClelland; moving away from a zero-tolerance response to terrorism to one that identifies and prioritizes the many security threats; developing non-military responses; and working with and protecting at-risk populations.

[58] Ibid., pp. 22–29, 38.
[59] Ibid., pp. 22–29.
[60] Ibid.
[61] Ibid.

Conclusion

Globalization has been facilitated by the exponential development of high-speed digital networks with ever-growing bandwidth. September 11 saw the utilization of those networks by the international terrorist group, al-Qaeda. The response of the USA to the September 11 attacks was to declare a war on terrorism. In so doing, it elevated 'terrorism' to being the main, if not, sole, security threat. It paid scant attention to other security threats like global warming, the proliferation of nuclear weapons and their technology, the development of long-range ballistic missiles, world poverty, natural disasters, infectious diseases, particularly HIV and AIDS, state failure, narcotics trafficking, gender,[62] and other forms of discrimination.

In the years to come, it is likely that the last ten years will be seen as a dark chapter in the development and enhancement of human rights. The issue then is whether it will be possible for the USA and its allies to rebuild their reputations as exponents of the rule of law and human rights. They need to set new foreign policy directions. These policies must 'manage and balance our increasing interdependence with our increasing vulnerability'.[63] If this is done then the preservation of human rights may, once again, be regarded by Western countries as central to all foreign policy considerations.

Bibliography

Books

Begg, Moazam (2006), *Enemy Combatant: A British Muslim's Journey to Guantanamo and Back*, London: Free Press.

Brown C.(ed.) (2003), *Lost Liberties: Ashcroft and the Assault on Personal Freedom*, New York: New York Press.

Burnside, Julian (2007), *Watching Brief*, Melbourne: Scribe Publications.

Grey, Stephen (2007), *Ghost Plane: The Untold Story of the CIA's Torture Program*, Carlton, Victoria: Scribe Publications.

---

[62] Mary Robinson, 'Connecting Human Rights, Human Development, and Human Security', in *Human Rights in the 'War on Terror'*, Richard Ashby (ed.).

[63] Ibid., p. 311.

Henoff, N. (2003), *The War on the Bill of Rights and the Gathering of Resistance*, New York: Steven Stories Press.

Horne, Donald (2001), *Looking for Leadership: Australia in the Howard Years*, Melbourne: Viking Penguin Books.

Kilcullen, David (2009) (ed.), *The Accidental Gorilla*, Carlton, Victoria: Scribe Publications.

McCoy, Alfred (2006), *A Question of Torture*, New York: Metropolitan Books/Henry Holt and Company LLC.

Obama, Barack (2006/2009), *The Audacity of Hope*, Melbourne: The Text Publishing Company.

Robertson, Geoffrey (1999/2009), *Crimes against Humanity: The Struggle for Global Justice*, Melbourne: Penguin Books.

Sales, Leigh (2007), *Detainee 002: The Case of David Hicks*, Melbourne: Melbourne University Press.

Sanger, David (2009), *The Inheritance*, London: Bantam Press.

Stafford Smith, Clive (2007), *Bad Men: Guantanamo Bay and the Secret Prisons*, London: Weidenfeld and Nicholson.

Wilkie, Andrew (2004), *Axis of Deceit*, Melbourne: Black.

Articles in Books and Journals

Charlesworth, Hilary, 'What's Law Got to do with the War', in *Why the War Was Wrong*, Raimond Gaita (ed.) (2003), pp. 35–60. Melbourne: Text Publishing Company.

Coghlan, Peter, 'War and Liberation', in *Why the War was Wrong*, Raimond Gaita (ed.) (2003), pp. 113–45. Melbourne: Text Publishing Company.

Freeman, Michael, 'Order, Rights and Threats: Terrorism and Global Justice', in *Human Rights in the 'War on Terror'*, Richard A. Wilson (ed.) (2005), pp. 1–35, New York: Cambridge University Press.

Goldman, Julianna and Nichols Hans, 'Obama, Singh Talks to Shape "Indispensable Partnership"', retrieved 12/11/2010 from: http://www.bloomberg.com.news/2010-11-07/obama-singh-talks-in-delhi-to-shape-century-s-indispensable-partnership-.html

Goldstone, Richard, 'The Tension between Combating Terrorism and Protecting Civil Liberties', in *Human Rights in the 'War on Terror*, Richard A. Wilson (ed.) (2005), pp. 157–68, New York: Cambridge University Press.

Hicks, Neil, 'The Impact of Counter Terrorism', in *Human Rights in the 'War on Terror'*, Richard A. Wilson (ed.) (2005), pp. 209–24. New York: Cambridge University Press.

Manne, Robert, 'Explaining the Invasion', in *Why the War was Wrong*, Raimond Gaita (ed.) (2003), pp. 8–34. Melbourne: Text Publishing Company.

Neirer, Aryeh, 'How Not to Promote Democracy and Human Rights', in *Human Rights in the 'War on Terror'*, Richard A. Wilson (ed.) (2005), p. 140, New York: Cambridge University Press.

Osiatynbski, Wiktor, 'Are Human Rights Universal in an Age of Terrorism', in *Human Rights in the 'War on Terror'*, Richard A. Wilson (ed.) (2005), pp. 295–307, New York: Cambridge University Press.

Peating, Stephanie, 'Canberra Declares War on the Language of Terrorism', *The Age*, 7 July 2009.

Robinson, Mary, 'Connecting Human Rights, Human Development, and Human Security', in *Human Rights in the 'War on Terror'*, Richard A. Wilson (ed.) (2005), pp. 308–16, New York: Cambridge University Press.

Scarlet, Jeff, 'Jesus Killed Mohammed: The Crusade for a Christian Military', *Harpers Bizarre,* May 2009.

Syrota, George, 'The Definition of 'Terrorist Act' in Part 5.3 of the Commonwealth Criminal Code', *University of Western Australia Law Review*, 33, 2007, pp. 307–50.

5

Globalization and Its Effects on the Emerging Jurisprudence on the Right to Education in South Africa and Nigeria

Avinash Govindjee
Elijah Adewale Taiwo

INTRODUCTION

The term 'globalization' is one of the most fashionable buzzwords of contemporary political, economic, and academic debate.[1] Since the end of the Cold War in the late 1980s, the term has assumed a greater profile in political, economic, policy, and popular discourse.[2] As such, the 'era of globalization' is fast becoming the preferred term

---

[1] See Isaac E. Ukpokolo, 'Globalization and the Search for Cultural Philosophy for Contemporary Africa', *Nigeria and Globalization Discourses on Identity Politics and Social Conflict*, in Duro Oni, Suman Gupta, Tope Omoniyi, Efurosibina Adegbija, and Segun Awonusi (eds) (Lagos: Centre for Black and African Arts and Civilization, 2004), p. 275; See also, W. J. Morgan, 'Globalization and State Socialism: End of Illusions or New Educational Opportunities?', in *Widening Access to Education as Social Justice: Essays in Honor of Michael Omolewa*, Akpovire Oduaran and Harbans S. Bhola (eds) (Dordrecht: Springer/UNESCO Publishing, 2006), p. 95.

[2] Cyril Obi and Iwebunor Okwechime, 'Globalization and Identity Politics: The Emerging Patterns of Inter-ethnic Relations in Nigeria's Niger Delta', in *Nigeria and Globalization Discourses*, Oni *et al.*, p. 347. It is observed that the concept of 'globalization' is presented as a new phenomenon that had roots in earlier periods, but has come up again since the early 1980s, sweeping everything before it, marking a distinctly new epoch in the world history,. See Yusufu Bala Usman, 'What Exactly is Globalization?', Keynote Address delivered at the 40th Annual

for describing the current times.[3] In this context, Khor submits that globalization has become the defining process of the present age and is perhaps the most widely discussed phenomenon today.[4] Globalization is about an increasingly interconnected and interdependent world and this has many important dimensions—economic and social, political, environmental, cultural, as well as religious.[5] The various dimensions affect people, institutions, and countries in one way or the other, positively or negatively. However, the economic aspect of globalization is perceived to be at the heart of the whole process of globalization. It receives greater attention, especially in view of its rapid pace and force in shaping the world economy.[6]

Just as the concept 'globalization' occupies an important place in the global discourse, education also forms a major force in economic, intellectual, social, and cultural empowerment in contemporary times.[7] It occupies a major item on the international agenda. Reports from organizations such as the United Nations Educational, Scientific, and Cultural Organization (UNESCO), the World Bank and the Organization for Economic Cooperation and Development (OECD) attest to the crucial role of education in economic development throughout the world.[8] As is evident from the various human rights instruments that guarantee the right to education, the importance of education cuts across national, regional, and international boundaries. It is universal. It forms an important part of social development and, therefore, is indispensable in the development of any country. Education is of utmost importance because no country can

---

Conference of the Nigerian Association of Law Teachers (Lagos: Nigerian Institute of Advanced Legal Studies, 16–19 May 2004), p. 5.

[3]   See Ukpokolo, 'Globalization and the Search for Cultural Philosophy', p. 275.

[4]   See Martin Khor, *Globalization and the South: Some Critical Issues* (Ibadan: Spectrum Books, 2000), p. 1.

[5]   See Mike I. Obadan, 'International Trade and Globalization: The Socio-Political and Economic Realities for Nigeria', in *Foreign Investment Promotion in A Globalized World*, D. A. Guobadia and P. T. Akper (eds) (Lagos: NIALS, 2006), p. 184.

[6]   Ibid.

[7]   See Brian Burtch, 'Education, Law and Social Justice', in *Widening Access to Education as Social Justice*, Oduaran and Bhola (eds), p. 91.

[8]   See Association of University Teachers & Development Education Association, *Globalization and Higher Education (Guidance on Ethical Issues Arising from International Academic Activities)* (Forthcoming, London, 1999), p. 6.

ever sustain economic growth while perpetuating a high level of illiteracy. Thus, the issues of globalization, education, knowledge, skills, and development are of crucial importance in global debates in this age and are completely intertwined.

This contribution highlights how the concepts of globalization and human rights intersect with particular reference to the right to education in South Africa and Nigeria. The main focus of this chapter is on South Africa and Nigeria, and this will necessitate brief profiles of the two countries. The two countries are different not only in terms of political and social values and traditions, but the economies of the two countries as well as their demographic factors are also different. Nevertheless, these countries present themselves as two important factors to be reckoned with, within the African continent. This makes the discussions on the two countries apposite in this respect. While the main focus of this chapter is on South Africa and Nigeria, it will also draw on the experiences of other countries on the subject.

The chapter is divided into seven parts. Following this general introduction we examine the brief profiles of the two countries. In the third part, the chapter discusses the meanings of the two dominant terms 'education' and 'globalization'. The fourth part discusses the legal framework guaranteeing the right to education globally, while the fifth examines the right to education in South Africa and Nigeria. In the sixth part the impacts of globalization on the right to education in the two countries are assessed, while the conclusion forms the last part.

BRIEF PROFILES OF SOUTH AFRICA AND NIGERIA

South Africa

South Africa is a large country located at the foot of Africa, occupying an area of 1.2 million square kilometre and sharing common boundaries to the north with Namibia, Botswana, and Zimbabwe, and to the north-east with Mozambique and Swaziland. The Independent Kingdom of Lesotho is completely enclosed by South African territory.[9] Given the country's population of over 45 million, South Africa is

---

[9] See *Country Education Profiles on South Africa*, 2nd edn (Canberra: Commonwealth of Australia, 2004), p. 1.

the second most populated country in Africa. Almost 54 per cent of the population lives in urban areas.[10] With 86 per cent literacy level, South Africa has one of the highest rates of literacy in Africa. Notwithstanding this high rate of literacy, it is observed that more than 3 million people have no formal education in the country.[11]

The early contact of the territory now constituting present-day South Africa with the outside world was in 1652 when the Dutch East India Company came to the Cape with the intent of establishing a permanent fort to supply fresh produce for their ships en route to and from the East.[12] The country later came under British rule and in 1906 the British government decided to grant limited political autonomy to the various provinces that existed then, under what was termed 'responsible government'. In 1909, a draft constitution for the unification of the four provinces was submitted to the British Parliament which was adopted. On 31 May 1910, the Union of South Africa, a sub-governing dominion within the British Empire, came into being.[13]

The country had a long period of apartheid rule until the development of a new political system in the early 1990s and that system of governance impacted seriously on the educational system by creating inequality in the country.[14] However, the first democratic

---

[10] However, Seafield submits that over half of the South African population lives in rural areas with 68 per cent of the total rural population living in abject poverty. She asserts that very little profit-based agricultural activity takes place in rural areas and subsistence farming is limited. The incidence of illiteracy and lack of basic resources is compounded in rural areas. See Lucrecia Seafield, 'South Africa: The interdependence of All Human Rights', in *Human Rights under African Constitutions: Realizing the Promise for Ourselves*, Abdullahi Ahmed An-Na'im (ed.) (Philadelphia: University of Pennsylvania Press, 2003), p. 296.

[11] Ibid.

[12] Ibid.

[13] Ibid., pp. 296–97.

[14] In this regard, Professor Berger posits that like most injustices in contemporary South Africa, educational inequality can be traced easily back to apartheid. Shortly after the National Party victory in 1948, the architects of apartheid implemented a formalized system of race-based education. Codified in the Bantu Education Act of 1953 and the Extension of the University Education Act, national education policy was an integral part of apartheid's dehumanizing segregation. He submits further that even after the country's first elections in 1994 and school desegregation, the lingering effects of such policies are visible in poor schooling for students of all ages. See Eric Berger, 'The Right to Education under the South African Constitution', *Columbia Law Review*, 103, 2003, p. 616.

parliament was elected in April 1994 and a new constitution was adopted which, with amendments, became the current 1996 South African Constitution.[15] The 1996 South African Constitution is the supreme law in the country and it expressly provides for the right to education, among other rights.[16] The constitution also provides that when interpreting the Bill of Rights, a court must consider international law. In this context, recognition shall be given to the various international instruments that guarantee human rights, and, in our context, the right to education.[17]

Nigeria

The Federal Republic of Nigeria occupies an area of 924,000 square kilometre in the west of Africa. With the population of about 144 million, Nigeria is the most populous country in Africa. It operates a presidential system of government with the federal government at the centre and 36 component states. While the official language is the English language, there are also over 250 languages stemming from the diverse ethnic groups in the country.[18] Nigeria was also colonized by the British. The early contacts of the British with the territories

---

[15] See *Country Education Profiles on South Africa*, p. 1.

[16] See Section 2 of the constitution which provides for the supremacy of the constitution and Section 29 which guarantees the right to education. South Africa is divided into nine provinces with the country's legislative capital and the seat of Parliament in Cape Town. The administrative capital is Pretoria, where the government departments are based. South Africa's Supreme Court of Appeal sits in Bloemfontein and the Constitutional Court in Johannesburg. The country has eleven different official languages (Afrikaans, English, isiNdebele, isiXhosa, isiZulu, Sepedi, Sesotho, Setswana, siSwati, Tshivenda, and Xitsonga) with different religious denomination reflecting many and varied origins of its population. The country has a hybrid government structure with strong powers vested in the Central Government and some federal characteristics, with provinces having limited legislation making functions. These facts and figures are taken from 'South Africa in Brief', *The Constitution of the Republic of South Africa*, 4th edn, (Juta's Pocket Statutes, 2006), pp. v–viii; See also, Lucrecia Seafield, 'South Africa: The Interdependence of All Human Rights', p. 295.

[17] See Section 39 of the constitution.

[18] The dominant ethnic groups are the Hausa in the north, Ibo in the south-east, and Yoruba in the soutwest. See Chinonye Obiagwu and Chidi Anselm Odinkalu, 'Nigeris: Combating Legacies of Colonialism and Militarism', in *Human Rights under African Constitutions*, Abdullahi Ahmed An-Na'im (ed.), p. 212.

that constitute modern Nigeria were in the early nineteenth century and the contacts were initially with the inhabitants of the coastal areas of Lagos, Benin, Bonny, Brass, Degema, and Calabar for trading purposes.[19]

Lagos was ceded to the British Crown under a Treaty of Cession in 1861. Through this treaty Lagos became a British Colony, with English law introduced in the colony.[20] Other parts of the country were subsequently acquired as British Protectorates and English law was also introduced in those areas.[21] The annexation of Lagos in 1861 could be regarded as the real beginning of the British colonial conquest of Nigeria.[22] The territory was ruled under the Southern and Northern Protectorates with the colonial administrative capital in Lagos. In 1914, the British government amalgamated the two protectorates, thus bringing all the ethnic nationalities into one political union called Nigeria.[23]

Nigeria eventually got political independence on 1 October 1960, and became a republic within the Commonwealth in 1963. Post-independence, the country came under long years of military rule that impacted adversely on all sectors. The education sector in particular was seriously neglected. The prolonged military rule

---

[19]   The first consul was appointed sometimes in 1849. Consular courts were established in reaction to the failure of the indigenous/customary courts to effectively settle the trade disputes between the indigenes, British and other foreign traders. See Akintude O. Obilade, *The Nigerian Legal System* (Ibadan: Spectrum Law Publishing, 1990), pp. 17–18.

[20]   By virtue of the Supreme Court Ordinance No. 11 of 1863, the first Supreme Court of the colony was established in Lagos. The court was conferred with civil and criminal jurisdiction. In 1866, the British merged her colonies in West Africa and placed them under one government then known as the Government of the West African Settlements. Such territories consisted of Lagos, the Gold Coast, Sierra Leone, and Gambia. Appeals from the courts established then for Lagos lay to the West Africa Court of Appeal from where appeal lay to the Judicial Committee of the Privy Council. See Obilade, *The Nigerian Legal System*, p. 18.

[21]   They were the Northern and Southern Protectorates. These protectorates, together with the Lagos Colony were amalgamated in 1914 to form the modern Nigeria.

[22]   See B. C. Uweru, 'Repugnancy Doctrine and Customary Law in Nigeria: A Positive Aspect of British Colonialism', *African Research Review*, 2(2), 2008), p. 290.

[23]   Obiagwu and Odinkalu, 'Nigeria: Combating Legacies of Colonialism and Militarism', p. 212.

further impacted heavily on the laws and institutions existing for the defence of human rights. However, on 29 May 1999, the country returned to a civilian regime with a constitutional apparatus put in place to sustain the rule of law and human rights. The country adopted a new constitution with this reversion. This constitution recognizes some fundamental rights in Chapter 4 while other categories of rights, such as the right to education, are provided for in Chapter 2 as fundamental objectives and directive of the state policy.

DEFINING 'EDUCATION' AND 'GLOBALIZATION'

As the words 'education' and 'globalization' are dominant in this chapter, it is necessary to examine their meanings before proceeding further.

Education

The word 'education' does not lend itself to precise definition since it is very susceptible to time and place.[24] Bhola corroborates this contention by stating that the term 'education' is not easy to define.[25] For any definition of the term to be satisfactory, it has to relate closely to the social structure, economy and politics of the particular country.[26] However, in view of its multifaceted nature, education can be defined in different ways, broadly and in a narrow sense. When defined in a broad sense it encompasses 'all activities by which a human group transmits to its descendants, a body of knowledge and skills and a moral code which enable that group to subsist'.[27] In this sense, education is primarily concerned with the transmission to the younger generation of the skills necessary to effectively undertake the tasks of daily living and with the inculcation of the social,

---

[24] W. O. Lester Smith, *Education in Great Britain* (Oxford: Oxford University Press, 1949), p. 1.

[25] See H. S. Bhola, 'Access to education: A Global Perspective', in *Widening Access to Education as Social Justice,* Oduaran and Bhola (eds), p. 55.

[26] See Smith, *Education in Great Britain*, p. 2.

[27] See Amadou-Mahtar M'Bow, 'Introduction', in *The Child's Rights to Education*, G. Mialaret (ed.) (Paris: Unesco, 1979), p. 11.

cultural, religious, and philosophical values held by the particular community.[28]

Education in the broad sense further impacts upon the entire process of social life by means of which individuals and social groups learn to develop consciously for themselves, and for the benefit of the national and international communities, the whole of their personal capacities, attitudes, aptitudes, and knowledge.[29] Education can, in turn, be more narrowly defined to refer to formal or professional instruction imparted within a national, provincial, or local education system, whether private or public.[30] It is generally the case that the term 'education' is used in international instruments to refer to formal institutional instruction.[31]

The General Conference of the UNESCO has defined the term 'education' to mean 'all types and levels of [formal] education, and includes access to education, the standard and quality of education, and the conditions under which it is given'.[32] Talking philosophically, John Newsom described education as a political issue, for it is concerned with a child's relationship to the world both as a child and as a future adult.[33] He submits that 'to deny a child the best education for his particular needs is to deprive him of something as essential to his proper growth as any of the things which help him to grow to his full physical stature ...'[34] Delbruck submits that international legal instruments normally

---

[28]   Douglas Hodgson, *The Human Right to Education* (Dartmouth: Ashgate, 1998), p. 3.

[29]   See Article 1(a) of the Recommendation Concerning Education for International Understanding, Cooperation and Peace and Education Relating to Human Rights and Fundamental Freedoms 1974. See also, Hodgson *The Human Right to Education*, p. 3.

[30]   M'Bow, 'Introduction', p. 11.

[31]   Hodgson, *The Human Right to Education*, p. 4.

[32]   Article 1(2) of the UNESCO Convention against Discrimination in Education, 1960.

[33]   Politics according to him is not only the science and art of government, but the deeper study of man's relation with other men in society. See John Newsom, *The Child at School* (Harmonsworth & Middlesex: Penguin Books, 1950), p. 12.

[34]   Ibid., p. 15. It is submitted, however, that although children are the main beneficiaries, the right to education belongs to all individuals. See Article 26(1) of the UDHR, 1948, which provides that everyone has the right to education.

use the term 'education' in two senses. First, education as the provision of basic skills, and second, education as the development of the intellectual, spiritual, and emotional potential of the young person, or, in other words, the broader development of his or her personality.[35]

In this chapter, we will adopt the definition postulated by Verheyde due to its comprehensive nature. He defines education as

> ... the process of developing the child's personality, talents, mental and physical abilities; developing the child's respect for human rights, fundamental freedoms and maintenance of peace, respect for his or her parents, national values of his or her country and those of other civilizations; developing the child's ability to participate in a free society in the spirit of mutual tolerance; and developing the child's respect for other civilizations, cultures, religions, sexes and for natural environment.[36]

Globalization

It is important to mention that 'globalization' as a concept is somewhat imprecise. As a result, discussions about globalization are often conducted without any consensus being feasible.[37] However, various writers and scholars have attempted working definitions of the term 'globalization'. It is submitted that, as a concept, 'globalization' refers both to the compression of the time and space of social relations, and to the intensification of consciousness of the world existing as a whole.[38]

[35] See J. Delbruck, 'The Right to Education as an International Human Rights', *German Yearbook of International Law*, 35, 1992, pp. 94, 99; see also, Mieke Verheyde, 'Article 28: The Right to Education', in *A Commentary of the United Nations Convention on the Rights of the Child*, A. Alen, J. Vande Lanotte, E. Verhellen, F. Ang, E. Berghmans, and M. Verheyde (eds) (Leiden: Martinus Nijhoff Publishers, 2006), p. 11.

[36] Verheyde, 'Article 28: The Right to Education', n. 35, p. 12; see also, Articles 28(1) and 29(1) of the CRC.

[37] E. O. Esiemokhai, M. O. Adeleke, and O. S. Kuteyi, 'Globalization and the Right to Democracy and Good Governance: The Best Practices' Paper presented at the 40th Annual Conference of the Nigerian Association of Law Teachers, (Lagos: Nigerian Institute of Advanced Legal Studies, 16–19 May 2004), p. 1.

[38] Morgan, 'Globalization and State Socialism', p. 96.

One simple definition is that globalization increases the range of economic, political, and social powers and influence beyond national and even continental boundaries and identities.[39] In this context, Morgan posits that

> ... globalization's characteristics are spatial reorganization of production system and labor markets, the spread of industrial organization and manufacture across borders, technological revolutions in computers, telecommunications, and transport, the spread and dominance of market forces, the reemergence of laissez-fare as an economic orthodoxy, and the substantial migration of peoples. It also claims the emergence of a borderless world in which global communications and a relentless trend towards a monoculture absorbs or even erases national cultures.[40]

Bala Usman equally alludes to this fact when he submits that

> ... globalization is, basically, the intensification, ... of the interconnection and interdependence between all parts of the world, particularly at the levels of the economy and communications, such that former national barriers to the movement of information, finance, goods, services, and entrepreneurship, are being drastically reduced, and everybody now has to compete with everybody, in what has now become a global village and a single market.[41]

The concept is further defined as 'a process of integrating economic decision making such as the consumption, investment and saving process all across the world'.[42] Globalization is seen as a process of shifting autonomous economies into a global market, that is, the systemic integration of autonomous economies into a global trading environment.[43]

It is submitted that the key elements of the process of globalization are: the interconnection of sovereign nations through trade

---

[39] It is observed that in its most extreme form, the concept of globalization predicts the end of the national economy and the end of the nation-state as the primary unit of political organization and loyalty. See ibid.

[40] Ibid.

[41] See Yusufu Bala Usman, 'What Exactly is Globalization?', Keynote Address delivered at the 40th Annual Conference of the Nigerian Association of Law Teachers (Lagos: Nigerian institute of Advanced Legal Studies, 16–19 May 2004), p. 5.

[42] See Mike Kwanashie, 'The Concept and Process of Globalization', *Central Bank of Nigeria Economic and Financial Review*, 36(4), 1998, p. 341.

[43] Ibid.

and capital flows; harmonization of the economic rules that govern relationships between foreign nations; creation of structures to support and facilitate dependence and interconnection; and creation of a global market place.[44] Obadan also submits that globalization is about an increasingly interconnected and interdependent world, and this has many important dimensions such as economic and social, political and environment, cultural and religious.[45] Simply put, therefore, globalization is a process of breaking down the national barriers to international influences and the integration of countries into the international world order.[46]

Globalization is further defined as 'a process by which different regions of the world are pulled together through an expanding network of exchanges of peoples and ideas and cultures as well as goods and services across vast distances'.[47] It is submitted that one of its positive aspects is that it enables goods and services to get to states in every part of the world, with shipping, airfreight and business travels facilitating participation in the global economy.[48] In this context, Khor asserts as follows:

> Perhaps the most important and unique feature of the current globalization process is the 'globalization' of national policies and policy making mechanisms. National policies (including economic, social, cultural and technological areas) that until recently were under the

[44] Emmanuel E. Okon, 'Foreign Investment and National Security in Developing Countries under the Globalized Environment: The Nigerian Perspective', Paper presented at the Round Table on International Trade and Globalization: Challenges for Nigeria (Lagos: Nigerian Institute of Advanced Legal Studies, 18 June 2002), p. 7.

[45] See Obadan, 'International Trade and Globalization', p. 1.

[46] See Shishi M. John, Isa Yakubu, and Abdulkarim A. Kana, 'Globalization, Democracy and Good Governance in Nigeria- the Best Practices', Paper Presented at the 40th Annual Conference of the Nigerian Association of Law Teachers (Lagos: Nigerian Institute of Advanced Legal Studies, 16–19 May 2004), p. 7. In spite of these positive aspects of globalization process, it is submitted that there is the need to still preserve the independence and sovereignty of states. See also, Esiemokhai et al., 'Globalization and the Right to Democracy and Good Governance', p. 2.

[47] See A. U. Iwara, 'Identity Politics, Globalization and Socio-Political Engineering in Nigeria', in *Nigeria and Globalization Discourses*, Oni et al., p. 20.

[48] See Esiemokhai et al., 'Globalization and the Right to Democracy and Good Governance', p. 7.

jurisdiction of states and people within a country have increasingly come under the influence of international agencies and processes or of big private corporations and economic/financial players. This has led to the erosion of national sovereignty and narrowed the ability of governments and people to make choices from options in economic, social and cultural policies.[49]

According to Aina, the key components of the globalization process are constituted as follows: the emergence of a time–space-compressed interdependent world; the emergence of a new world order, that is, a shift from a bipolar to a unipolar world; the emergence of a new international division of labour in context of the polarized global economy seeking to integrate all local economies through trade liberalization and deregulation, and so on; the emergence of new flow of persons, cultures, ideas, and funds (finances); the merger and spread of new technologies, particularly IT, and their trans-nationalization and integration; and the increasing significance of knowledge and information for production, culture, and the economy.[50]

Multinational corporations (MNCs) play a dominant role in the process of globalization through their investments, production, and trade.[51] Similarly, economic philosophies as propounded by the World Trade Organization (WTO), and the conditionality of the World Bank and the International Monetary Fund (IMF) that goes with it, greatly influences the idea of globalization.[52] These bodies therefore play dominant roles at the global level and this chapter will assess how their policies have impacted generally on human rights and, particularly, on the right to education.

---

[49] Martin Khor, *Globalization and the South: Some Critical Issues* (Ibadan: Spectrum Books, 2000), p. 5.

[50] Aina, Tade A., 'From Colonization to Globalization: Reflections on Issues in Transformation and Democratic Development in Africa', in *Globalization and Sustainable Human Development in Nigeria*, Aina Tade *et al.* (eds) (Lagos: University of Lagos, 2002), p. 14; see also, Awonusi Segun, 'Globalization and Hegemonic English in Nigeria: Identity Conflicts and Linguistic Pluralism', in *Nigeria and Globalization Discourses*, in Oni *et al.*, pp. 85–86.

[51] See Asbjorn Eide, 'Interdependence and Indivisibility of Human Rights', in *Human Rights in Education, Science and Culture: Legal Developments and Challenges*, Yvonne Donders and Vladimir Volodin (eds) (Paris/Hampshire/ Burlington: Ashgate/UNESCO Publishing, 2007), p. 47.

[52] See Iwara, 'Identity Politics, Globalization and Socio-Political Engineering', p. 21.

THE GLOBAL GUARANTEE OF THE RIGHT TO EDUCATION

The right to education is described as an empowerment right.[53] This is because the right to education is necessary for exercising and enjoying other rights. The enjoyment of a number of civil and political rights, such as freedom of information and the right to vote, depends on a minimum level of education. Also, economic, social, and cultural rights, such as the right to choose work or to take part in cultural life, can also only be exercised meaningfully once a minimum level of education has been achieved.[54] The relationship between the right to education and other rights shows the interdependency between all human rights. This interdependency is significant for a nation's development since lack of basic education affects an individual's quality and standard of life.[55] Education is important because it prepares learners for life, politically and economically.[56] It also serves a positive social function in helping to build values such as tolerance and respect for human rights.[57] Therefore, the importance of education in the society cannot be overemphasized. [58]

However, since the Second World War there has been a global emphasis on human rights, which led to the passing of the Universal Declaration of Human Rights (UDHR) in 1948 and the signing

---

[53] F. Coomans, 'The Core Content of the Right to Education', in D. Brand and S. Russell (eds), *Exploring the Core Content of Socio-Economic Rights: South African and International Perspectives* (Pretoria: Protea Book House, 2002), p. 160.

[54] G. Veriawa and F. Coomans, 'The Right to Education', in *Socio-economic Rights in South Africa*, D. Brand and C. Heyns (eds) (Pretoria: Pretoria University Law Press, 2005), p. 57.

[55] Brand and Russell, *Exploring the Core Content of Socio-Economic Rights*, p. 160.

[56] Malherbe asserts this in the following words: '… the virtues of education in preparing learners for life, for meaningful interaction with other human beings, for constructive civic and political involvement, and for successful economic participation stand beyond reason'. See R. Malherbe, 'The Constitutional Framework for Pursuing Equal Opportunities in Education', *Perspectives in Education*, 22(3), 2004, p. 10.

[57] S. Khoza (ed.), *Socio-Economic Rights in South Africa*, 2nd edn (Cape Town: Community Law Centre, UWC, 2007), p. 412.

[58] Judicial opinions also attest to the importance of education in the society. See *Brown v. Board of Education of Topeka*, 347 US 438 (1954), where it was held that, today, education is perhaps the most important function of state and local governments. See also, *Jones v. The Queen*, [1986] 2 SCR 284; and *G. v. An Bord* [1980] IR 32.

of the international covenants on civil and political rights, and on economic, social and cultural rights. These have been reflected in regional human rights treaties and human rights guarantees contained in national constitutions.[59] The UDHR, the International Covenant on Civil and Political Rights (ICCPR), 1966 and the International Covenant on Economic, Social and Cultural Rights (ICESCR), 1966 constitute the International Bill of Rights. Collectively, they provide for the right to education at global level.[60] The UDHR for instance states that the right to education is for all people and states further that elementary education shall be free and compulsory while higher education shall be accessible to all on the basis of merit.[61]

Between 1976 (when the ICESCR was ratified) and 1990, a series of international covenants and conventions were promulgated that provide a comprehensive legal basis for the protection of the right to education. The Convention on the Rights of the Child (CRC), 1989, for example, contains a comprehensive set of legally enforceable commitments concerning the rights to education.[62] The convention reaffirms the right of every child to free and compulsory primary schooling, and states

[59] Avinash Govindjee, 'Lessons for South African Social Assistance Law from India: Part 1—The Ties that Bind: The Indian Constitution and Reasons for Comparing South Africa with India', *Obiter*, 26(3), 2005, pp. 575–76.

[60] See Article 26, UDHR; Articles 13 and 14, ICESCR, and Article 19(2), ICCPR, which, though not expressly providing for the right to education, is wide to encompass the right to education. Tracing the origin of the right to education, Dlamini submits that:

[61] Article 26 of the UDHR, 1948.

> [T]he idea of a right to education can be traced back to the traditional concept of the natural duty of parents to take care of and bring up their children. This parental responsibility gradually and increasingly became associated with furthering the development and needs of children instead of conforming to the wishes of the parents. Emphasis has shifted towards formal education as an indispensable part of upbringing. Today this right is considered as primarily the right of all children to be educated. The duty to provide education has shifted from parents to society. Owing to the possibility of parents failing to exercise this power because of ignorance or selfishness, compulsory education, funded by the state up to a minimum age, has become the norm.

See C. R. M. Dlamini, 'Culture, Education, and Religion', in *Rights and Constitutionalism: The New South African Legal* Order, D. van Wyk, J. Dugard, B. de Villiers, and D. Davis (eds) (Cape Town: Juta & Co, 1994), p. 581.

[62] See Articles 28, 29, 30, and 31 of the CRC.

further that higher levels of education shall be accessible to all without discrimination of any kind.[63] It also protects the child from exploitative work that might interfere with the child's education.[64] Similarly, the African Charter on Human and Peoples' Rights (ACHPR), 1981 states that 'every individual shall have a right to education'.[65] Thus, the right to education is given wide recognition in a number of important international and regional human rights instruments.[66]

Right to Education in South Africa and Nigeria

Both the South African and the Nigerian Constitutions recognize the right to education. The Constitution of the Republic of South Africa, 1996, for instance, provides that everyone has the right to a basic education, including adult basic education;[67] and to further education that the state, through reasonable measures, must make progressively available and accessible.[68] The constitution provides, further, that everyone has the right to receive education in the official language or languages of his/her choice in public educational institutions,[69] as well as the right to establish and maintain independent educational institutions.[70]

[63] Both South Africa and Nigeria have ratified this convention.

[64] See Article 32 of the CRC.

[65] Article 17 of the ACHPR.

[66] See Article 10 of the Convention on the Elimination of Discrimination Against Women (CEDAW) 1979; Articles 23, 24, and 29 of the Convention on the Rights of the Child (CRC) 1989; Article 17 of the African Charter on Human and Peoples' Rights (ACHPR), 1981; the African Charter on the Rights and Welfare of the Child, 1990; the UNESCO Convention Against Discrimination in Education, 1960; the World Declaration on Education for All—Meeting Basic Learning Needs, adopted by the World Conference on Education for All on 9 March 1990; the European Convention, 1953; the American Declaration of the Rights and Duties of Man, 1948, among others. Apart from the human rights law, other laws such as refugee law, humanitarian law, migration law, and trade law equally regulate education. See Tomasevski, K., 'Has the Right to Education a Future within the United Nations? A Behind-the-Scenes Account by the Special Rapporteur on the Right to Education 1998–2004', *Human Rights Law Review*, 5(2), 2005, p. 224.

[67] Section 29(1)(a) of the South African Constitution, 1996.

[68] Section 29(1)(b) of the South African Constitution, 1996.

[69] Section 29(2) of the South African Constitution, 1996.

[70] Section 29(3) of the South African Constitution, 1996.

In Nigeria, the 'right' to education is guided by Section 18 of the Constitution of the Federal Republic of Nigeria (CFRN), 1999, which provides that government shall direct its policy towards ensuring that there are equal and adequate educational opportunities at all levels.[71] The section states further that government shall strive to eradicate illiteracy and shall, as and when practicable, provide free education at all levels.[72] In terms of the two constitutions as well as relevant regional and international human rights documents, 'education' is seen as a right that the state must endeavour to protect. The states have obligations to implement the right to education as postulated in the constitutions and other human rights instruments.

However, many years after the adoption of the Universal Declaration of Human Rights and several other international, regional, and national instruments that guarantee the right to education, the realization of this right remains elusive, especially in the developing countries. Dall asserts that more than 100 million school-age children still have no access to any kind of basic education service across the globe.[73] He states further that 960 million adults are still illiterate while more than one-third of the world's adults have neither access to printed knowledge nor technical skills to help them adapt to their societies' social and economic conditions.[74] In addition, millions of children and adults fail to

---

[71] Section 18(1) of the CFRN, 1999.

[72] Section 18(3)(a) to (d) of the CFRN 1999; In furtherance of these constitutional mandates, the Government launched the Universal Basic Education (UBE) Programme in 2004. Prior to this new programme, the Universal Primary Education (UPE) programme introduced by the Obasanjo-led military government in the 1970s was in operation. The UBE Act, 2004 and the Child's Rights Act, 2003 provide the legal framework for the implementation of the UBE programme, which makes basic education free and compulsory. See I. Igbuzor, 'The State of Education in Nigeria', Keynote Address delivered at a Round Table organized by Civil Society Action Coalition on Education for All (CSACEFA) (Abuja, 3 July 2006), p. 3, available at http://www.dawodu.com/igbuzor14.htm (accessed on 14 August 2008).

[73] S. Dall, 'Children's Right to Education: Reaching the Unreached', in J. R. Himes (ed.), *Implementing the Convention on the Rights of the Child* (The Hague/London/Boston: UNICEF & Martinus Nijhoff Publishers, 1995), p. 143.

[74] Ibid.

complete the basic education programmes they start; and millions more enter schools, but do not learn enough to meet their basic learning needs.[75]

However, at almost 5.5 per cent of gross domestic product, South Africa is seen as having one of the highest rates of government investment in education in the world.[76] Despite these commitments, and an all-inclusive educational policies developed by the Department of Education, it is observed that many schools in the country fall far short of the basic requirements for adequate education.[77] According to Berger, most schools (especially in rural areas) lack the resources to provide students with the education they need to participate effectively in a democratic capitalist society.[78] Pupil-to-teacher ratios in most rural schools are as high as 51 to 1, while many school buildings are in weak condition needing repairs. Most schools do not have safe drinking water within walking distance, toilets or telephones, and are badly overcrowded.[79] The 2001 Census revealed that 4.5 million South Africans aged 20 years and older did not have a formal education and another 4 million people had primary schooling only, thereby corroborating this position.[80]

In Nigeria, it is observed that poor government policies have led to drastic reductions in government spending/budget on education. The consequences of this include poor salaries for teachers, degradation of education facilities at all levels, and strikes in the universities and schools.[81] According to the Millennium Development Goals Report, the literacy level in Nigeria has steadily

[75] Ibid.

[76] See *The 2006/07 South African Yearbook*, p. 195; The 2008 budget also allocates R121.1 billion to education. See Tucker, 'Every Child in School, Every Day', in Education Law Project (Johannesburg: Centre for Applied Legal Studies), available at http://www.law.wits.ac.za/cals (accessed on 15 September 2008).

[77] See Eric Berger, 'The Right to Education under the South African Constitution', *Columbia Law Review*, 103 2003, pp. 614, 661.

[78] Ibid., pp. 619–20.

[79] Ibid.

[80] See 'The Right to Education, 5th Economic and Social Rights Reports Series 2002/2003 Financial Year', South African Human Rights Commission (21 June 2004), p. xiii.

[81] See Igbuzor, 'The State of Education in Nigeria'.

deteriorated, especially within the 15 to 24 years age bracket.[82] The report states further that by 1999 the overall literacy rate had declined to 64.1 per cent from 71.9 per cent in 1991. The trend was in the same direction for male and female members of the 15 to 24 years age bracket. Among males, the rate declined from 81.35 per cent in 1991 to 69.8 per cent in 1999, while the decline among females was from 62.49 per cent to 59.3 per cent during the same period.[83]

Similarly, the UNESCO Education for All (EFA) Global Monitoring Report on Sub-Saharan Africa gave the frightening figure of 33 million children of school age still not enrolled in school in the region.[84] Nigeria, together with six other countries, had more than 1 million out-of-school children each.[85] This is further corroborated by the UNICEF Report[86] which observes that Nigeria is lagging behind in the Millennium Development Goals (MDGs) that aim to ensure that children everywhere in the world are able to complete a full course of good quality education at all levels by 2015.[87]

While it is acknowledged that many issues dealing with the adequacy of education in any particular country are mainly of policy, financial, or pedagogical nature, this chapter seeks to examine the contributory effect of globalization on this issue. It will evaluate the actual impact of the concept on the right to education as postulated in both national and international human rights instruments. In a globalized world, this issue becomes more relevant in view of the

---

[82] See 'Nigeria Millennium Development Goals 2005 Report, National Planning Commission' (Abuja, 2005), p. 14.

[83] Ibid.

[84] 'UNESCO Education For All Global Monitoring Report, Regional Overview: Sub-Saharan Africa' (2008), p. 2, available at: http://www.efareport.unesco.org (accessed on 14 August 2008).

[85] Others are Burkina Faso, Cote d'Ivoire, Ethiopia, Kenya, Mali, and Niger.

[86] See Victor, 'Nigeria Lagging Behind in MDGs—UNICEF', *The Punch Newspaper*, 12 August 2008, availableat http://www.punchng.com/Articl. aspx?theartic=Art20080812273179 (accessed on 12 August 2008).

[87] The world adopted eight Millennium Development Goals in 2000. These goals represent a common vision for reducing poverty by 2015 and provide clear objectives for significant improvement in quality of people's lives. Learning and education are recognized as the heart of all development and consequently, of this global agenda. See http://www.un.org/Pubs/chronicle/2007/issue4/0407p37. html (accessed on 13 August 2008).

attendant questions of who should provide education, for whom, how, with what content, and under what conditions. Further, in the context of globalization, education appears to be treated in terms of market shares and competitive prices as if it were any ordinary economic service. The introduction of user fees in schools, and the privatization and commercialization of education that globalization may engender could adversely impact on the concept of education as a right.

IMPACT OF GLOBALIZATION ON THE RIGHT TO EDUCATION

Globalization underlies structural dynamics that drive social, political, economic, and cultural processes around the world.[88] It has a visible impact on social and economic development everywhere. It presumably gives everyone an equal chance, if each individual improves his or her educational levels. It is observed that the overall levels of education have increased throughout the world on account of globalization.[89] Although education is the major tool for incorporation into the "knowledge society" and technological economy, it is globalization which brings education to the forefront.[90]

It is observed that globalization increases the range of economic, political, and social powers and influence beyond national and even continental boundaries and identities. In its most extreme form, it is posited that the concept of globalization predicts the end of national economy and the end of the nation state as the primary unit of political organization and loyalty.[91] Thus, globalization's characteristics are spatial reorganization of production systems and labour markets, the spread of industrial organization and manufacture across borders, technological revolutions in computers, telecommunications, and transport, the spread and dominance of market forces, the re-emergence of laissez-faire as an economic orthodoxy, and the

---

[88] Nelly P. Stromquist, 'The Impact of Globalization on Education and Gender: An Emergent Cross-National Balance', *Journal of Education*, 37, 2005, p. 7.

[89] Ibid., p. 12.

[90] Ibid., p. 15.

[91] Morgan, 'Globalization and State Socialism', p. 96.

substantial migration of peoples.[92] It also claims the emergence of a borderless world in which global communications and a relentless trend towards a monoculture absorbs or even erases national cultures.[93]

The implications of globalization are enormous. The weakness of the nation state in the face of global flows of money, goods, and services is seen as constituting the final nail in the coffin of effective state intervention in political economy.[94] Tilly submits that rights (or publicly enforceable claims) would certainly be at risk in such a world, asserting that rights come into being as a result of negotiations that produce contracts to which authorities (historically governments) are always parties. Without authorities, no rights exist. Citizenships and democracy depend on the maintenance of such rights. In general, a state's capacity to pursue social policies, including workers' rights, has depended on the power of enforcement.[95] The globalization of economic activities and the creation of powerful transnational corporations are now undermining the capacity of states to pursue effective social policies.[96]

However, it is submitted that globalization is not a neutral process in which developed and developing countries have equal participation. It is observed that the odds are heavily tilted in favour of the industrialized world, given that the current participation of Africa in world trade is only 2 per cent.[97] It is not therefore entirely surprising that many people in Africa tend to have a negative perception of globalization and such economic philosophies as are propounded by the World Trade Organization (WTO) and the conditionality of

---

[92] Ibid.; Ohmae argues thus: 'Inevitably, the emergence of the interlinked economy brings with it an erosion of national sovereignty as the power of information directly touches local communities, academic, professional, and social institutions, corporations and individuals. It is this borderless world that will give participating economies the capacity for boundless prosperity.' See Kenichi Ohmae, *The Borderless World: Power and Strategy in the Interlinked Economy* (London: Fontana Paperbacks, 1991), p. 269.

[93] Morgan, 'Globalization and State Socialism', p. 96.

[94] Ibid.

[95] Tilly, C., 'Globalization threatens Labor's Rights', *International Labour and Working Class History*, 47, 1995, p. 23; see also, Morgan, 'Globalization and State Socialism', pp. 96–97.

[96] Tilly, 'Globalization threatens Labor's Rights', p. 23.

[97] See Iwara, 'Identity Politics, Globalization and Socio-Political Engineering', p. 21.

the World Bank and the International Monetary Fund (IMF) that goes with it.[98]

The pertinent question, therefore, is this: What is globalization doing to education in South Africa and Nigeria? In other words, what is the impact of globalization on the right to education in South Africa and Nigeria? In addressing this question, two particular concepts emerge: 'education-as-a-right' and 'education-as-a-trade-service'. While human rights proponents advocate the notion of education as a right, globalization on the other hand brings about the idea of education-as-a-trade-service. In this context, Tomasevski submits that proponents of globalization object to education being provided by the government. In that version, they contend that education should be traded just like any other service and its financing by the government would be defined as an illegal state subsidy.[99]

However, on the other hands, human rights advocates portray the right to education as defined in international human rights treaties whereby most, if not all, education would be provided or at least financed by the government.[100] In the world of globalization, education is described in terms of market shares and competitive prices, with university education, in particular, traded like any other service.[101] It is in this context that it is submitted that the two notions, 'education-as-a-right' and 'education-as-a-trade-service' do not overlap. They describe two different worlds which coexist in parallel.

In a globalized world, education appears to be treated in terms of market shares and competitive prices as if it were any ordinary economic service. Globalization also encourages competition, and the free flow of ideas, information, and human capital. It is, however, argued that globalization facilitates the migration of highly trained human capital from less developed countries to the developed countries with the resultant consequence of 'brain drain' being experienced. The introduction of user fees in schools, and the

---

[98] Ibid.
[99] See Tomasevski, 'Has the Right to Education a Future Within the United Nations?', p. 207.
[100] Ibid.
[101] Ibid., pp. 207–08.

privatization and commercialization of education (which may be facilitated by globalization) could adversely impact on the meaningful realization of the right to education.[102]

Tomasevski therefore submits that the advent of trade in education services has challenged the very notion that education exists as a human right.[103] She argues that most ministries of education in the OECD countries often monitor the ranking of their countries in the global assessments of educational performance. She asserts that ministries of education in developing countries are likely to be influenced by the World Bank's education strategy, which is not informed by human rights law.[104]

It is submitted that the contemporary processes of globalization have changed the framework for the implementation of the system of human rights as a whole in fundamental ways.[105] Eide asserts that the present direction of globalization has been strongly influenced by the neo-liberal ideology.[106] The ideology opposes an active role of the state in social and economic affairs, claiming that such intervention will negatively affect the economy of the country as a whole.[107] The adherents of these ideologies often argue that societies are best served by the survival of the fittest, notwithstanding that such policies lead to vastly increased inequality and encourage great hardship due to

---

[102] See, generally, Stromquist, 'The Impact of Globalization on Education and Gender', pp. 17–23.

[103] See Tomasevski, 'Has the Right to Education a Future Within the United Nations?', p. 224.

[104] Ibid.

[105] See Asbjorn Eide, 'Interdependence and Indivisibility of Human Rights', p. 40.

[106] According to Eide, the extreme versions of neo-liberal ideologies, the recent versions of laissez-faire policies that had wide support in the dominant economic circles during the middle and later part of the nineteenth century in Great Britain and the United States, and which have had a revival in recent years. The ideology opposes an active role of the state in social and economic affairs, claiming that such intervention will negatively affect the economy of the country as a whole. See Eide, ibid., p. 37; Historically, education has been public education. But neo-liberals want to break what they called 'the monopoly of the state' and to increase the supply of education through non-governmental stakeholders and, more important, through privatization, which means bringing private capital into education for profit-making, which ostensibly will be to the benefit of both the learner and purveyor of teaching. See Bhola, 'Access to Education: A Global Perspective', p. 56.

[107] See Eide, 'Interdependence and Indivisibility of Human Rights', p. 37.

lack of social prevention of poverty. They argue that those who survive will ultimately benefit from a future richer society resulting from the achievements of the most capable and creative.[108] We submit, however, that such convictions are in stark contrast to the human rights system adopted since the Second World War.[109]

In the most problematic forms, neo-liberal ideology requires privatization of public enterprises, deregulation of the economy, blanket liberalization of trade and industry, massive tax cuts, strict control on labour, reduction of public expenditures, particularly social spending, and downsizing of government, expansion of international markets, and removal of controls on global financial flows.[110] It is asserted that these have facilitated the enormous growth in the size and reach of multinational corporations, whose power has increased greatly in comparison to the power of states and their governments. It is argued that in this process, the IMF and the World Bank have moved to centre stage as guardians of the global economic order, by imposing criteria for credit and grants that are essential to development.[111]

It is observed that during the 1980s and part of the 1990s, the IMF and the World Bank pursued a rigid neo-liberal approach. One of its most negative aspects, directly relevant to the core concern of UNESCO's right to education, was the World Bank policy calling for introduction of school fees even at primary school level, in direct conflict with Article 13 of the ICESCR, which requires primary education to be free and compulsory for all.[112] In addition to Article 13 of the covenant, Article 2(1) also imposes obligations on the state parties to ensure full realization of the rights in the covenant. The article provides:

> Each State Party to the present Covenant undertakes to take steps, individually and through international assistance and co-operation, especially economic and technical, to the maximum of its available resources, with a view to achieving progressively the full realization of the rights recognized in the present Covenant by all appropriate means, including particularly the adoption of legislative measures

---

[108] Ibid.
[109] Ibid.
[110] Ibid., p. 40.
[111] Ibid.
[112] Ibid.

Under international law, the primary responsibility for human rights rest with the government. States are required to respect the freedoms and fulfil the rights of their citizens. States are never entitled to abdicate from their human rights obligations, be it in the context of international trade and regulations, international investment agreements, or in any other way. Human rights hold priority in all such relations.[113]

Bhola submits that globalization is both the context and the condition of all education today, all around the world.[114] It is submitted that the current path of globalization must change. Too few from the developing world currently share in the benefits of globalization.[115] Too many in this world have no voice in the design of globalization or any influence on its course. Everywhere, globalization has widened the social divide.[116] It is posited that globalization must be reinvented to have a 'human face' and must be made to serve all people both in the developed and the developing world.[117]

It is submitted that globalization is a theory born of the neo-liberal ideology of 'market over politics' and free market without social responsibility. It is submitted that development under globalization has led to a world governed by 'profit over people', dispensing altogether with the whole idea of culturally rich, humanistic societies that live in peace, advance the grand project of civilization, and fulfil the destiny of humankind.[118] Bhola submits further that in its concrete manifestations development under globalization has brought about a transfer of wealth from poor to rich nations, and from poor people within nations to their rich compatriots; technology has created environmental disasters and widespread displacement among

---

[113] Ibid.

[114] See Bhola, 'Access to Education: A Global Perspective', p. 45.

[115] It is submitted that the shift of funds from the south to the north means that fewer resources can be used at the country level, for either infrastructural investments or social welfare concerns. National budgets are currently defined first in terms of what must be assigned to the payment of external debt. For instance, Alhaji Atiku Abubakar, a former Nigeria vice president noted that in the late 1970s, Nigeria borrowed $2 billion from the international community. By 2004, it had paid about $28 billion and still has an outstanding debt of nearly $30 billion. See Stromquist, 'The Impact of Globalization on Education and Gender', p. 10.

[116] See Bhola, 'Access to Education: A Global Perspective', p. 45.

[117] Ibid.

[118] Ibid., p. 51.

labourers struggling to eke out a living; the state has withdrawn from education and health services; and people unable to buy those services are left without them.[119]

It is also observed that the current model of education in the Third World is reinforced by the frames and forces of globalization, which have very nearly succeeded in establishing a new division of labour in the globalized world, with knowledge-based high-paying jobs in developed countries, and low-skill services and assembly jobs in developing countries. The educational implication of this new division of labour is that the Third World does not need much more than basic education for the preparation of its low-skilled labourers and, indeed, cannot really afford to become a knowledge-producing, knowledge-using region.[120]

The Western free-market, neo-liberal model of development is inappropriate for most Third World countries since it largely serves the interests of a small aristocracy while neglecting the poor and the poorest of the poor in informal subsistence economies.[121] The educational systems that are in place do keep a small portion of the formal economy going, but even here things are regressing as the state withdraws from its responsibility to provide public education. The World Bank's structural adjustment policies have provided cover to states to withdraw from their responsibility to provide at least basic education for all children.[122] University education has languished in most Third World countries. Only the rich can 'buy' good education from private academics at home and universities

---

[119] Ibid.

[120] Ibid., p. 53.

[121] Ibid., p. 54.

[122] To ensure payment of the external debt, international financial institutions have promoted the implementation of major changes in the economies of debtor countries. There is consensus that these structural adjustment programmes (SAPs) constitute the primary mechanism through which globalization has affected people in developing countries. SAPs establish the economic priorities of countries and shape their government programmes for debt repayment in order to qualify those countries for new lines of credit. Such programmes usually call for opening national economies to global trade, engaging in government austerity, and engaging in privatization of state enterprises. See Stromquist, 'The Impact of Globalization on Education and Gender', p. 10; See also, Bhola, 'Access to Education: A Global Perspective', p. 54.

abroad.[123] This is particularly true of Nigeria where there are many private universities, private secondary and private primary schools with very exorbitant school fees that are beyond the reach of average citizens.

Tomasevski therefore advises that one should look into the effects of IMF and World Bank poverty reduction strategy papers on the accessibility of education to see if an increase in education fees is part of the package of measures agreed between the government concerned and the IMF. It is equally important to know whether financial and other forms of assistance or compensatory measures are available for underprivileged persons and groups to safeguard continued access to education as a human right.[124] In a number of African countries, it is found that state monopoly on education is coming to an end. In addition, there is the tendency to involve the private (business) sector in the funding and building of schools. The privatization of education is supported, and sometimes even imposed, by the IMF and the World Bank (which are agents of globalization) within the framework of structural adjustment programmes.[125]

In terms of regional and international human rights instruments, primary education shall be free and compulsory. It is, therefore, submitted that primary education must enjoy priority with respect to resource allocation, because it deals with the fundamental basis for a person's development and the development of society as a whole. It is the responsibility of the state to provide for primary education and to maintain education services. Government cannot waive that responsibility by giving more concessions to the private sector, or stimulating public–private partnerships for financing the education infrastructure.[126] In terms of Article 13 of the ICESCR, states have the principal responsibility for the direct provision of education in

---

[123]   See Bhola, 'Access to Education: A Global Perspective', p. 54.

[124]   Tomasevski, K, 'Report on the Mission to Uganda', UN Doc. E/CN.4/2000/6/ Add.1, paras 29–34; see also, F. Coomans, 'Content and Scope of the Right to Education as a Human Right and Obstacles to Its Realization', in *Human Rights in Education, Science and Culture*, Donders and Volodin (eds), pp. 200–01.

[125]   For this development, see, UNESCO Sources, No. 102, June 1998, pp. 12–13; see also, Coomans, 'Content and Scope of the Right to Education as a Human Right', p. 223

[126]   Ibid., p. 201.

most circumstances.[127] States have the immediate duty to provide primary education for all.[128] For those states that have not yet realized compulsory and free primary education, there is an 'unequivocal obligation' to adopt and implement a detailed plan of action as provided for in Article 14.[129]

As a reaction to the lack of government resources available for education, a number of African countries decided to embark upon a new strategy.[130] For instance, in 1998, African ministers of education agreed that the time had come to put an end to the state monopoly of education. Under pressure from and encouraged/supported by the IMF and the World Bank, a strategy of cost-sharing in public–private partnership is now promoted.[131] Partners include the government on the one hand and international donors, the private sector, and communities on the other. For African countries, this strategy means, for example, that non-governmental organizations (NGOs) and local communities should make up for the state's failings.[132] It is submitted that privately funded education benefits the better-off, who can afford it, with the consequences of excluding disadvantaged groups. Thus, state failure to provide for education might have a negative impact on equality of opportunity for children in all sectors of society.[133]

Governments present all kinds of reasons as justifications for having or introducing school fees for children of compulsory school age. These include a lack of sufficient public schools compared to the number of private schools that charge fees, lack of government funding of public schools and the need to cut public

---

[127] Committee on Economic, Social and Cultural Rights, 'General Comment No. 13 on the Right to Education (Article 13 of the covenant)', CESCR 21st Session, December, UN Doc. E/C.12/1999/10, para. 48.

[128] Ibid., para. 51.

[129] Committee on Economic, Social and Cultural Rights, 'General Comment No. 11: Plans of Action for Primary Education, (Article 14)', UN Doc. E/C.12/1999/4, para. 9.

[130] Coomans, 'Content and Scope of the Right to Education as a Human Right', p. 209.

[131] See, generally, K. Tomasevski, *Education Denied-Costs and Remedies* (London and New York: Zed Books, 2003), pp. 71–77.

[132] Coomans, 'Content and Scope of the Right to Education as a Human Right', pp. 209–10.

[133] K. Watkins, *The Oxfam Education Report* (Oxford: Oxfam, 2000), p. 149.

spending for education as a consequence of structural adjustment programmes.[134]

Furthermore, another serious effect of globalization on the developing countries is the issue of mobility of labour and its consequential effect of brain drain in the academic institutions. The term 'brain drain' is often used to describe the movement of high-level experts from developing countries to industrialized nations.[135] As the state of the universities has deteriorated in the developing countries, academics have sought employment opportunities outside their continents, consequently draining institutions of their faculty members. Many public institutions in Nigeria have lost significant numbers of their key faculty members to universities and other commercially oriented institutions in the developed countries.

Also, the idea of globalization has facilitated regional migration, that is, academic migration to regional and neighbouring countries, and brought about serious shortages of high-level faculty in some countries in which Nigeria and South Africa are inclusive. Many academic departments have lost their pre-eminent faculty to regional universities in other parts of Africa and other continents of the world. Academics and professionals in Nigeria have migrated to other countries, most notably, the USA, South Africa, Botswana, Saudi Arabia, and European countries.[136] Reports also indicate that many academics from South Africa are equally migrating to Australia, Britain, Canada, the USA, and other developed countries.[137]

However, in Africa, South Africa appears to be the biggest beneficiary of the exodus of scholars from other African countries, especially Nigeria. This is attributable to the idea of globalization which encourages free flow of skill and knowledge coupled with the

---

[134] See K. Tomasevski, *School Fees as Hindrance to Universalizing Primary Education*, Background study for EFA Global Monitoring Report 2003–2004, (27 June 2003), pp. 81–82.

[135] D. Teferra and P. G. Altbach, *African Higher Education* (Bloomington & Indianapolis: Indiana University Press, 2003), p. 11.

[136] According to Munzali Jibril, it is estimated that there are at least 10,000 Nigerian academics and 21,000 Nigerian doctors in the United States alone. See Teferra and Altbach, *African Higher Education*, pp. 12, 495.

[137] It is ironic; however, that while several African countries complain about the loss of their highly skilled labour to South Africa, South Africa itself bemoans its loss of talent to other countries. Ibid., p. 12.

fact that the South African job market provides better salary packages in the continent.[138] Though the idea of globalization facilitates movement from one country to the other, the causes of migration, whether regional or international, are complex.[139]

It is observed that the impact of globalization on the right to education has been both positive and negative. It is contended that the positive impacts of globalization are enormous and have contributed to a significant increase in the level of education throughout the world by opening new avenues for access to education at different levels. On the other hand, globalization has been criticized for its adverse effects on the developing countries. Writing on the inequality created by the globalization process, Khor argues as follows:

> Globalization is a very uneven process, with unequal distribution of benefits and looses. This imbalance leads to polarization between the few countries and groups that gain, and the many countries and groups in society that lose out and are marginalized. Globalization, polarization, wealth concentration and marginalization are therefore linked through the same process ... the uneven and unequal nature of the present globalization process is manifested in the fast growing gap between the world's rich and poor people and between developed and developing countries, and in the large differences among nations in the distribution of gains and losses.[140]

However, globalization also has its advantages. It is submitted that globalization contributes to developments in science and technology, communications, and, in particular, information processing, which have substantially changed the structure of the global system and can have many beneficial consequences for human rights. While during the last two decades they might have resulted in many negative consequences, developments in communications and information processing may be turned to the advantage of a

---

[138] Ibid.

[139] The reasons why scholars migrate or decide to stay abroad are products of a complex blend of economic, political, social, cultural, and psychological factors. The impact and chemistry of each factors varies from country to county and individual to individual and fluctuates with time, even for the same individual. See Teferra and Altbach, *African Higher Education*, p. 12.

[140] See Khor, *Globalization and the South: Some Critical Issues*, pp. 9–10.

holistic approach to human rights.[141] Globalization is a plus in the sense that the spectacular advances in Western science and technology, and consequently in telecommunication and transportation, have effected a virtual annihilation of time and distance, leading to an acceleration of world history and an intensification of processes (economic, social, cultural, and political) within, between, and among nations.[142]

It is also submitted that one of the positive aspects of globalization is that it enables goods and services to filter through to states in every part of the world. Shipping, airfreight, and business travels facilitate participation in the global economy.[143] Further, there are problems that citizens of a state may not be able to solve without external assistance; this also constitutes a positive contribution on the part of globalization.

In addition, international cooperation, through the transfer of information, knowledge, and technology, that globalization engenders, is essential to the effective realization of the right to education in the less developed countries.[144] It has been repeatedly observed that the right to education is an economic necessity upon which the development of developing countries depends.[145] The gap between educational facilities in industrialized countries and those in developing countries demands an active policy of academic cooperation which would assist in contributing to the implementation of the right to education.[146]

Since its inception in 1945, the United Nations has recognized the necessity of international cooperation in solving international problems of an economic, social, cultural, or humanitarian character.[147] Article 55 of the United Nation Charter provides, *inter alia*, that the United Nations shall promote 'international cultural and educa-

---

[141] See Eide, 'Interdependence and Indivisibility of Human Rights', p. 41.

[142] See Bhola, 'Access to Education: A Global Perspective', p. 50.

[143] Esiemokhai *et al.*, 'Globalization and the Right to Democracy and Good Governance', p. 7.

[144] Hodgson, *The Human Right to Education*', p. 213.

[145] Ibid., pp. 213–14.

[146] M. Nowak, 'The Right to Education', in *Economic, Social and Cultural Rights*, A. Eide (ed.) (1995), pp. 189, 198.

[147] Article 1(3) of the United Nations Charter.

tional co-operation'. The United Nations General Assembly and the General Conference of the UNESCO have therefore been active in promoting the exchange of human and material resources between states.[148]

In summary, in the context of globalization, because of workers' need to compete for the few good jobs globalization creates, the demand for educational expansion has to increase. Parents realize education is an asset in modern society and invest, to the extent of their financial means, in schooling for their children. As a result, enrolments are rising across countries.[149] Much of the expansion of education in several countries has taken place through increased parental share of schooling costs. In a number of countries, students even in the primary level of education pay fees to attend public schools. Thus, school fees operate as a major obstacle to the universalization of primary education. In addition, globalization encourages privatization and liberalization of schooling. It is observed that international financial institutions have insisted on the introduction of user fees, and cost-sharing and privatization of education. This means treating education as a mere commodity in the market place, leading to some loss of the human right to education.[150]

CONCLUSION

This chapter argues that under international and national human rights documents, education is seen as a right with corresponding obligations on states to provide fundamental education. It has been observed that the impact of globalization in this arena has been both positive and negative. The positive impacts of globalization are enormous and have contributed to a significant increase in the level of education throughout the world by opening new avenues for access to education at different levels. Globalization also encourages competition, and the free flow of ideas, information, and human capital. The consequence of this free flow of human capital is the migration

---

[148] Hodgson, *The Human Right to Education*, p. 212.
[149] See Stromquist, 'The Impact of Globalization on Education and Gender', p. 17.
[150] Ibid., p. 18.

of highly trained human capital from less developed countries to developed countries. This has resulted in a brain drain in the developing countries. It is also observed that the introduction of user fees in schools, and the privatization and commercialization of education (which may be facilitated by globalization) adversely impacts upon the meaningful realization of the right to education. Globalization, with its notion of education as a trade commodity, doubtless undermines the concept of education as a right that states are obliged to provide. If states are to religiously adhere to the strict notion of free market advocated by globalization, the right to education as guaranteed in both the South African and Nigeria Constitutions become meaningless.

Under international law, the primary responsibility for human rights realization rests with the government. States are required to respect the freedoms and fulfil the rights of their citizens. States are never entitled to abdicate their human rights obligations. Human rights must hold priority. It is, therefore, suggested that the current path of globalization, which has effectively widened the social divide, must change. It is further suggested that globalization must be reinvented to exhibit a human face, and must be made to benefit both the developed and developing countries.

BIBLIOGRAPHY

Books

Hodgson, D. (1998), *The Human Right to Education*, Dartmouth: Ashgate.

Khor, M. (2000), *Globalization and the South: Some Critical Issues*, Ibadan: Spectrum Books.

Khoza, S. (ed.) (2007), *Socio-Economic Rights in South Africa* (2nd edn), Cape Town: Community Law Centre, University of Western Cape.

Newsom, John (1950), *The Child at School*, Harmonsworth and Middlesex: Penguin Books.

Smith, W. O. Lester (1949), *Education in Great Britain*, Oxford: Oxford University Press.

Obilade, A. O. (1990), *The Nigerian Legal System*, Ibadan: Spectrum Books.

Ohmae, K. (1991), *The Borderless World: Power and Strategy in the Interlinked Economy*, London: Fontana Paperbacks.

Teferra, D. and P. G. Altbach (2003), *African Higher Education*, Bloomington and Indianapolis: Indiana University Press.

Tomasevski, K. (2003), *Education Denied-Costs and Remedies*, London and New York: Zed Books.

Watkins, K. (2000), *The Oxfam Education Report*, Oxford: Oxfam.

Articles in Books and Journals

Berger, E., 'The Right to Education under the South African Constitution', *Columbia Law Review*, 103, 2003, p. 614.

Bhola, H. S., 'Access to Education: A Global Perspective', in *Widening Access to Education as Social Justice: Essays in Honor of Michael Omolewa*, Akpovire Oduaran and Harbans S. Bhola (eds) (2006), Dordrecht, the Netherlands: Springer/UNESCO Publishing.

Burtch, B., 'Education, Law and Social Justice', in *Widening Access to Education as Social Justice: Essays in Honor of Michael Omolewa*, Akpovire Oduaran and Harbans S., Bhola (eds) (2006), Dordrecht, the Netherlands: Springer/UNESCO Publishing.

Coomans, F., 'The Core Content of the Right to Education', in *Exploring the Core Content of Socio-Economic Rights: South African and International Perspectives*, Danie Brand and Sage Russell (eds) (2002), Pretoria: Protea Book House.

Coomans, F., 'Content and Scope of the Right to Education as a Human Right and Obstacles to Its Realization', in *Human Rights in Education, Science and Culture*, Yvonne Donders and Vladimir Volodin (eds) (2007), Ashgate/UNESCO Publishing.

Dall, S., 'Children's Right to Education: Reaching the Unreached', in *Implementing the Convention on the Rights of the Child*, J. R. Himes (ed.) (1995), The Hague/London/Boston: UNICEF & Martinus Nijhoff Publishers.

Delbruck, J., 'The Right to Education as an International Human Right', *German Yearbook of International Law*, 35, 1992, p. 94.

Dlamini, C. R. M., 'Culture, Education, and Religion', in *Rights and Constitutionalism: The New South African Legal Order*, D. van Wyk, J. Dugard, B. de Villiers, and D. Davis (eds) (1994), Cape Town: Juta & Co.

Eide, A., 'Interdependence and Indivisibility of Human Rights', in *Human Rights in Education, Science and Culture: Legal Developments and Challenges*, Yvonne Donders and Vladimir Volodin (eds) (2007), Paris/Hampshire/Burlington: Ashgate/UNESCO Publishing.

Govindjee, A., 'Lessons for South African Social Assistance Law from India: Part 1—The Ties that Bind: The Indian Constitution and Reasons for Comparing South Africa with India', *Obiter*, 26(3), 2005, p. 575.

Iwara, A. U., 'Identity Politics, Globalization and Socio-Political Engineering in Nigeria', in *Nigeria and Globalization Discourses on Identity Politics and Social Conflict*, Duro Oni, Suman Gupta, Tope Omoniyi, Efurosibina Adegbija, and Segun Awonusi (eds) (2004), Lagos: Centre for Black and African Arts and Civilization.

Kwanashie, M., 'The Concept and process of Globalization', *Central Bank of Nigeria Economic and Financial Review*, 36(4), 1998, p. 341.

Malherbe, R., 'The Constitutional Framework for Pursuing Equal Opportunities in Education', *Perspectives in Education*, 22(3), 2004, p. 9.

Morgan, W. J., 'Globalization and State Socialism: End of Illusions or New Educational Opportunities?', in *Widening Access to Education as Social Justice: Essays in Honor of Michael Omolewa*, Akpovire Oduaran and Harbans S. Bhola (eds) (2006), Dordrecht, the Netherlands: Springer/UNESCO Publishing.

Obadan, M. I., 'International Trade and Globalization: The Socio-Political and Economic Realities for Nigeria', in *Foreign Investment Promotion in A Globalized World*, D. A. Guobadia and P. T. Akper (eds) (2006), Lagos: NIALS.

Obi, C. and I. Okwechime, 'Globalization and Identity Politics: The Emerging Patterns of Inter-ethnic Relations in Nigeria's Niger Delta', in *Nigeria and Globalization Discourses on Identity Politics and Social Conflict*, Duro Oni, Suman Gupta, Tope Omoniyi, Efurosibina Adegbija, and Segun Awonusi (eds) (20040, Lagos: Centre for Black and African Arts and Civilization.

Obiagwu, C. and C. A. Odinkalu, 'Nigeris: Combating Legacies of Colonialism and Militarism' in *Human Rights Under African Constitutions: Realizing the Promise for Ourselves,* Abdullahi Ahmed An-Na'im (ed.) (20030, Philadelphia: University of Pennsylvania Press.

Seafield, L. 'South Africa: The Interdependence of All Human Rights', in *Human Rights under African Constitutions: Realizing the Promise for Ourselves*, Abdullahi Ahmed An-Na'im (ed.) (2003), Philadelphia: University of Pennsylvania Press.

Segun, A., 'Globalization and Hegemonic English in Nigeria: Identity Conflicts and Linguistic Pluralism', in *Nigeria and Globalization Discourses on Identity Politics and Social Conflict*, Duro Oni, Suman Gupta, Tope Omoniyi, Efurosibina Adegbija, and Segun Awonusi (eds) (2004), Lagos: Centre for Black and African Arts and Civilization.

'South Africa in Brief', *The Constitution of the Republic of South Africa* (4th edn), Juta's Pocket Statutes (eds) (2006).

Stromquist, N. P., 'The Impact of Globalization on Education and Gender: An Emergent Cross-National Balance', *Journal of Education*, 37, 2005, p. 7.

Tade, A., 'From Colonization to Globalization: Reflections on Issues in Transformation and Democratic Development in Africa', in *Globalization and Sustainable Human development in Nigeria*, Aina Tade *et al.* (eds) (2002), Lagos: University of Lagos.

Tilly, C., 'Globalization threatens Labor's Rights', *International Labour and Working Class History*, 47, 1995, p. 1.

Tomasevski, K., 'Has the Right to Education a Future Within the United Nations? A Behind-the-Scenes Account by the Special Rapporteur on the Right to Education, 1998–2004', *Human Rights Law Review*, 5(2), 2005, p. 205.

Ukpokolo, I., 'Globalization and the Search for Cultural Philosophy for Contemporary Africa', in *Nigeria and Globalization Discourses on Identity Politics and Social Conflict*, Duro Oni, Suman Gupta, Tope Omoniyi, Efurosibina Adegbija, and Segun Awonusi (eds) (2004), Lagos: Centre for Black and African Arts and Civilization.

Uweru, B. C., 'Repugnancy Doctrine and Customary Law in Nigeria: A Positive Aspect of British Colonialism', *African Research* Review, 2(2), 2008, p. 286.

Verheyde, M., 'Article 28: The Right to Education', in *A Commentary of the United Nations Convention on the Rights of the Child*, A. Alen, J. Vande Lanotte, E. Verhellen, F. Ang, E. Berghmans, and M. Verheyde (eds) (2006), Leiden: Martinus Nijhoff Publishers.

Veriawa G. and Coomans, F., 'The Right to Education', in *Socio-economic Rights in South Africa*, Danie Brand and Christof Heyns (eds) (2005), Pretoria: Pretoria University Law Press.

Papers Presented at Meetings/Conferences

Esiemokhai, E. O., M. O. Adeleke, and O. S. Kuteyi, 'Globalization and the Right to Democracy and Good Governance: The Best Practices', paper presented at the 40th Annual Conference of the Nigerian Association of Law Teachers, Lagos, 16–19 May 2004.

Igbuzor, I., 'The State of Education in Nigeria', Keynote Address delivered at a Round Table organized by Civil Society Action Coalition on Education for All, Abuja, 3 July 2006.

John, S. M., Yakubu, and A. A. Kana, 'Globalization, Democracy, and Good Governance in Nigeria—the Best Practices', paper presented at the 40th Annual Conference of the Nigerian Association of Law Teachers, Lagos, 16–19 May 2004.

Okon, E. E. 'Foreign Investment and National Security in Developing Countries under the Globalized Environment: The Nigerian Perspective', paper presented at the Round Table on International Trade and Globalization: Challenges for Nigeria, Lagos,, 18 June 2002.

Usman, Y. B. 'What Exactly is Globalization?', Keynote Address delivered at the 40th Annual Conference of the Nigerian Association of Law Teachers, Lagos, 16–19 May 2004.

Official Documents/Reports

Association of University Teachers & Development Education Association, (1999), *Globalization and Higher Education (Guidance on Ethical Issues arising from International Academic Activities)*, London.

Country Education Profiles on South Africa (2nd edn), Canberra: Commonwealth of Australia, 2004.

'Recommendation Concerning Education for International Understanding, Cooperation and Peace and Education Relating to Human Rights and Fundamental Freedoms', 1974.

'The Right to Education', 5th Economic and Social Rights Reports Series, 2002/2003 Financial Year, South African Human Rights Commission, 2004.

'Nigeria Millennium Development Goals, 2005 Report', Abuja, Nigeria: National Planning Commission, 2005.

K. Tomasevski, 'Report on the Mission to Uganda', UN Doc. E/CN.4/2000/6/Add.1.

K. Tomasevski, 'School Fees as Hindrance to Universalizing Primary Education', Background Study for EFA Global Monitoring Report, 2003–2004.

Online Documents

Tucker, 'Every Child in School, Every Day', Education Law Project, Johannesberg: Centre for Applied Legal Studies, available at http://www.law.wits.ac.za/cals (accessed 15 September 2008).

UNESCO Education for All Global Monitoring Report, Regional Overview: Sub-Saharan Africa, available at http://www.efareport.unesco.org.

Victor, S., 'Nigeria Lagging Behind in MDGs—UNICEF', *The Punch Newspaper*, available at http://www.punchng.com/Articl.aspx?theartic=Art20080812273179 (accessed 8 December 2008).

Legal Cases

Brown v. *Board of Education of Topeka*, 347 US 438 (1954).
Jones v..*The Queen*, [1986] 2 SCR 284.
G. v. *An Bord*, [1980] IR 32.

6

Emergence of the Human Right to Water in an Era of Globalization and Its Implications for International Investment Law

Owen McIntyre

INTRODUCTION

It is often assumed by those opposed to the involvement of the private sector in the provision of water and sanitation services, particularly those concerned about private sector involvement in developing countries, that the recognition of the human right to water ought to operate to hinder such involvement.[1] However, while the practical application of the right to water should help to ensure that certain aspects of social protection, relating particularly to affordability, equality of access, restrictions on disconnection, public participation, and quality of supply, are respected and protected, for example, by means of their inclusion in contracts concluded between public authorities and private companies for the provision of water-related services, the normative requirements emerging from this right do not per se restrict the privatization of

[1] See, for example, Henri Smets, 'Economics of Water Services and the Right to Water', in *Fresh Water and International Economic Law*, Edith Brown Weiss, Laurence Boisson de Chazournes and Nathalie Bernasconi-Osterwalder (eds) (Oxford: Oxford University Press, 2005), pp. 177–83; Bronwyn Morgan, 'Turning Off the Tap: Urban Water Service Delivery and the Social Construction of Global Administrative Law', *European Journal of International Law*, 17, 2006, p. 215.

water services. In fact, the only statement of international declarative law impacting directly on private sector participation in this area is the one included in the 2001 Bonn Recommendations, adopted by 118 states at the Bonn International Conference on fresh water, to the effect that 'private sector participation should not be imposed on developing countries as a conditionality for funding'.[2] Indeed, the emergence of the human right to water may serve to facilitate private investment in water services by identifying broadly accepted standards of service and social safeguards, which private investors can factor into their investment decisions and which make it difficult for public authorities to alter the regulatory environment arbitrarily.

The inclusion of water and sanitation targets among the Millennium Development Goals (MDGs) has highlighted the need to mobilize private investment in order to have any realistic chance of meeting such targets. For example, it is quite clear that a number of key UN agencies envisage a significant role for private sector water providers in making progress towards the MDG target.[3] It is telling that the World Panel on Financing Water Infrastructure, which was convened by the UN secretary general, chaired by Michel Camdessus, a former president of the World Bank, and made up of representatives of international financial institutions, banks, and businesses involved in funding private investments in the water sector, adopted a report providing unqualified support for the existence of right to water.[4] In addition, the CEOs of at least two leading water multinationals, Suez and Véolia, have expressly recognized the universal nature of the right of access to water.[5]

---

[2] See http://www.water2001.de/outcome/BonnRecommendations/Bonn_Recommendations.pdf (accessed 12 October 2009).

[3] See, UNDP, *Human Development Report 2006. Beyond Scarcity: Power, Poverty and the Global Water Crisis* (New York: Palgrave Macmillan, 2006), p. 77; *Water in a Changing World*, 3rd UN World Water Development Report (Paris/London: UNESCO / Earthscan, 2009), pp. 9, 62–63, 262, 287.

[4] J. Winpenny, *Financing Water for All: Report of the World Panel on Financing Water Infrastructure* (Kyoto: World Water Council, 2003). See, Smets, 'Economics of Water Services and the Right to Water', p. 175. See also, Paul van Hofwegen, *Report of the Task Force on Financing Water for All* (Marseilles: World Water Council (WWC Publications), 2006).

[5] Smets, 'Economics of Water Services and the Right to Water', pp. 175–76.

Though the level of private sector water service provision remains relatively small in percentage and numerical terms, estimated in 2001 at no more than 5 per cent globally and covering no more than 300 million individuals,[6] Morgan points out that 'a remarkable 7,300 per cent increase on 1974–1990 private-sector investment levels in water services occurred between 1990 and 1997', and that 'intergovernmental activities in relation to water since then have intensified and continue to incorporate the private sector as a key partner in their vision.'[7]

Though Morgan also notes that the rate of increase in private sector involvement may have peaked, Schreiber, writing in 2008 and citing sources from 2006 and 2007,[8] notes 'a vast increase in the amount of water privatization contracts between states and investors resulting in roughly 10 percent of global water consumers today receiving their water from private enterprise'.[9] Of course, private sector involvement in the provision of water and sanitation services may take a range of forms depending, for example, on whether assets or operations, or both, move from the public to the private sector, on how much ownership or control is transferred to the private sector, on what types of functions the private company performs, and on how long the arrangement is due to last.[10] The form of privatization employed in any particular instance will have obvious implications for the nature and extent of state regulation required so as to meet the social objectives of the human right to water, for the private

---

[6] UNDP, '2nd UN World Water Development Report' (New York: UNESCO, Paris and Berghahn Books, 2006).

[7] Bronwyn Morgan, 'Turning Off the Tap: Urban Water Service Delivery and the Social Construction of Global Administrative Law', 17/1 *European Journal of International Law*, 17(1), 2006, p. 218.

[8] Naren Prasad, 'Privatisation Results: Private Sector Participation in Water Services After 15 Years', *Development Policy Review*, 24, 2006, p. 669; Charles Mann, 'The Rise of Big Water', *Vanity Fair*, May 2007, p. 122.

[9] Will Schreiber, 'Realizing the Right to Water in International Investment Law: An Interdisciplinary Approach to BIT Obligations', *Natural Resources Journal*, 48, Spring 2008, p. 434.

[10] See Melina Williams, 'Privatization and the Human Right to Water: Challenges for the New Century', *Michigan Journal of International Law*, 28, 2007, p. 493; Violeta Petrova, 'At the Frontiers of the Rush for Blue Gold: Water Privatization and the Human Right to Water', *Brook. Journal of International Law*, 31, 2006, p. 584.

operator's incentive to invest in infrastructure so as to improve or extend the services provided, for its ability to recoup capital invested, and, consequently, for the availability of financing.

Of course, states retain primary responsibility for ensuring that the actions of private service operators do not compromise the realization of the human right of access to water and sanitation. Under the obligation 'to protect', states are obliged to ensure equal and affordable access to water and sanitation services, which might require that they establish and maintain an appropriate regulatory system for private sector providers based on, *inter alia*, independent monitoring, genuine public participation, and effective penalties for non-compliance.[11] Under the obligation 'to fulfil', states are required to consider the requirements of equity and affordability, which might involve legislating for appropriate pricing policies or the introduction of a system of income supplements for socially disadvantaged groups.[12] In addition, under the obligation 'to respect', General Comment 15 includes a requirement for states to take steps to prevent its citizens or companies based within its jurisdiction violating the right of access to water in other states.[13] This requirement might be addressed in a number of ways, such as by providing financial and technical support for building the necessary capacity for the public sector in other states in which its companies operate to perform the regulatory tasks required.

However, it is increasingly important to understand the mechanisms by means of which emerging human rights requirements relating to access to water and sanitation services might apply to and influence the behaviour of private sector providers, especially those operating in developing countries. There is a wide range of such mechanisms, including standards for water services provision developed by international bodies, various policies and codes of conduct adopted voluntarily by key transnational operators, an ongoing UN initiative to clarify the options for ensuring that transnational corporations respect human rights requirements, and the increasing

---

[11] See Committee on Economic, Social and Cultural Rights, 'General Comment No. 15, The Right to Water (Articles 11 and 12 of the International Covenant on Economic, Social and Cultural Rights)', paras 23 and 24, UN Doc E/C.12/2002/11, (2002) [hereafter, General Comment 15].

[12] General Comment 15, paras. 25–29.

[13] General Comment 15, para. 33.

significance of human rights factors in the practice and jurisprudence of international investment law.

CORPORATE OBLIGATIONS

Despite recent interest in the idea of extending the application of key international human rights norms so as to apply directly to corporations,[14] which could make the requirements of the human right to water central to arrangements for the privatization of water and sanitation services, it is clear that such norms could only as yet dictate corporate behaviour where individual corporations have voluntarily agreed to abide by codes of conduct that explicitly or implicitly require compliance with international human rights norms.[15] The UN Global Compact is a high-profile initiative that aims to encourage the adoption of such instruments and provides ten core principles that, while not referring explicitly to water rights or entitlements, do provide that companies should comply with international human rights norms, which might be argued to include a right to water and sanitation.[16] Indeed, Williams points out that the corporate code of conduct of at least one large transnational water services company expressly alludes to the UN Global Compact, thereby indirectly accepting international human rights obligations at the corporate level.[17] Though such acceptance remains voluntary and is not accompanied by any formal oversight or enforcement mechanisms, voluntary corporate policies or codes of conduct are increasingly likely to be linked to various forms of governmental assistance for corporations operating abroad. In a 2009 report, the special representative of the secretary general (SRSG) on the issue of human rights and transnational corporations and other business

---

[14] See generally, Steven R. Ratner, 'Corporations and Human Rights: A Theory of Legal Responsibility', *Yale Law Journal*, 111, 2001, p. 443.

[15] See generally, Sean D. Murphy, 'Taking Multinational Corporate Codes to the Next Level' *Columbia Journal of Transnational Law*, 43, 2005, p. 389.

[16] See Williams, 'Privatization and the Human Right to Water', pp. 488–91.

[17] Rheinisch-Westfälisches Elektizitätswerk Aktiengesellschaft [Rhenish-Westphalian Electric Power Company] (RWE) 'AG Corporate Code of Conduct' (Essen: RWE AG, 2005) pp. 7–8. See, Williams, 'Privatization and the Human Right to Water', p. 488, who also points out that RWE is listed as a participant in the UN Global Compact.

enterprises notes that 'a growing number of States are adopting corporate social responsibility (CSR) policies ... In some cases, access
to official assistance, such as export credit or investment insurance,
may be linked to companies having a CSR policy, participating in
the United Nations Global Compact, or confirming their awareness
of the OECD Guidelines'.[18]

The OECD Guidelines for Multinational Enterprises represent
another legally non-binding initiative that might operate to support
application of key elements of the human right to water to private
companies. They consist of recommendations providing voluntary
principles and standards for responsible conduct for multinational
corporations operating in or from states that adhere to the OECD
declaration and cover business conduct in such areas of relevance
to the implementation of the human right to water as human
rights, environment, information disclosure, combating bribery,
and consumer interests.[19] Though voluntary, it is significant that
the guidelines benefit from a formal monitoring apparatus as each
of the 40 adhering states is required to set up a National Contact
Point (NCP) responsible for the promotion of the guidelines at the
national level and for handling all enquiries and matters related to
the guidelines in that specific state, including the investigation of
complaints made about a company operating in, or headquartered
in, that state.

There is a clear trend in the declarative practice of states towards
extending responsibility for respecting human rights to private companies involved in the provision of private services. For example,
the Draft Declaration on Guaranteed Access to Essential Services,[20]
proposed by France in the context of the 2002 World Summit on

[18] United Nations, Human Rights Council, 'Promotion of All Human Rights,
Civil, Political, Economic, Social and Cultural Rights, Including the Right to
Development, Business, and Human Rights: Towards operationalizing the "protect, respect and remedy" Framework', p. 8, para. 21 UN Doc. A/HRC/11/13
(2009).

[19] See Organization for Economic Cooperation and Development, 'OECD
Guidelines for Multinational Enterprises', 21 June 1976, available at
http://www.oecd.org/dataoecd/56/36/1922428.pdf (revised 2000) (accessed on
12 October 2009).

[20] See, further, Bronwyn Morgan, 'The Regulatory Face of the Human Right to
Water', *Journal of Water Law*, 15(5), 2004, pp. 181–82.

Sustainable Development held in Johannesburg, relates to essential services indispensable for a dignified life, expressly including drinking water and sanitation,[21] and would apply equally to both public and private sector providers. The draft declaration regards as central to the practical implementation of the right to access essential services the provision of an adequate and appropriate regulatory framework and, to this end, it appends to the right 'key principles of a code of sustainable management that would regulate the provision of such access'.[22] However, this approach emphasizes the role of the state in regulating private service providers, rather than extending international human rights obligations per se so as to apply directly to private business entities.

In respect of the development of an appropriate regulatory framework for private sector water service providers, which is informed by international human rights law and widely accepted by states and leading private operators, the adoption in 2007 of three sets of guidelines by Technical Committee 224 of the International Standards Organization (ISO) represents a significant step.[23] The guidelines set standards for service activities relating to the provision of drinking water supply and sewerage services, which apply equally to both public and private actors, both as service provider and user. With thirty-five participating countries and seventeen observer countries involved in their development and adoption, in liaison with a range of interested international organizations, including the World Health Organization, the World Bank and the International Water Association, and with leading industry interests, the ISO guidelines must at least enjoy the indeterminate status of 'soft law' under international law and are likely to prove influential in determining an acceptable level of service provision where a dispute arises with a private sector provider, such as in the context of investment arbitration proceedings.

Of potentially far greater significance in this regard is that the ongoing UN initiative on the issue of human rights and transnational corporations and other business entities is developing

---

[21] Draft Declaration, Article 1.
[22] Morgan, 'The Regulatory Face of the Human Right to Water', p. 181.
[23] On the background to this ISO initiative, see generally, ibid., pp. 182–83. See also Morgan, 'Turning Off the Tap', pp. 224–27.

practical recommendations for operationalizing a framework for ensuring that private corporations respect human rights. As part of this initiative, the UN Sub-Commission on the Promotion and Protection of Human Rights had approved in August 2003 the ill-fated draft norms on the Responsibilities of Transnational Corporations and Other Business Entities with Regard to Human Rights,[24] which had sought to compel transnational corporations to comply with certain human rights obligations, traditionally applying only to state actors.[25] Recognizing the very significant role played by non-state corporate actors,[26] the draft norms sought to augment rather than replace state responsibilities with corporate obligations.[27] The document went on to list the key economic, social, and cultural rights by which it purported to bind such corporations, including 'in particular the rights to development, adequate food and drinking water, the highest attainable standard of physical and mental health, adequate housing'.[28] Thus, the UN draft norms promised to do much to ensure that private sector water service providers respect the right of access to water services and, thereby, to contribute significantly to the general realization of the right. However, the legal status, and thus the true normative value, of the draft norms was always in question.[29] At the request of the Human Rights Commission, the Economic and Social Council of the United Nations affirmed in 2004 that the

---

[24] ECOSOC, Commission on Human Rights, Sub-Commission on the Promotion and Protection of Human Rights, 'Norms on the Responsibilities of Transnational Corporations and Other Business Entities with Regard to Human Rights', UN Doc. E/CN.4/Sub.2/2003/12/Rev.2 (2003). See, further, David Weissbrodt and Muria Kruger, 'Norms on the Responsibilities of Transnational Corporations and Other Business Enterprises with Regard to Human Rights', *American Journal of International Law*, 97, 2003, p. 901.

[25] Ibid.

[26] See, further, John H. Knox, 'Horizontal Human Rights Law', *American Journal of International Law*, 102(1), 2008, p. 19.

[27] Article H, para. 19.

[28] Article E, para. 12.

[29] On the drafting history and legal status of the UN Draft norms, generally, see Larry Catá Backer, 'Multinational Corporations, Transnational Law: The United Nations' Norms on the Responsibilities of Transnational Corporations as a Harbinger of Corporate Social Responsibility in International Law', *Columbia Human Rights Law Review*, 37, 2006, p. 287.

draft norms 'have no legal standing' and thus that they represented nothing more than aspirational standards.[30] Indeed, in 2005 John Ruggie was appointed as the SRSG on the issue of human rights and transnational corporations and other business enterprises with a broad mandate to re-examine this entire issue, and he concluded in a 2006 interim report that 'the flaws of the Norms make that effort a distraction from rather than a basis for moving the Special Representative's mandate forward'.[31] Indeed, in April 2009 he further concluded that recent confusion in respect of business and human rights was due to the draft norms, which 'so co-mingled the respective responsibilities of States and companies that it was difficult if not impossible to disentangle the two'.[32] Therefore, it seems safe to assume that the UN draft norms are well and truly a dead initiative in their current form.

In 2008, the SRSG proposed a new approach for understanding the issue of human rights and transnational corporations, based on the 'protect, respect, and remedy' policy framework. The framework is described as resting on three complementary pillars: '… the State duty to protect against human rights abuses by third parties, including business, through appropriate policies, regulation, and adjudication; the corporate responsibility to respect human rights, which in essence means to act with due diligence to avoid infringing on the rights of others; and greater access by victims to effective remedy, judicial and non-judicial'.

Though much of the detail of this policy framework continues to be elaborated through the ongoing work of the SRSG, this approach appears already to enjoy considerable support from the Human

---

[30] See Williams, 'Privatization and the Human Right to Water', pp. 490–91.

[31] United Nations Economic and Social Council, 'Interim Report of the Special Representative of the Secretary-General on the Issue of Human Rights and Transnational Corporations and Other Business Enterprises', UN Doc. E/CN.4/2006/97 (2006), para. 69. See Williams, 'Privatization and the Human Right to Water' See, further, John Gerard Ruggie, 'Business and Human Rights: The Evolving International Agenda', (2007) 101 *American Journal of International Law*, 101, 2007, pp. 826–27. See Knox, 'Horizontal Human Rights Law', pp. 41–42.

[32] United Nations Human Rights Council, UN Doc. A/HRC/11/13 (2009), p. 16, para. 58.

Rights Council[33] and among states, leading business entities, and civil society.[34]

In respect of the state's duty to protect, the SRSG's 2009 report states that this requires each state to ensure the protection of rights 'against other social actors, including business, who impede or negate those rights' and that it 'applies to all recognized rights that private parties are capable of impairing, and to all types of business enterprises'.[35] The SRSG makes it clear that this duty relates to a standard of conduct rather than a standard of result and explains that states 'may be considered in breach of their obligations where they fail to take appropriate steps to prevent it [abuse] and to investigate, punish, and redress it when it occurs'.[36] In respect of the corporate responsibility to respect, the SRSG's report states that, in addition to the need to comply with all applicable national law, companies must at a minimum have regard to the one 'social norm' which 'has acquired near-universal recognition by all stakeholders, namely the corporate responsibility to respect human rights, or, put simply, to not infringe on the rights of others'.[37] He goes on to explain that in order to satisfy the corporate responsibility to respect, which 'exists independently of State duties and variations in national law',[38] and encompasses 'all internationally recognized human rights',[39] 'what is required is an ongoing process of human rights due diligence, whereby companies become aware of, prevent, and mitigate adverse human rights impacts'.[40] Also, as water privatizations will often involve commitments on the part of companies to invest in water infrastructure, which usually involves huge capital costs, it is significant that the SRSG views the due diligence obligation to respect human rights

---

[33] United Nations Human Rights Council, 'Report of the Special Representative of the Secretary-General on the Issue of Human Rights and Transnational Corporations and Other Business Enterprises', UN Doc. A/HRC/8/5 (2008). See UN Doc. A/HRC/11/13, p. 3, para. 1.

[34] UN Doc. A/HRC/11/13, pp. 3–4, paras 3–5.

[35] Ibid., pp. 6–7, para. 13.

[36] Ibid., p. 7, para. 14.

[37] Ibid., p. 13, para. 46.

[38] Ibid., p. 14, para. 48.

[39] Ibid., p. 14, para. 52.

[40] Ibid., p. 14, para. 49.

as applying to banks and other lenders. [41] Such lenders or investors would obviously include international financial institutions (IFIs) or multilateral development banks (MDBs) supporting private sector investment in water. In respect of the provision of greater access by victims of human rights violations to effective remedy, the SRSG's report outlines the role of the state obligation 'to take appropriate steps to investigate, punish and redress corporate-related abuse of the rights of individuals within their territory and/or jurisdiction'[42] (as distinct from the individual right to remedy recognized in a number of international and regional human rights conventions), and highlights the emphasis placed by some international and regional human rights bodies, in elaborating upon the nature of this state obligation, on 'ensuring that effective remedial processes exist for abuses by private companies carrying out "State functions"'.[43] The report also outlines the role of non-judicial mechanisms, such as grievance mechanisms established at the company, national, or international levels, and proposes a set of principles which should underpin all such mechanisms.[44]

Therefore, while undoubtedly immensely constructive, and much more in keeping with the traditionally accepted precepts of international law,[45] the 'protect, respect, and remedy' framework currently being pursued by the SRSG is rather softer in terms of the nature of the human rights obligations that it seeks to impose on private business entities than the ill-fated UN draft norms. However, due it's more legally cautious and considered approach and its greater emphasis on the practical and extra-legal extension of such obligations, it is likely to have a more profound impact on the day-to-day operations of private sector water and sanitation service providers. For example, the SRSG's commitment to exploring the significance of international human rights obligations for the negotiation and

---

[41]   Ibid., p. 18, para. 73.

[42]   Ibid., p. 21, para. 87.

[43]   Ibid., p. 21, para. 89.

[44]   Ibid., p. 23, para. 99. Originally proposed under the SRSG's 2008 Report, UN Doc. A/HRC/8/5, para. 92.

[45]   A number of commentators have highlighted the hazards associated with proposals to place human rights duties directly on private actors, particularly businesses.

application of investment and trade agreements is likely to prove significant for water services companies operating in developing states.

A number of commentators, most notably Knox, highlight the hazards associated with proposals to place human rights duties directly on private actors, particularly businesses. In particular, he points out that, while 'international law has the *legal* capacity to place direct horizontal duties on all private actors not to violate one another's human rights', 'what it lacks is the *practical* and *political* capacity to *enforce* those duties'.[46] Knox argues that very significant practical considerations 'militate toward leaving private violations of human rights to domestic law',[47] particularly as 'the obligation of States to *ensure* the right goes beyond merely avoiding direct violation ... [I]t requires affirmative action to secure the right, or make it safe from loss or interference', based on a requirement 'that governments use due diligence to ensure that human rights are protected from private interference'.[48]

However, he readily concedes that 'powerful reasons argue against leaving private violations *entirely* to domestic law', as 'domestic governments may fail to prevent it [a private actor] from interfering with other's human rights', thus indicating 'the need to use international law where domestic institutions are inadequate' and providing 'international human rights law with a crucial, albeit limited, role in specifying, placing, and enforcing private duties'.[49]

INTERNATIONAL INVESTMENT LAW

Recent developments in international investment law, the body of rules that functions to provide protection to private sector investors operating in foreign jurisdictions against arbitrary interference with their property or business interests by the sovereign actions of host states, suggest that this area may offer some clarity in respect of the requirements imposed by the human right to water on host states and private actors in cases of water services privatization. Though inviting foreign investment in formerly public water and sanitation services is frequently intended to improve the quality and coverage

---

[46] Knox, 'Horizontal Human Rights Law'.
[47] Ibid., p. 20.
[48] Ibid., p. 21. (Original emphasis.)
[49] Ibid., p. 20. (Original emphasis.)

of such services, and thus to further the realization of the human right to water, it is quite clear that this body of law can function to restrict the development and application of human rights norms. There remains considerable scope for foreign investors to rely on international investment rules to challenge human-rights-inspired regulatory measures taken by host states before international investment tribunals. Though, in principle, 'in such cases states should be able to invoke their human rights obligations under international treaties in defense of their regulatory measures since states have an obligation to protect human rights under both customary and conventional international law',[50] the situation is complicated by 'deficiencies in the clarity of the substantive norms protecting human rights on the one hand and foreign investments on the other hand' as well as by a lack of 'interfaces between the supervision mechanisms of international investment law and international human rights'.[51]

The rules on the protection of foreign investors are principally set out in a complex and extensive web of bilateral investments treaties (BITs) and regional investment treaties (RITs). Over 2,300 BITs have now been concluded between states, of which over 1,700 are currently in force.[52] Such agreements will normally provide for, *inter alia*, the fair and equitable treatment of investors, the payment of compensation in the event of direct or indirect expropriation of the investment, and mandatory dispute settlement before an investment arbitration tribunal. General international law in respect of indirect, regulatory expropriation remains somewhat unclear. Obviously, states enjoy the freedom, as a function of the fundamental principle of state sovereignty, to regulate commercial enterprises, including regulation for economic and social purposes, and in many instances non-discriminatory and bona fide regulation will be regarded as falling within the accepted 'police powers' of states and therefore perfectly

---

[50] Surya P. Subedi, *International Investment Law: Reconciling Policy and Principle* (Oxford/Portland: Hart Publishing, 2008), p. 168.

[51] Ursula Kriebaum, 'Privatizing Human Rights—The Interface between International Investment Protection and Human Rights', *Transnational Dispute Management* 1, 3(5), 2006, pp. 3–4.

[52] UNCTAD Research Note, 'Recent developments in International Investment Agreements', UNCTAD/WEB/ITE/IIT/2005/1, pp. 1 and 7, cited by Kriebaum, 'Privatizing Human Rights', p. 2.

lawful and not incurring the liability of the host state.[53] On the other hand, international tribunals have found that international rules on expropriations may 'cover non-discriminatory regulation that might be said to fall within an exercise of a state's so-called police powers'.[54] Kriebaum reports that the jurisprudence of international arbitral tribunals in regulatory expropriations is, somewhat confusingly, dominated by two opposed theoretical approaches. Under the 'sole effects' doctrine, in determining whether an indirect expropriation has occurred, the tribunal will only consider the effect of the governmental measure on the investment and will entirely disregard the purpose of the measure.[55] In contrast, under the 'police powers' doctrine, the tribunal will also consider a range of other factors including, in particular, the purpose of the measure.[56] Clearly, where the police powers doctrine is employed, particularly in its more extreme form, the regulatory capacity of host states in the area of human rights protection would be very considerable and the protection offered to foreign investors significantly reduced. Though Kriebaum favours the intermediate approach adopted in *Tecmed*, whereby the tribunal first examined the impact of the measure on the investment and then assessed whether that impact was proportional to the measure's stated public purpose,[57] she confirms that a 'binary system' appears to operate in terms of these theoretical approaches and that 'it is impossible to predict which strand a tribunal will follow and which outcome it will reach' so that, under relevant customary and general

---

[53] Kriebaum, 'Privatizing Human Rights', p. 15.

[54] North America Free Trade Agreement (NAFTA), *Pope & Talbot* v. *Canada* (Award, 26 June 2000), 7 ICSID Reports 69. See also, NAFTA, *SD Myers Inc.* v. *Govt. of Canada* (Partial Award, 13 November 2000), 40 ILM (2001) 1408. See, further, Kriebaum, 'Privatizing Human Rights', p. 16.

[55] Kriebaum, 'Privatizing Human Rights', citing NAFTA, *Metalclad Corp.* v. *United Mexican States* (Award, 30 August 2000), 5 ICSID Reports 226.

[56] Kriebaum, 'Privatizing Human Rights', citing at p. 18, NAFTA, *Methanex Corporation* v. *USA*, (Final Award, 3 August 2005) and UNCITRAL, *Saluka Investments BV* v. *Czech Republic*, (Partial Award, 17 March 2006), which emphasized the fact that measures were for a public purpose commonly accepted as being within the police powers of states in order to find no expropriation, as an 'extreme form of the police powers doctrine', and ICSID, *Tecnicas Medioambientales Tecmed SA* v.*United Mexican States*, (29 May 2003, 43 ILM (2004) 133, as an 'intermediate approach'.

[57] Ibid., pp. 18, 20.

international law, 'neither investors nor states are in a position to foresee the consequences of their actions'.[58]

In addition, the principle of 'fair and equitable treatment', whether included under a BIT or invoked under customary international law, might operate to restrict the capacity of host states to legislate for the realization of human rights. Subedi points out that the scope of this 'cardinal principle of foreign investment law' has recently been expanded 'in a broad manner to catch a wide variety of state activities that have detrimental consequences for foreign investors'.[59] In this regard, he cites the International Centre for the Settlement of Investment Disputes (ICSID) tribunal case of *Enron* v. *Argentina*, where the tribunal concluded that 'a key element of fair and equitable treatment is the requirement of a "stable framework for the investment"' and stated further that 'this interpretation has been considered "an emerging standard of fair and equitable treatment in international law"'.[60] In respect of the legal capacity of host states to take measures for the realization of human rights, such as the human right to water, Subedi is keen to ensure that 'investment tribunals do not unduly stretch the protection under the principle to include all sorts of governmental activities, of both omission and commission', in a manner inconsistent with the established tenets of general international law.[61] He notes that this is an absolutely central issue in recent investment arbitration cases.[62]

However, as already noted, the specific rules applying to the protection of foreign investors are usually set out in the BITs and RITs,

---

[58] Ibid., p. 20.

[59] Subedi, *International Investment Law*, p. 173. He points out, at p. 172, that 'traditionally the principle of fair and equitable treatment is supposed to be concerned with the obligation not to deny justice in criminal, civil or administrative adjudicatory proceedings in accordance with the principle of due process embodied in the principal legal systems of the world'.

[60] *Enron Corporation and Ponderosa LP* v. *Argentine Republic,* ICSID Case No. ARB/01/3, Award of 22 May 2007, para. 260. See Subedi, *International Investment Law,* p. 172.

[61] Subedi, *International Investment Law*, p. 172.

[62] Ibid., p. 175. Indeed, he further points out, at p. 174, that 'the expansion of the principle of fair and equitable treatment was one of the reasons given by Bolivia for its withdrawal from ICSID in May 2007, along with the allegation that ICSID tribunals have tailored the principle of fair and equitable treatment in favour of foreign corporations.'

negotiated between the host state(s) and the home state(s) in which the investor is based. In addition, the investor and the host state will normally conclude an investment contract, particularly in the case of infrastructure projects or concessions relating to the provision of public services, such as water supply or sanitation services, which typically 'provide far higher levels of protection to investors than typical commercial contracts by insulating them from future changes in the domestic law of the host country'.[63] Such 'stabilization clauses' provide that 'the law in force in the host state at the time the contract takes effect is the law that will apply to the terms of the contract, regardless of future changes in the legal regime of the host country'.[64] A stabilization clause has been similarly described as one which 'purports to obligate the State to maintain, for a long-term period, the regulatory framework that applies to the investment at the time the investment is made'[65] and might function 'to frustrate the protection of human rights in the country'.[66] Van Harten further describes stabilization clauses as 'a legal mechanism to secure the economic interests of an economic combine against the danger posed by the right of a self-governing people to determine their future'.[67] Likewise, Subedi observes that 'such provisions are liable not only to limit the sovereignty of states but also undermine the object and purpose of future international human rights and environmental treaties'[68] and questions the consistency of such provisions with the principles of economic sovereignty and the right of economic self-determination of states, which he describes as 'serious contenders to qualify as principles of *jus cogens*, which override all other rules, whether treaty-based or otherwise'.[69] However, he explains that 'due to the narrow commercial focus of international investment or commercial arbitration tribunals, adequate attention

---

[63] Ibid., p. 171.
[64] Ibid.
[65] Gus Van Harten, 'The Public–Private Distinction in the International Arbitration of Individual Claims Against the State', *International and Comparative Law Quarterly*, 56, 2007, p. 381.
[66] Ibid., p. 382.
[67] Ibid.
[68] Subedi, *International Investment Law*, p. 171.
[69] Ibid., p. 170.

to such competing principles of international law has not been given in resolving investment disputes', nor to 'this actual and potential conflict'.[70]

At any rate, such stabilization clauses have been enforced by arbitral tribunals and have formed the principal basis of arbitration awards.[71] Indeed, even in the *Methanex* case, cited by Kriebaum as an example of an investment arbitration tribunal applying a radical police powers doctrine, the NAFTA tribunal stated categorically thus: 'As a matter of general international law, a non-discriminatory regulation for a public purpose ... is not deemed expropriatory or compensable *unless specific commitments had been given by the regulating government to the then putative foreign investor contemplating investment that the government would refrain from such regulation.*'[72]

Therefore, international investment arbitration tribunals would appear to be quite prepared to apply stabilization clauses so as to restrict the exercise of the otherwise legitimate police powers of host states, even perhaps where such exercise is intended to further the realization of human rights in line with the international obligations of host states.

The enforceability against host states in international law of such stabilization clauses, or of any other contractual clauses entered into with investors, may be greatly enhanced through the inclusion of so-called 'umbrella clauses' in investment treaties. According to Van Harten, 'many treaties contain such clauses, which typically provide for the States Parties to "respect" or "observe" or "abide by" all of their obligations and commitments to foreign investors'.[73] Such clauses have

---

[70] Ibid., p. 172. See also, Kriebaum, 'Privatizing Human Rights', p. 22.

[71] Van Harten, 'The Public–Private Distinction in the International Arbitration of Individual Claims', p. 384, cites the example of *Texaco Overseas Petroleum Co. & California Asiatic Oil Co.* v. *Government of the Libyan Arab Republic* (Merits) (19 January 1977), 17 *ILM* 4. See also, *AGIP SpA* v. *People's Republic of Congo* (Merits) (30 November 1979) 1 ICSID Rep. 306; 21 *ILM* 726, para. 85.

[72] *Supra*, n. 56, Part IV – Chapter D, p. 4, para. 4. See Kriebaum, 'Privatizing Human Rights', p. 19. (Emphasis added.)

[73] Kriebaum, 'Privatizing Human Rights', p. 388, citing Anthony C. Sinclair, 'The Origins of the Umbrella Clause in the International Law of Investment Protection', *Arbitration International*, 20, 2004, pp. 412–13.

been relied upon by arbitral tribunals[74] and may be interpreted broadly as one which 'transforms a breach of contract by the State into an outright violation of the treaty'.[75] Therefore, international investment law might well be expected to operate to insulate and exempt foreign investors from the effect of regulatory measures introduced by host states, subsequent to the agreement of a water services concession, for the purposes of ensuring the realization of the human right to water.[76]

However, it is interesting to note that the concept of a human right of access to water and sanitation would appear to have received solid, if implicit, support in recent statements of international arbitration tribunals engaged in the settlement of investor–state disputes over water and sanitation service contracts. The ICSID, the most commonly used arbitration institution in investor–state cases,[77] has reversed its previous position to refer pointedly to the human rights implications of such contracts while weighing the element of public interest at stake in the particular dispute in question. In the course of a very high profile and controversial dispute over the privatization of water services in the Bolivian city of Cochabamba, an ICSID arbitral tribunal decided in January 2003[78] that, without the agreement of the parties to the dispute, it did not have jurisdiction to grant a request from interested third parties to, *inter alia*, attend the proceedings and to have access to all submissions made to the tribunal.[79] Further, the tribunal did

---

[74] See *SGS Société Général de Surveillance* v. *Philippines* (Jurisdiction) (29 January 2004), 16 *World Trade and Arbitration Materials* 91, cited in Van Harten, 'The Public–Private Distinction in the International Arbitration of Individual Claims', p. 389.

[75] Ibid., p. 388.

[76] On the essentially regulatory nature of measures required for the practical implementation of key elements of the human right to water, see generally, Bronwyn Morgan, 'The Regulatory Face of the Human Right to Water', pp. 179–86.

[77] Kyla Tienhaara, 'Third Party Participation in Investment-Environment Disputes: Recent Developments', *Review of European Community and International Environmental Law*, 16(2), 2007, p. 230.

[78] ICSID Case no. ARB/02/3 *Aguas del Tunari SA* v. *Republic of Bolivia*, Letter from the president of the Tribunal Responding to the Petition (29 January 2003).

[79] ICSID Case no. ARB/02/3 *Aguas del Tunari SA* v. *Republic of Bolivia*, Petition of La Coordinadora Para la Defensa del Agua y Vida, La Federation Departmental Cochabamba de Organizaciones Regantes, Sempa Sur, Friends of the Earth Netherlands, Oscar Olivera, Omar Fernandez, Father Luis Sanchez, and Congressman Jorge Alvarado to the Arbitral Tribunal (29 August 2002).

not believe that any useful purpose could be served by permitting the petitioners to make submissions at that particular point.[80] This decision suggests that the tribunal was not at that time prepared to accord much significance to the public interest aspects, and by inference to the human rights elements, of the dispute. However, in a landmark decision in May 2005, concerning a petition from five NGOs to participate as *amici curiae* in investor–state proceedings concerning a water distribution and sewage services contract in Argentina, the ICSID would appear to have recognized that the provision of water and sanitation services inevitably involves questions of human rights.[81] In assessing the appropriateness of the subject matter of the case for *amicus curiae* submissions,[82] the ICSID reasoned that:

> The factor that gives this case particular public interest is that the investment dispute centers around the water distribution and sewage systems of a large metropolitan area, the city of Buenos Aires and surrounding municipalities. Those systems provide basic public services to millions of people and as a result may raise a variety of complex public and international law questions, *including human rights consideration.*[83]

This position was followed, almost verbatim, by an arbitral tribunal composed of the same members in a March 2006 decision concerning a petition to submit an *amicus* brief in very similar proceedings from an NGO and three named individuals, variously described as having expertise in law, human rights, and sustainable development.[84] It seems logical to conclude that the tribunal could only have had in mind the emerging concept of the human right

[80] See, further, Tienharra, 'Third Party Participation in Investment-Environment Disputes', p. 234.

[81] ICSID Case no. ARB/03/19, *Aguas Argentinas S.A., Suez, Sociedad General de Aguas de Barcelona S.A. and Vivendi Universal S.A.* v. *The Argentine Republic,* Order in Response to a Petition for Transparency and Participation as Amicus Curiae (19 May 2005).

[82] The tribunal considered three basic criteria in considering whether to exercise its power to accept *amicus* submissions: *a*) the appropriateness of the subject matter of the case; *b*) the suitability of a given non-party to act as *amicus curiae* in that case; and *c*) the procedure by which the *amicus* submission is made and considered. Ibid., para. 17.

[83] Ibid., para. 19. (Emphasis added.)

[84] ICSID Case no. ARB/03/17, *Aguas Provinciales de Santa Fe S.A., Suez, Sociedad General de Aguas de Barcelona S.A. and InterAguas Servicios Integrales del Agua*

to water. In justifying the possibility of accepting *amicus* submissions from appropriate non-parties, which 'may be able to afford the Tribunal perspectives, arguments, and expertise that will help it arrive at a correct decision',[85] the tribunal distinguished the matters of public interest arising therein from the 'matters of public interest ... present in virtually all cases of investment treaty arbitration under ICSID jurisdiction'. What set this case apart from other 'ostensibly private litigation' before the ICSID was quite clearly the 'particular public interest' flowing from the fact that it involved the provision of water and sanitation services.[86]

Indeed, in the February 2007 decision of the ICSID tribunal in respect of the petition by five NGOs to make an *amicus curiae* submission in the proceedings of the case relating to the provision of water supply and sewage services in Buenos Aires, resubmitted in light of the tribunal's May 2005 Order,[87] the tribunal appreciated the potential impact that its final decision might have for the realization of elements of the human right to water for the millions of people within the area covered by the contract.[88] In response to the claimants' argument that the withdrawal from the claim of Aguas Argentinas SA (AASA), the former operator of the water and sewage system, changed the nature of the subject matter of the case, so that it no longer involved sufficient matters of public interest to make it appropriate for an *amicus* submission, the tribunal confirmed its finding of May 2005, stating that:

> Even if its decision is limited to ruling on a monetary claim, to make such a ruling the Tribunal will have to assess the international responsibility of Argentina. In this respect, it will have to consider matters involving the provision of 'basic public services to millions of people'. To do so, *it may have to resolve 'complex public and international law questions, including human rights considerations'* (Order of 19 May 2005, para. 19). It is true

---

S.A. v. *The Argentine Republic,* Order in Response to a Petition for Participation as *amicus curiae* (17 March 2006).

[85] Ibid., para. 20.

[86] Ibid., para. 18

[87] *Supra,* n. 82.

[88] ICSID Case No. ARB/03/19, *Suez, Sociedad General de Aguas de Barcelona S.A. and Vivendi Universal S.A.* v. *The Argentine Republic,* Order in Response to a Petition by Five Non-Governmental Organizations for Permission to Make an *Amicus Curiae* Submission (12 February 2007).

that the forthcoming decision will not be binding on the current operator of the water and sewage system of Buenos Aires. *It may nonetheless have an impact on how that system should and will be operated.*[89]

This statement clearly anticipates the possibility that consideration of human rights requirements might result in a tribunal decision that stipulates basic standards of water and sanitation service provision that any contracted private operator ought to meet, irrespective of any standards set out in a concession contract. Further, the tribunal recognized the potential significance of its own pending final decision in this case for the identification of minimum acceptable standards of water and sanitation service provision generally, and thus for the implementation of core elements of the human right to water: 'More generally, because of the high stakes in this arbitration and the wide publicity of ICSID awards, one cannot rule out that *the forthcoming decision may have some influence on how governments and foreign investor operators of the water industry approach concessions and interact when faced with difficulties.*'[90]

At the very least, the tribunal acknowledged the potential significance of its decision in this case for ensuring basic standards in the case of water services privatization involving foreign investors. However, taken at its broadest, this statement could also amount to recognition of the importance of ICSID practice for the application and development in international law of the human right to water.

The ICSID took a similar approach in another decision in February 2007, allowing a petition by five NGOs to make an *amicus* submission in the course of an investor–state dispute concerning a private sector lease contract for water supply in Tanzania.[91] In seeking to establish their credentials for making an *amicus* submission, the petitioners emphasized their interests, *inter alia*, in 'ensuring that the constitutional and environmental rights of the Tanzanian people are secured and realized by all',[92] in 'issues relating to access

---

[89] Ibid., para. 18. (Emphasis added.)

[90] Ibid. (Emphasis added.)

[91] ICSID Case no. ARB/05/22, *Biwater Gauff (Tanzania) Ltd. V. United Republic of Tanzania*, Procedural Order no. 5 (2 February 2007).

[92] Ibid., para. 11(a), regarding the Lawyers' Environmental Action Team (LEAT).

to water, especially for the poor and women',[93] and in using 'international law, institutions and processes to protect the environment, human health and human rights'.[94] Also, they included among the reasons for their petition the fact that 'this arbitration process goes far beyond merely resolving commercial or private conflicts, but rather has a substantial influence on the population's ability to enjoy basic human rights'[95] and 'raises a number of issues of vital concern to the local community in Tanzania, and a wide range of potential issues of concern to developing countries (and indeed all countries) that have privatized, or are contemplating a possible privatization of, water or other infrastructure services'.[96] In considering the petitioners' related request to have access to the key arbitration documents, the tribunal described the petitioners' proposed role in the proceedings, stating that 'it is envisaged that the Petitioners will address broad policy issues concerning sustainable development, environment, *human rights and governmental policy*'.[97] In response to the claimant's argument that sufficient issues of public interest do not arise in the present case as the claimant has exited Tanzania and the operator is defunct, the tribunal, finding for the petitioners, found that 'this is not determinative of the issue, since any decision by the Arbitral Tribunal *still has the potential to impact upon the same wider interests*'.[98]

The recognition by ICSID tribunals of the relevance of human rights considerations in international investment disputes concerning water services, though implicit, is significant in terms of the recognition of the human right to water in general international law, especially as the

---

[93] Ibid., para. 11(c), regarding the Tanzania Gender Networking Programme (TGNP).

[94] Ibid., para. 11(d), regarding the Center for International Environmental Law (CIEL). The petitioner NGOs are further described, in para. 20, as having 'specialized interests and expertise in human rights, environmental and good governance issues locally in Tanzania, and *in the multiple critical inter-relationships between international investment law and sustainable development at the international level*'. (Emphasis added).

[95] Ibid., para. 14.

[96] Ibid., para. 12.

[97] ICSID Case no. ARB/05/22, *Biwater Gauff (Tanzania) Ltd.* v. *United Republic of Tanzania*, Procedural Order no. 5 (2 February 2007), para. 64. (Emphasis added.)

[98] Ibid., para. 53 (Emphasis added).

incidence of investor–state disputes has risen significantly in recent years.[99] Also, human rights considerations are increasingly likely to be raised before investment dispute tribunals in the light of the trend towards allowing non-disputant third party participation where such disputes raise serious questions of public interest.[100] As examples of this trend, Tienhaara lists the 2001 decision of the United Nations Commission on International Trade Law (UNCITRAL) ad hoc arbitral tribunal to accept *amicus curiae* briefs in the claim made under Chapter 11 of NAFTA[101] in the *Methanex* case[102] and the subsequent 2003 statement of the Free Trade Commission of NAFTA on third party participation in Chapter 11 Disputes;[103] the new format 'model' bilateral investment treaties (BITs) adopted by Canada in 2003[104] and by the USA in 2004[105] expressly providing for third party participation in investment dispute proceedings; the adoption of new ICSID Rules of Procedure for Arbitration Proceedings in 2006;[106]

[99] Tienhaara, 'Third Party Participation in Investment-Environment Disputes', p. 230.

[100] Ibid., pp. 231–38.

[101] North American Free Trade Agreement (17 December 1992), 32 *ILM* 289.

[102] *Methanex Corp.* v. *United States of America,* Decision of the Tribunal on Petitions from Third Parties to Intervene as *amici curiae* (15 January 2001). See further, Sagarika Saha, 'Methanex Corporation and the USA: The Final NAFTA Tribunal Ruling', *Review of European Community and International Environmental Law*, 15(1), 2006, p. 110; Howard Mann, 'Opening the Doors, At Least a Little: Comment on the *Amicus* Decision in *Methanex* v. *United States*', *Review of European Community and International Environmental Law*, 10(2), 2001, p. 241. It is worth noting that the case involved a challenge by a Canadian investor to a Californian measure aimed at protecting ground water from contamination through the phasing out of a petroleum additive and that the non-disputant *amicus* briefs permitted in *Methanex* concerned environmental arguments additional to the public health arguments raised by the parties to the dispute. Clearly, similar public health and environmental grounds could lend support to elements of the human right to water.

[103] Statement of the Free Trade Commission on Non-Disputing Party Participation (Montreal, 1 October 2003).

[104] The Canadian model Foreign Investment Promotion and Protection Agreement (FIPA) is available at www.dfait-maeci.gc.ca/tna-nac/documents/2004-FIPA-model-en.pdf (accessed on 12 October 2009).

[105] The US Model BIT is available at www.state.gov/documents/organization/29031.doc. (accessed on 12 October 2009).

[106] ICSID Convention, Regulations and Rules (ICSID, April 2006), available at www.worldbank.org/icsid/basicdoc/basicdoc.htm (accessed on 12 October 2009).

and the 2006 decision of UNCITRAL that its Working Group II on International Arbitration and Conciliation should commence work on revision of the UNCITRAL arbitration rules in respect of, *inter alia*, third party intervention and disclosure of awards.[107] One might add to this list the binding interpretative note adopted by the NAFTA parties in 2001 providing public access to relevant documents submitted to or issued by NAFTA Chapter 11 tribunals and the making public of awards.[108]

Though the aforementioned ICSID decisions do not make it clear on precisely what sources of law the tribunals have based the conclusion that they are entitled or required to consider questions of human rights requirements or entitlements, it is clear that in deliberating on such investment disputes the tribunals may generally have regard to rules contained under 'the ICSID Convention, multilateral investment treaties, bilateral investment treaties (including separate investment chapters in "economic integration agreements"), customary international law, general principles of law, specific agreements or decisions, and national legislation'.[109]

In his painstaking empirical study of the sources of law applied by ICSID tribunals, Fauchald explains that 'the instrument referring the case to ICSID arbitration often determines the rules to be applied. Otherwise, Article 42(1) of the ICSID Convention applies [which provides that] "the Tribunal shall apply the law of the Contracting State party to the dispute ... *and such rules of international law as may be applicable*"'.[110]

Further, in examining the approach of ICSID tribunals to the application of customary international law and general principles of law in particular, he observes that:

> ICSID tribunals may be faced with the application of customary international law and general principles of law where there is a reference

[107] UNCITRAL, 39th Session (June/July 2006).

[108] Notes of Interpretation of Certain NAFTA Provisions (31 July 2001). See Nathalie Bernasconi-Osterwalder and Edith Brown Weiss, 'International Investment Rules and Water: Learning from the NAFTA Experience', in *Fresh Water and International Economic Law*, Weiss *et al.* (eds), pp. 286–87.

[109] Ole Kristian Fauchald, 'The Legal Reasoning of ICSID Tribunals—An Empirical Analysis', (2008)19/2 *European Journal of International Law.* 19(2), pp. 301–64, page 2 of 74 of online version. (References omitted).

[110] Ibid. (References omitted, emphasis added.)

to such rules in a relevant treaty, where the treaty does not address the issue in question, *i.e.,* where there is a legal *lacuna* in the treaty, and where customary international law replaces a clause in a treaty (*i.e.,* it develops after the treaty has been concluded).[111]

In respect of the first situation just listed, he notes that it is 'quite common to include clauses referring to customary international law in relevant treaties',[112] including, for example, Article 1131(1) of NAFTA. Therefore, the tribunals may be inferring the human rights dimension in the aforecited cases from a variety of legal sources, including customary international law and general principles of law as listed in Article 38(a)(c) of the Statute of the International Court of Justice. Thus it would be open to ICSID tribunals to identify and apply elements of the human right to water as leading-edge principles and concepts of customary or general international law. By appearing to interpret and apply the applicable law in a manner consistent with the key parameters of the human right to water, the ICSID approach is entirely consistent with paragraph 35 of General Comment 15 which provides that 'agreements concerning trade liberalization should not curtail or inhibit a country's capacity to ensure the full realization of the right to water'.

Clearly, it is not difficult to imagine a situation where a poor state, desperate to gain access to the capital and expertise of a foreign private sector water services operator, might be tempted to limit its policy options, at least in respect of that particular investor, in exchange for such private investment. Indeed, ample evidence suggests that such stabilization clauses are very much more prevalent in investor contracts with poorer states.[113] Where a stabilization clause is included in a water services concession contract, the state's freedom to introduce subsequent measures intended to ensure the realization of the human right to water would appear to be severely limited, and this situation would be exacerbated where an umbrella clause is included in the relevant investment treaty. This suggests that one potentially effective means of facilitating the adoption of such national

---

[111]   Ibid., p. 6 of 74 of online version. (References omitted).

[112]   Ibid., p. 7 of 74 of online version. (References omitted).

[113]   See, SRSG Report (22 April 2009). See also, United Nations, Human Rights Council, 'Promotion of All Human Rights, Civil, Political, Economic, Social and Cultural Rights, Including the Right to Development, Business, and Human Rights: Towards operationalizing the "protect, respect and remedy" Framework', p. 11, para. 32, UN Doc. A/HRC/11/13 (2009).

measures by host states would involve the inclusion of an express reference to human rights considerations, or at least to the human right to water, in bilateral or regional investments treaties. After all, a number of international investment disputes based on BITs have already arisen concerning water services concessions.[114] Such a reference might recognize or make limited exceptions for the requirements of the human right to water.[115] However, in addition to introducing considerable uncertainty into investment treaties, due to the substantive uncertainty of the requirements inherent in the concept, such a treaty provision could only impact on concession contracts concluded subsequent to entry into force of the treaty. It remains, however, an approach that human rights groups might advocate to states that have declared support for the concept, whenever such states are negotiating or reviewing bilateral investment treaties, especially with developing countries. Equally, host states negotiating water services concession contracts with foreign investors might seek inclusion of such a limited exception to any stabilization clause. At any rate, the inclusion of an express reference to, or exceptions for, considerations relating to the human right to water in bilateral or regional investments treaties would be entirely consistent with the exhortations of the Committee on Economic, Social, and Cultural Rights (CESCR) in Article 35 of General Comment 15, which provides in full:

> States parties should ensure that the right to water is given due attention in international agreements and, to that end, should consider the development of further legal instruments. With regard to the conclusion and implementation of other international and regional agreements, States parties should take steps to ensure that these instruments do not adversely impact upon the right to water. Agreements concerning trade liberalization should not curtail or inhibit a country's capacity to ensure the full realization of the right to water.

Ultimately, states seeking foreign private investment in water services that are seriously committed to ensuring the realization of the

---

114   The *Aguas del Tunari* dispute, ICSID Case no. ARB/02/3, is based on the BIT between the Netherlands and Bolivia; the *Aguas del Aconquija* dispute, ICSID Case no. ARB/97/3, is based on the BIT between France and Argentina; and the *Azurix* dispute, ICSID Case no. ARB/01/12, is based on the 1991 BIT between the USA and Argentina.

115   See, for example, the 2007 Norwegian Model BIT.

human right to water would be well advised to introduce measures setting out the appropriate regulatory framework prior to conclusion of any concession contract. It is telling that the UN SRSG should recently report that 'as a next step, the Special Representative is exploring the feasibility of developing guidance on "responsible contracting" for host Government agreements in relation to human rights.'[116]

CONCLUSION

A human-rights-related dispute might typically arise in the context of water services privatization where the privatized service is not operated in accordance with human rights requirements, for example, where the operator fails to extend the service to all those that require it or where those unable to pay for the service are denied access to a minimum quantity of water. Though the emergence of the human right of access to water is unlikely, at least under international law, to impose specific obligations directly on private entities involved in the provision of water supply and sanitation services, the concept would appear recently to have received implicit support in the statements of international arbitration tribunals engaged in the settlement of investor–state disputes over water and sanitation service contracts. The ICSID, the most commonly used arbitration institution in investor–state cases, has on a number of occasions pointedly referred to the human rights implications of water and sanitation concession contracts while weighing the element of public interest at stake in the particular dispute in question. The tribunals of ICSID have appreciated that their decisions may be expected to influence the practice of states in framing legal and contractual arrangements for the participation of the private sector in water services and, thus, their potential impact on the realization of . elements of the human right to water for the millions of people living within areas covered by such contracts. Such recognition by ICSID tribunals, though implicit, is significant on a number of levels in terms of the recognition of the human right to water in general international

---

[116] United Nations, Human Rights Council, 'Promotion of All Human Rights, Civil, Political, Economic, Social and Cultural Rights, Including the Right to Development, Business, and Human Rights: Towards operationalizing the "protect, respect and remedy" Framework', p. 12, para. 36, UN Doc. A/HRC/11/13 (2009).

law. The incidence of investor–state disputes has risen significantly in recent years and human rights considerations are increasingly likely to be raised before investment dispute tribunals in the light of the trend towards allowing non-disputant third party participation where such disputes raise serious questions of public interest.

Irrespective of how the acknowledged human rights considerations are to be taken account of in international investment disputes, one potentially effective means of facilitating the adoption of national measures intended to ensure the realization of the human right to water by host states would involve the inclusion of an express reference to human rights considerations, or at least to the human right to water, in bilateral or regional investments treaties. Human rights groups might advocate the inclusion of certain limited exceptions to states that have declared support for the concept, whenever such states are negotiating or reviewing bilateral investment treaties, especially with developing countries. Equally, host states negotiating water services concession contracts with foreign investors might seek inclusion of such a limited exception to any stabilization clause employed. The opportunities for effective intervention by advocates of the human right to water during the negotiation and conclusion of international investment treaties are patently obvious. In seeking to build on the advances hinted at by ICSID tribunals, such advocates need only to refer to the examples of a state's violation of the obligation to fulfil the right to water listed under paragraph 44(c) (vii) of General Comment 15, which include the 'failure of a State to take into account its international legal obligations regarding the right to water when entering into agreement with other States or with international organizations'.

BIBLIOGRAPHY

Articles in Books and Journals

Bernasconi-Osterwalder, Nathalie and Edith Brown Weiss, 'International Investment Rules and Water: Learning from the NAFTA Experience', in *Fresh Water and International Economic Law*, Edith Brown Weiss, Laurence Boisson de Chazournes, and Nathalie Bernasconi-Osterwalder (eds) (2005), p. 263, Oxford: Oxford University Press.

Catá Backer, Larry, 'Multinational Corporations, Transnational Law: The United Nations' Norms on the Responsibilities of Transnational Corporations as a

Harbinger of Corporate Social Responsibility in International Law', *Columbia Human Rights Law Review*, 37, 2006, p. 287.

Fauchald, Ole Kristian, 'The Legal Reasoning of ICSID Tribunals: An Empirical Analysis', *European Journal of International Law*, 19(2), 2008, pp. 301–64.

Knox, John H., 'Horizontal Human Rights Law', *American Journal of International Law*, 102(1), 2008, p. 1.

Kriebaum, Ursula, 'Privatizing Human Rights: The Interface Between International Investment Protection and Human Rights', *Transnational Dispute Management*, 3(5), 2006, p. 1.

Mann, Charles, 'The Rise of Big Water', *Vanity Fair*, May 2007, p. 122.

Morgan, Bronwyn, 'The Regulatory Face of the Human Right to Water', *Journal of Water Law*, 15(5), 2004, pp. 179–86.

Morgan, Bronwyn, 'Turning Off the Tap: Urban Water Service Delivery and the Social Construction of Global Administrative Law', *European Journal of International Law*, 17, 2006, p. 215.

Murphy, Sean D., 'Taking Multinational Corporate Codes to the Next Level', *Columbia Journal of Transnational Law*, 43, 2005, p. 389.

Petrova, Violeta, 'At the Frontiers of the Rush for Blue Gold: Water Privatization and the Human Right to Water', *Brook. Journal of International Law*, 31, 2006, p. 577.

rasad, Naren, 'Privatisation Results: Private Sector Participation in Water Services After 15 Years', *Development Policy Review*, 24, 2006, p. 669.

Ratner, Steven R., 'Corporations and Human Rights: A Theory of Legal Responsibility', *Yale Law Journal*, 111, 2001, p. 443.

Ruggie, John Gerard, 'Business and Human Rights: The Evolving International Agenda', *American Journal of International Law*, 101, 2007, p. 819.

Schreiber, Will, 'Realizing the Right to Water in International Investment Law: An Interdisciplinary Approach to BIT Obligations', *Natural Resources Journal*, 48, Spring 2008, p. 431.

Sinclair, Anthony C., 'The Origins of the Umbrella Clause in the International Law of Investment Protection', *Arbitration International*, 20, 2004, p. 411.

Smets, Henri, 'Economics of Water Services and the Right to Water', in *Fresh Water and International Economic Law*, Edith Brown Weiss, Laurence. Boisson de Chazournes, and Nathalie Bernasconi-Osterwalder (eds) (2005), Oxford: Oxford University Press.

Subedi, Surya P. (2008), *International Investment Law: Reconciling Policy and Principle*, Oxford / Portland: Hart Publishing.

Tienhaara, Kyla, 'Third Party Participation in Investment-Environment Disputes: Recent Developments', *Review of European Community and International Environmental Law*, 16(2), 2007, p. 230.

Van Harten, Gus, 'The Public-Private Distinction in the International Arbitration of Individual Claims Against the State', *International and Comparative Law Quarterly*, 56, 2007, p. 371.

Van Hofwegen, Paul (2006), *Report of the Task Force on Financing Water for All*, Marseilles: World Water Council (WWC Publications).

Weissbrodt, David and Muria Kruger, 'Norms on the Responsibilities of Transnational Corporations and Other Business Enterprises with Regard to Human Rights', *American Journal of International Law*, 97, 2003, p. 901.

Williams, Melina, 'Privatization and the Human Right to Water: Challenges for the New Century', *Michigan Journal of International Law*, 28, 2007, p. 469.

UN Documents

Committee on Economic, Social and Cultural Rights, 'General Comment no. 15, The Right to Water (Articles 11 and 12 of the International Covenant on Economic, Social and Cultural Rights)', paras 23 and 24, UN Doc. E/C, 12/2002/11, 2002.

ECOSOC, Commission on Human Rights, Sub-Commission on the Promotion and Protection of Human Rights, 'Norms on the Responsibilities of Transnational Corporations and Other Business Entities with Regard to Human Rights', UN Doc. E/CN.4/Sub.2/2003/12/Rev.2, 2003.

UNCTAD, 'Recent Developments in International Investment Agreements', Research Note, UNCTAD/WEB/ITE/IIT/2005/1.

UNDP, '2nd UN World Water Development Report', Paris, 2006.

UNDP, 'Human Development Report 2006: Beyond Scarcity: Power, Poverty and the Global Water Crisis', New York, 2006, p. 77.

UNDP, 'Water in a Changing World: 3rd UN World Water Development Report', Paris/London: UNESCO / Earthscan, 2009.

UNESCO, 'Interim Report of the Special Representative of the Secretary-General on the Issue of Human Rights and Transnational Corporations and Other Business Enterprises', UN Doc. E/CN.4/2006/97, 2006.

United Nations, Human Rights Council, 'Report of the Special Representative of the Secretary-General on the Issue of Human Rights and Transnational Corporations and Other Business Enterprises', UN. Doc. A/HRC/8/5, 2008.

United Nations, Human Rights Council, 'Promotion of All Human Rights, Civil, Political, Economic, Social and Cultural Rights, Including the Right to Development, Business and Human Rights: Towards Operationalizing the "Protect, Respect And Remedy" Framework', para. 21, UN Doc. A/HRC/11/13, 2009.

Official Documents/Reports

North American Free Trade Agreement (17 December 1992), 32 *ILM* 289.

Organization for Economic Cooperation and Development, 'OECD Guidelines for Multinational Enterprises', 21 June 1976, available at http://www.oecd.org/dataoecd/56/36/1922428.pdf (revised 2000) (accessed 12 October 2009).

Rheinisch-Westfälisches Elektizitätswerk Aktiengesellschaft [Rhenish-Westphalian Electric Power Company] (RWE) (2005), *AG Corporate Code of Conduct*, p. 7, Essen: RWE AG.

Winpenny, J. (2003), *Financing Water for All: Report of the World Panel on Financing Water Infrastructure*. Kyoto: World Water Council.

7
Interface between the Third Generation Human Rights and Good Governance in a Globalized World

M. Abdul Hannan

INTRODUCTION

In the most general sense, human rights are understood as rights that belong to any individual as a consequence of being human, independently of acts of law.[1] It has become routine to speak of different 'generations' of human rights.[2] According to the current terminology, human rights of the first generation are 'negative' human rights, or civil liberties, which enjoin states to abstain from interfering with personal freedom. Freedom and security of a person or freedom of speech are paradigmatic examples of this class of rights. When referring to human rights of the second generation or 'positive' rights, what is meant are economic or social rights, such as the right to work or the right to social security, which entitle individuals or collectives to the provision of certain goods or social services. Lastly, human rights of the third generation are highly complex composite rights like the right to development, the right to peace, and the right to a clean environment.

---

[1] M. Abdul Hannan is Associate Professor, Department of Law and Justice, University of Rajshahi, Bangladesh. Marek Piechowiak, 'The Concept of Human Rights and their Extra-legal Jurisdiction', in *An Introduction to the International Protection of Human Rights: A Textbook*, Raija Hanski and Markku Suksi (eds) (Åbo: Institute for Human Rights, 1997), p. 3.

[2] Following French lawyer K. Vasak, 'A 30-Year Struggle', *The UNESCO Courier*, November 1977, p. 29.

Third generation human rights are sometimes called 'solidarity rights'. None of these rights has solid legal foundations in a legal instrument of worldwide applicability. At the regional level, however, the African Charter on Human and Peoples' Rights (AfCHPR) has proclaimed the right to development[3] and the right to peace and security,[4] as well as the right to a 'general satisfactory environment'.[5]

THE THREE RIGHTS

Right to Development

The right to development, the intellectual authorship of which is attributed to the Senegalese lawyer Keba Mbaye,[6] was first affirmed in a number of resolutions of the Human Rights Commission (HRCion). In Resolution 5 (XXXV) of 2 March 1979 the commission 'reiterated' that the right to development was a human right. A more stringent note was struck by the General Assembly (GA) of the United Nations (UN), which, by Resolution 36/133 of 14 December 1981, characterized the right to development as an 'inalienable' human right. Eventually, the GA adopted a Declaration on the Right to Development by Resolution 41/128 of 4 December 1986. Article 1 of that declaration provides as follows: 'The right to development is an inalienable human right by virtue of which every human person and all peoples are entitled to participate in, contribute to, and enjoy economic, social, cultural, and political development, in which all human rights and fundamental freedoms can be fully realized.' Clearly, this text mirrors the earlier text of Article 28 of the Universal Declaration of Human Rights (UDHR), 1948.

---

[3] African Charter of Human and Peoples Rights (hereafter, AfCHPR), Article 22.
[4] AfCHPR, Article 23.
[5] AfCHPR, Article 24.
[6] 'Le droit au developement comme un droit de l'homme' (1972), p. 503. African authors have contributed a great deal to clarifying the meaning and scope of the right to development. See in particular: G Abi-Saab, 'The Legal Formulation of a Right to Development', in *The Right to Development at the International Level*, R. J. Dupuy (ed.) (Alphen aan den Rijin: Sijthoff & Noordhoff, 1980), p. 159; M. Bedjaoui, 'The Right to Development', in *International Law Achievements and Prospects* (Paris and Dordrecht: UNESCO and Martinus Nijhoff, 1991), p. 1177.

As defined in the GA Resolution 41/128, the right to development appears as an aggregate right that draws its substance from other instruments that set forth human rights and fundamental freedoms with binding effect.[7] Because of its extremely wide scope, it met with a large amount of scepticism, on the part of Western states in particular. At the Vienna World Conference on Human Rights in 1993, the USA for the first time accepted the concept of a right to development. Thereafter, for many years, working groups established by the HRCion have attempted to clarify in more detail its legal connotations. To date, all these efforts have proved of no avail. The latest resolution of the GA on the issue, adopted on 19 December 2006, again extends the mandate of a working troop (Resolution 61/169).[8] It reflects almost all of the world's economic and social problems. Probably the time-honoured French adage applies here as well: *Qui trop embrace mal eternity*, which is tantamount to saying that whoever pursues too ambitious a goal, will eventually end up with empty hands.[9] In recent years, emphasis has shifted to the fight against poverty. Ambitious goals were defined by the UN Millennium Declaration[10] and confirmed by the 2005 World Summit Outcome.[11] However, political declarations alone do not generate economic resources. The objective of the Millennium Declaration to halve poverty by 2015 can hardly be reached.

Right to Peace

The right to peace is the second component of the third generation human rights. It also grew up within the HRCion, where it was first proclaimed in 1976. The next stage was reached when the GA in 1978 adopted the Declaration on the Preparation of Societies for

---

[7] For a recent appraisal see, B. A. Andreassen and S. P. Marks (eds), *Development as a Human Right* (Harvard: Harvard University Press, 2006); U. Baxi, 'The Development of the Right to Development', in *Human Rights: New Dimensions and Challenges*, J Symonides (ed.) (Aldershot and Paris: Ashgate and UNESCO, 1998), p. 99.

[8] See also Human Rights Committee (HRC), Res. 4/4, 30 March 2007.

[9] N. J. Udombana, 'The Third World and the Right to Development: Agenda for the Next Millennium' (2000), 22 *HRQ* 753.

[10] GA Res. 55/2, 8 September 2000, para. 19.

[11] GA Res. 60/1, 16 September 2005, para. 19; see also HRC Res. 2/2, 27 November 2006.

Life in Peace,[12] which affirmed that 'every nation and every human being ... has the inherent right to life in peace'. The process of standard-setting came to its culmination in 1984 with the adoption of the Declaration on the Right of Peoples' to Peace.[13] In the vote, not fewer than thirty-four states abstained even though the resolution solemnly proclaims 'that the peoples of our planet have a sacred right to peace'. After the demise of the communist regimes in Central and Eastern Europe, interest in this 'right' faded away.[14] In recent years, however, resolutions of the GA have again referred to the sacred right to peace of the peoples of our planet.[15] The observer, nonetheless, fails to perceive any elements of operational particularization.

Right to a Clean Environment

The right to a clean or healthful environment, by contrast, has lost nothing of its original attractiveness.[16] It was mentioned for the first time in the concluding declaration adopted by the UN Conference on the Human Environment, held in June 1972 in Stockholm. Principle 1 of that declaration starts out in a politically correct fashion with the words: 'Man has the fundamental right to freedom, equality and adequate conditions of life, in an environment of a quality that permits a life of dignity and well-being,'[17]

The only truly legal text that has embraced this proposition in broad terms is the AfCHPR, which in Article 24 sets forth a right to a 'general satisfactory environment'. Mostly, however, a somewhat more cautious attitude has prevailed. Governments are quite aware of the necessity to reconcile environmental concerns with other concerns of public policy. Thus, the Rio Declaration on Environment and Development of 14 June 1992[18] qualifies the relationship between humankind and

---

[12] GA Res. 33/73, 15 December 1978.

[13] GA Res. 39/11, 12 November 1984.

[14] In praise of this right see A. Nastase, 'The Right to Peace', in Bedjaoui, 'The Right to Development', pp. 1219–31.

[15] GA Res. 57/216, 18 December 2002 (adopted with 116 votes in favour to 53 against, with 14 abstentions).

[16] P. Sands, *Principles of International Environmental Law*, 2nd edn (Cambridge: Cambridge University Press, 2003), pp. 293–97.

[17] See also GA Res. 45/94, 14 December 1990.

[18] (1992) 31 ILM 876.

its environment by stating that 'human beings ... are entitled to a healthy and productive life in harmony with nature'. The declaration refrains from speaking of a 'right' to a clean environment; rather, the duties of states to protect the natural environment are stressed. A total departure from an anthropocentric approach can be found in the World Charter for Nature, adopted by the GA on 28 October 1982 (GA Resolution 37/7), which asserts that nature—and with it humankind as a part of nature—'shall be respected'. In recent years, the language has generally become even more guarded. It has been recognized that protection of the environment constitutes a challenge to humankind as a whole. Nobody can expect that others will assume the burden that everyone has to struggle with. The Johannesburg Declaration of the World Summit on Sustainable Development reaffirmed 'our commitment to sustainable development' (paragraph 1).[19] Thus, a realistic assessment has rightly replaced the euphoric rhetoric of the early years. In its Ogoniland decision of 27 October 2001,[20] the African Commission on Human and Peoples' Rights (AfHPRCion) was able to make a forceful application of Article 24 of the AfCHPR. In that case, the right showed its usefulness for extreme instances, where the mishandling of environmental issues is obvious and permits of no justification.

UNCERTAINTIES OF THE THIRD GENERATION RIGHTS

All human rights of the third generation are surrounded by grave uncertainties regarding their holders, the duty- bearers, and their substance.[21]

Holders of the Rights

According to the Declaration on the Right to Development, for instance, the right is vested in human beings and peoples alike, whereas the African Charter assigns it to peoples alone. As far as the

---

[19] Adopted on 4 September 2002. Available at http://www.un.org/esa/sustdev.doc-uments/WSSD_POI_PD/English/POI_PD.htm (accessed December 2007).

[20] *The Social and Economic Rights Centre and the Centre for Economic and Social Rights* v. *Nigeria*, 155/96, 27 October 2001.

[21] See C. Tomuschat, 'Human Rights in a World-Wide Framework' (1985), 45 HJIL 547, pp. 568–72.

right to peace is concerned, a glaring divergence is obvious. Whereas the Declaration on the Preparation of Societies for a Life in Peace mentions nations and human beings side by side, the Declaration on the Right of Peoples to Peace confines itself to acknowledging the right of peoples to peace. As already pointed out, the right to a satisfactory environment is mentioned as a right of peoples only by the African Charter. Thus, the relevant instruments do not maintain a consistent line. Generally, no great care is taken to specify on whom the benefits connected with the rights are bestowed—individuals or collective entities. This amply demonstrates that the actual effects expected of the rights are not connected with their specific characteristics as rights under positive international law.

Duty Bearers

According to the ordinary understanding of the essence of a right, a duty must exist as its corollary. Rights embody claims that another person is legally required to fulfil. Right and duty are just two sides of one and the same coin. In this regard, third generation rights have great weaknesses. Pursuant to the Declaration on the Right to Development, it is in particular states that have to strive for development by taking the steps necessary for that purpose. Translated into concrete terms this means that peoples are pitted against states, a dichotomy whose legal implications are difficult to grasp. On the one hand, the relevant propositions could mean that peoples have rights against their own governments, which is in fact the tendency pursued by the Declaration of Algiers, a legal text drawn up by a private group of legal scholars in 1978;[22] or they could be interpreted to express the idea that poorer states have entitlements vis-à-vis other states, that is, the international community. All this, however, does not fit easily into the traditional concept of international law where the international community as such has yet to find its proper place.

Content

It is even more difficult to gain a clear picture of the content of third generation rights. Generally, all of the rights under discussion

[22] See A. Cassese (ed.), *Pour un droit des Peuples. Essais sur la Declaration d'Alger* (Paris: Berger-Levrault, 1978).

are extremely wide in scope. They do not set out specific measures and steps to be taken by states or governments, but enunciate comprehensive goals. As indicated by the Declaration on the Right to Development, development means a state of affairs permitting everyone to enjoy to their full extent 'all' rights and freedoms. Thus, development has a variety of components and constitutes an ideal situation that rests on a multitude of factual and legal elements, many of which are not under the control of governments alone. Similar considerations apply to peace. Peace in the world depends on a wide array of factors, and it can be said that the entire system of the United Nations was established to ensure, in the first place, international peace and security. The effectiveness of the international mechanisms geared to ensure the peaceful settlement of international disputes and to prevent wars from occurring is not enhanced by the creation or the recognition of a right of individuals or peoples to peace. The right to a clean and healthful environment, too, belongs to the same category of broadly framed rights, the content of which encompasses almost anything that has some bearing on the sate of the environment. Agenda 21, the plan of action adopted by the Rio Conference in June 1992, constitutes in its printed version a book of no fewer than 400 pages.[23] It is in this plan of action that the requirements of a healthy environment are spelled out in detail. However, it appears that no one has a legal right to demand that the many steps described therein be taken, since there exist no corresponding legal obligations, Agenda 21 having been conceived of as a political commitment only.[24]

It is highly significant that not a single one of the rights of the third generation has to date received a clear profile. The fact that neither the holders of these rights, nor the corresponding duty bearers, nor the substance of the rights, have been unequivocally identified cannot simply be explained as accidental shortcomings that could without any difficulty be remedied by investing more lawyers' skills and intelligence. The inference that must be drawn is obvious. It would be more correct to define third generation rights not as true rights, but rather as agreed objectives that the

---

[23] UN Doc. A/CONF 151/26/Rev 1, vol. I, 14 June 1992.
[24] Christian Tomuschat, *Human Rights between Idealism and Realism* (Oxford: Oxford University Press, 2008), p. 59.

international community has pledged to pursue. Even so, they do not lose their juridical significance. They remain important sign-posts that mark the paths the international community should embark upon in conceiving and carrying out policies for the welfare of humankind as a whole. Indeed, individual human rights need a general framework of favourable conditions within which they can prosper. Any war threatens to lead to a total denial of individual rights by death and destruction. Although a state of affairs where everyone enjoys all the rights guaranteed by the UDHR and the two covenants of 1966[25] certainly guarantees peace, and in most instances also development, it has emerged that these macro condi-tions cannot be ensured from the micro perspective of individual human rights. There is a clear necessity to work on both levels, establishing mechanisms for the vindication of individual rights, but attempting at the same time to ensure peace, development, and a clean and healthful environment on a global level where the issues related to these fields of action are tackled directly in all their complexity. It is the recognition that human rights need a friendly and favourable environment that may also explain other initiatives that have sprung up in recent years. They are not placed under a heading of human rights, but they are all designed to build up that framework of security that is essential for individual rights to take their full effect.

DEMOCRACY AND GOOD GOVERNANCE

Democracy

Democracy may not be a panacea for all ills, but it has its origins in the political rights of the individual as laid down in all conventional instruments, and, on its part, it also contributes to stabilizing and strengthening human rights. Article 21 of the UDHR contains eve-rything that is conceivable in terms of political rights of the citizen in a democratic polity.

However, the word 'democracy' itself was carefully avoided. Concerning Article 25 of the International Covenant on Civil and

---

[25] International Covenant on Civil and Political Rights (ICCPR) and the International Covenant on Economic, Social and Cultural Rights (ICESCR).

Political Rights (ICCPR), which reflects almost textually the earlier provision, the same observation can be made. Although the rights of democratic participation are fully covered, one looks in vain for the word 'democracy'. In some other places, though, in a somewhat hidden fashion, democratic standards are referred to. In the limitation clauses complementing the rights set forth in Articles 14(1), 21, and 22 of the ICCPR, the requirements of a democratic society are mentioned as the criteria of the degree to which governmental interference may affect the substance of the rights concerned. Strangely enough, this yardstick makes no appearance in Article 19 of the ICCPR, the guarantee of freedom of speech, which constitutes the paradigm of a democratic right. On this point, Article 10(2) of the European Convention for the Protection of Human Rights and Fundamental Freedoms (ECHR) is more consistent. Whatever the reasons for the apparent lack of logic in the ICCPR may be, it is clear that in 1966 the UN had not yet evolved a coherent concept of democratic governance.[26]

In recent years, this state of affairs has changed dramatically. Democracy is now explicitly acknowledged as the only legitimate form of governance. The origins of this development go back once again to the HRCion. At its spring session in 1999, the commission adopted a resolution that affirmed in a fairly succinct way the basic principles of a democratic polity,[27] stressing in particular the interconnection between the democratic form of government and human rights by stating that 'democracy fosters the full realization of all human rights, and vice versa'. One year later, the HRCion expanded the text considerably and included almost all the rights that are granted to citizens in a liberal state.[28] It is remarkable that the journey of this text did not end in the HRCion, which in spite of its expertise was a subordinate body within the world organization, but found its way to the GA where it was reviewed and eventually approved with

---

[26] T. Franck, 'The Emerging Right to Democratic Governance' (1992). 86 AJIL 46; see further G. H. Fox and B. R. Roth (eds), *Democratic Governance and International Law* (Cambridge: Cambridge University Press, 2000); S. Wheatley, B De Meeester, and C Ryngaetrt, 'Democracy and International Law', 34, 2003, Netherlands Yearbook of International Law, p. 139.

[27] See GA Res. 1999/57, 27 April 1999, 'Promoting and Consolidating Democracy'.

[28] See GA Res. 2000/47, 25 April 2000, 'Promoting and Consolidating Democracy'.

only minor modifications.[29] A large majority supported this historic decision. A considerable number of states, however, abstained. The list of these abstentions is highly revealing. It includes the following countries: Bahrain, Bhutan, Brunei Darussalam, China, Cuba, Democratic Republic of the Congo, Honduras, Laos, Libya, Maldives, Myanmar, Oman, Qatar, Saudi Arabia, Swaziland, and Vietnam. Traditional monarchies march hand-in-hand with communist dictatorships and one or the other country whose ambassador may have received wrong instructions from its capital.[30]

Given the weight of these sixteen countries, it would be difficult to contend that democracy has become a binding standard under international customary law. China, in particulate, cannot be brushed aside in the same way as an isolated vote of the Maldives would be ignored. Nonetheless, the posture taken by a large and almost overwhelming group of nations is a clear indication of the importance the international community attaches to the necessary environment of human rights. Human rights are part of a system of mutually supportive elements. To rely on them alone does not suffice to protect the human being from encroachments on his/her rights. A proper constitutional structure must provide the foundations of a polity where a life in dignity and self-fulfilment becomes an actual opportunity for everyone.[31] The World Summit Outcome[32] opted for a compromise formulation in characterizing democracy as a universal 'value' (paragraph 135),[33] which leaves the issue of its legal classification

---

[29] GA Res. 55/96, 4 December 2000, 'Promoting and Consolidating Democracy'.

[30] For comments on this progressive development, see L. A. Sicilianos, 'Les Nations Unies et la Democratisation de l'Etat—Nouvelles Tendances', in R. Mehdi (ed.) *La Contribution des Nations Unies a la Democratisation de l'Etat* (Paris: Pedone, 2002), p. 13.

[31] See J. Donnelly, 'Human Rights, Democracy, and Development'. (1999) 21 *HRQ* 608, pp. 619–22.

[32] GA Res. 60/1, 16 September 2005.

[33] We reaffirm that democracy is a universal value based on the freely expressed will of people to determine their own political, economic, social and cultural systems and their full participation in all aspects of their lives. We also reaffirm that while democracies share common features, there is no single model of democracy, that it does not belong to any country or region, and reaffirm the necessity of due respect for sovereignty and the right of self-determination. We stress that democracy, development and respect for all human rights and fundamental freedoms are interdependent and mutually reinforcing.

widely open. Indeed, requests for democratic structures may become embroiled in fundamental controversies. Thus, the demands for a 'democratic and equitable international order', articulated in GA Resolution 61/160 (19 December 2006), were rejected by the Western group of states and some Latin American states, whereas the majority of Third World countries supported the motion. At the international level, claims for the introduction of 'democracy' more often than not boil down to a power struggle aimed at depriving Western countries of their structural majorities in world financial institutions. Yet the national model of 'one man, one vote' is not suitable for worldwide institutions. Subtle architectural gifts are needed to build such institutions in consonance with democratic tenets.[34]

At the European level, too, it was recognized that the complex mechanisms of the ECHR needed to be complemented by political monitoring efforts and expert advisory services in order to ensure the general framework within which human rights are located. For this purpose, the Venice European Commission for Democracy was founded in 1990. It has assisted, in particular, the new member states of the Council of Europe in building institutions that are permeated by a new spirit of democratic openness. Within the narrower context of the European Union, democracy figures prominently in the clause providing for structural homogeneity.[35]

Good Governance

The aforementioned considerations are also the background to two more recent developments that seek to build up a framework for securing the full enjoyment of human rights. It has been realized that a 'good life' depends not only on the basic principles upon which a system of government is predicated, but that the conduct of governmental elites and bureaucrats is a decisive factor in bringing the prevailing societal climate in a given state up to the level of the expectations raised by those principles.[36] In this regard, international

---

[34] See E. de Wet, 'The International Constitutional Order'. (2006) 55 *ICLQ* 51, pp. 63, 71.

[35] Treaty on European union (TEU), Article 6(1).

[36] M.K. Sinha, 'Human Rights and Good Governance'. (2006) 46 *IJIL* 539, p. 554, rightly affirms that the 'protection and promotion of human rights need a conducive and enabling environment'.

organizations and, in particular, the financial agencies of the international community have rightly started playing a role as defenders of the public interest. Since 1989, the World Bank has evolved a doctrine of 'good governance', which it has described in the following terms: 'Good governance is epitomized by predictable, open, and enlightened policy-making (that is, transparent processes); a bureaucracy imbued with a professional ethos; an executive arm of government accountable for its actions; and a strong civil society participating in public affairs; and all behaving under the rule of law.'[37]

Other institutions have followed suit. For the International Monetary Fund, it was an almost natural move to adopt similar strategies. It uses negotiations for orderly exchange arrangements according to Article IV of its statute to prevail upon member states to adjust their policies to the requirements of good governance. The African Development Bank also adopted a 'Policy on Good Governance' that lists exactly the same headings, namely, accountability, transparency, combating corruption, political participation of citizens, as well as legal and judicial reforms. This was done in response to the Grand Bay Declaration, adopted on 16 April 1999 by a summit meeting of the Organization of African Unity (OAU),[38] which affirms the interdependence of the principles of good governance, the rule of law, democracy, and development (paragraph 3). Likewise, the European Community included a clause to that effect in its latest agreement with the African, Caribbean and the Pacific (ACP) region states.[39] Recently, the doctrine of good governance received its definitive benediction by its inclusion in the UN Millennium Declaration[40] as well as in the World Summit Outcome.[41] It is clear that a framework of good governance, if actually established, leads to a significantly increased effectiveness of human rights.

HUMAN SECURITY

Almost at the same time that the World Bank evolved the concept of good governance, the United Nations Development Programme

---

[37] 'Governance: The World Bank's Experience', The World Bank (Washington, 1994), p. vii.

[38] http://ncb.intnet.mu/mfa/oau/decpl.htm (accessed December 2007).

[39] Cotonou Agreement, Article 9(3), 23 June 2000, OJ 2000 L 31/3, 15 December 2000.

[40] GA Res. 55/2, 8 September 2000, para. 13.

[41] GA Res. 60/1, 16 September 2005, paras 11, 21, 39.

(UNDP) framed the doctrine of 'human security'.[42] For many decades, the concept of security was understood exclusively in a military sense. It made its first appearance in the report of the Independent Commission on Disarmament and Security Issues (Palme Commission), issued in 1982.[43] After more than a decade, the UNDP took up the ideas contained therein. In its 1993 report it stressed that 'the individual must be placed at the centre of international affairs'.[44] Expanding the new concept, it attempted to give it a more fully substantiated content in its 1994 report, where, criticizing again the exclusive military use of the term in the past, it mentions seven aspects of what it understands by human security. Starting out with economic security (freedom from poverty), it refers additionally to food security (access to food), health security (access to healthcare and protection from diseases), environmental security (protection from pollution), personal security (physical protection against torture, war, and criminal attacks), community security (survival of traditional cultures), and political security (freedom from political oppression).[45]

It would appear that this new approach is largely the result of an overzealous bureaucracy, which has lost sight of the existing achievements in the field of human rights. Almost all of the security items mentioned in these reports are nothing other than a reflection of the rights enunciated in the two international covenants of 1966. Obviously, what human rights seek to achieve is freedom from want and from fear—the classical formulation laid down in the Atlantic Charter of 1941. There is no real need to coin new concepts. Instead, what seems to be necessary is to relate the activities undertaken by international organizations like the UNDP to the foundations as they were laid down many decades earlier in the treaties which, still today, constitute the groundwork of the entire gamut of international action in the field of human rights.

---

[42] F.O. Hampson and C.K. Penny, 'Human Security', in *The Oxford Handbook on the United Nations* T.G. Weiss and S. Daws (eds) (Oxford, Oxford University Press, 2006), p. 539; M. Zambelli, 'Putting People at the Centre of the International Agenda: The Human Security Approach', *Die Friedens-Warte*, 77, 2002, p. 173.

[43] The Independent Commission on Disarmament and Security Issues, *Common Security: A Blueprint for Survival* (New York: Simon and Schuster), 1982.

[44] 'Human Development Report', 1993, p. 2.

[45] Human Development Report, 1994, p. 22, 'New Dimensions of Human Security: Human Development Report', 1999, p. 36.

Nonetheless, the broad concept of human security should not be totally rejected. It highlights the function that institutions of the international community can discharge for the promotion and defence of human rights. Whoever speaks of human rights has in mind primarily the bilateral relationship between the state and its inhabitants, in particular its citizens. It is not clear, at first sight, what else can make a contribution with a view to making these rights a living reality. The jargon of 'human security' changes the perspective in a constructive way. What is referred to be not a situation of rights, which seems to be *a priori* a positive achievement, but a public interest task. Security is never an existing state of affairs: it is an objective that requires continuous efforts for its attainment. In this sense, also, a number of states, among them most prominently Canada and Norway,[46] have integrated the doctrine of human security as a primary aim in their foreign policy, albeit partly in a narrower sense as protection against violent threats.[47] Although the new motto does not usher in new content, it makes clear that the full enjoyment of human rights can only be achieved by structured efforts that view the looming challenge as a complex whole and not as a sequence of separate steps that can be taken independently from one another. The High-Level Panel on Threats, Challenges, and Change, entrusted with laying the intellectual groundwork for a fundamental overhaul of the UN, indeed took human security as its leitmotiv

---

[46] The first ministerial meeting of the Human Security Network, a group of fourteen countries, took place in May 1999 in Norway.

[47] The following definition of human security was adopted by that meeting, available at http://www.humansecuritynetwork.org/principles-e.php (accessed December 2007):

A commitment to human rights and humanitarian law is the foundation for building human security. Human security is advanced in every country by protecting and promoting human rights, the rule of law, democratic governance and democratic structures, a culture of peace and the peaceful resolution of conflicts. The international organizations created by states to build a just and peaceful worked order, above all the United Nations, in its role to maintain international peace and security as stated in the Charter, must serve the security needs of people.

Promoting sustainable human development, through the alleviation of absolute poverty, providing basic social services for all, and pursuing the goals of people-centre development, is necessary for building human security. Innovative international approaches will be needed to address the sources of insecurity, remedy the symptoms and prevent the recurrence of threats which affect the daily lives of millions of people.

for the integrated approach to international security that it adopted.[48] In response to its findings, the 2005 World Summit Outcome[49] has on the one hand approved the concept but has at the same time made clear that its exact meaning needs clarification (paragraph 143):

> We stress the right of people to live in freedom and dignity, free from poverty and despair. We recognize that all individuals, in particular vulnerable people, are entitled to freedom from fear and freedom from want, with an equal opportunity to enjoy all their rights and fully develop their human potential. To this end, we commit ourselves to discussing and defining the notion of human security in the General Assembly.

The term 'human security' highlights at the same time the factual conditions upon which real enjoyment of human rights is contingent. To establish a human-rights-friendly environment is much easier in a wealthy than in a poor nation. Rightly, therefore, the fight against poverty has in recent years become one of the central themes of discourse on human rights.[50] While there is broad agreement as to the aim to be achieved, opinions differ as to the most suitable avenue that should be followed. Under the influence of—perfectly legitimate—ideas about social justice, great emphasis has been placed on the action to be taken by governments. There is no denying the fact that public authorities must provide an essential contribution in the development process of any nation. But it should also be recognized that under conditions of freedom, societies themselves can do a lot to improve their living conditions.[51] Paternalism should not overshadow or eclipse private initiatives. It calls for political determination to find the appropriate balance between these two driving forces.

GLOBALIZATION

No excessive importance, therefore, should be attached to discussions about globalization and its negative impact on human rights.[52]

---

[48] UN Doc. 59/565, 2 December 2004.

[49] See GA Res. 60/1, 16 September 2005, para. 13.

[50] See GA Res. 55/2, 8 September 2000, para. 19.

[51] Rightly stated in the Millennium Declaration, wherein the list of fundamental values freedom occupies the first place (para. 6).

[52] See the rather polemical report for the UN Sub-Commission on the Promotion and Protection of Human Rights by J. Oloka-Onynango and Deepika Udagama, 'Globalization and its Impact on the Full Enjoyment of Human Rights' (UN

It is undeniable that humankind has entered into a new phase of its existence. National boundaries have lost the overriding significance they possessed at the time when the Iron Curtain divided Europe, with paradigmatic visibility in Berlin, although it should not be overlooked that a two-class society has emerged of which one part enjoys wide freedom of travel, while the other one remains stuck in its home countries. But it is inaccurate to see globalization as a project mainly driven by neo-liberals intent on abolishing the welfare state as it arose from the ashes of the Second World War and on re-colonizing the Third World.[53] To preserve the achievements of social justice is a duty of all responsible governments and opposing demands have to be balanced constantly. In a true democratic state, the yield of such balancing tests cannot ignore the needs of the large majority of the population. On the other hand, notwithstanding the many criticisms that may be directed at world economic and financial institutions, these institutions do not deserve to be accused of riding roughshod over the human rights of the populace in developing countries.

Contrary to the many critics of globalization, any impartial observer must note that the processes of change that it has brought about have yielded a broad range of positive results. No system of civilization remains unaffected by influences that it receives from outside. It is precisely the emergence of human rights at the centre of modern international law that should be welcomed as a victory over traditional state-centred conceptions of the world. One should not overlook, in particular, the impact that the UDHR has had on national constitutional systems. It is true that words must not be taken for hard facts. On the other hand, however, normative propositions that in official and high-ranking documents are repeated time and again will progressively shape the ways in which human

---

Doc. E/CM 4/Sub 2/2000/13, 15 June 2000). For a critical view see also P. O'Connell, 'On Reconciling Irreconcilables: Neo-liberal Globalization and Human Rights', 2007, 7 HRLR 483. All the relevant resolutions first by the HRCion (2001/32, 23 April 2001; 2003/23, 22 April 2003; 2005/17, 14 April 2005) and later by the HRC (4/5, 30 March 2007) were adopted against the opposition of the Western group of states.

53 Idowu William, 'African Legal Values and the Challenges of Globalization', 2005, 45 IJIL 354, p. 368, contends that globalization is 'the new name for colonialism by other means'.

beings think and argue. They may fail to be implemented for some time, they may be openly violated, but in the long run they will shape the ideological environment within which state power has to legitimate itself.

THE SHADOW OF TERRORISM

Just as war undermines and destroys human rights, so do terrorist attacks that indiscriminately target civilian populations. Peace, and law and order are needed for human rights to prosper. Rightly, therefore, the international community has decided to join forces to combat terrorist activities by preventive as well as repressive measures. The 2005 World Summit Outcome unequivocally condemned terrorism 'in all its forms and manifestations'.[54] There are no grounds that could justify resorting to terrorist activities.

At the same time, the international community has witnessed with growing concern that the fight against terrorism has taken a momentum that threatens well-established individual rights. To keep persons suspected of terrorist links imprisoned for long periods without trial,[55] to establish secret prisons where such persons are kept incommunicado, to apply methods of interrogation that the government concerned would never dare to apply to its own nationals,[56] to proceed to kill on the basis of vague evidentiary clues—all these reflect a mindset in which the life and personal integrity of a presumed enemy of their own national community counts for little, if

---

[54] GA Res. 60/1, 16 September 2005, para. 81

[55] A low point of judicial opportunism was reached with the decision of the US Court of Appeals for the District of Columbia of 2 December 2002 in *Al Odah* v.. *US*, 42 ILM (2003) 409 (pointing out that Guantanamo was under Cuban sovereignty). By contrast, in *A and Others* v. *Secretary of State for the Home Department*, 16 December 2004, 44 ILM (2005) 654, p. 682, Lord Nicholls of Birkenhead declared: 'Indefinite imprisonment without charge or trial is anathema in any country which observes the rule of law'.

[56] See, for instance, the aberrational advice given in a memorandum from Assistant Attorney General Jay S Bybee to White House Counsel Alberto R Gonzales 'Regarding Standards of Conduct for Interrogation', 1 August 2002 (2004) 98 AJIL 825. See in particular the opinion by the UN Special Reporter on Torture, M. Nowak, 'What Practices Constitute Torture? US and UN Standards', 2006, 28 *HRQ* 809.

anything at all.[57] The provisions on emergency situations contained in the universal and regional human rights instruments do not warrant such practices.[58] Accordingly, the Western world risks losing the moral authority that it gained after the Second World War by proclaiming the dignity of the human being as a sacred trust. If so-called 'national security' is elevated to the top of the hierarchy of values, the international human rights system falls apart.[59]

CONCLUSION

The human rights idea has lost nothing of its original impetus. Nobody wishes humankind to return to a situation where the individual would have to endure impotently the decisions of his/her government, unable to invoke any legal title to found his/her legitimate claims. But there is a growing awareness that human rights must be seen within the context of appropriate institutions. Human rights alone do not ensure effective enjoyment of human rights. They must be included in a network of institutions that are guided by the same philosophy. In that regard, the human rights movement returns to its sources. Jean Bodin and Thomas Hobbes placed their trust primarily in a government of unlimited authority.

It is certainly possible that there may be attempts in the future to use unorthodox strategies with a view to enforcing rights that are not capable of being enforced in the country of origin. It is, of course, much easier to guarantee human rights if the basic societal framework corresponds fully to the requirements of democracy and the rule of law. Today, the very idea of human rights contradicts such extremist solutions. But it is clear again that human rights cannot be seen in isolation.

---

[57] In its Opinion No 363/2005, International Legal Obligations of Council of Europe Member States in Respect of Secret Detention Facilities and Inter-State Transport of Prisoners, 18 March 2006, 2006, 27 *HRLJ* 122, the European Commission for Democracy through Law (Venice Commission) has reminded governments of their duty to respect the rule of law in the fight against terrorism. See also the Berlin Declaration of the International Commission of Jurists, 28 August 2004, 2005, 27 *HRQ* 350.

[58] A. Siehr, 'Derogation Measures under Article 4 ICCPR' (2004) 47 *GYIL* 544, p. 568.

[59] P. Hoffmann, 'Human Rights and Terrorism', 2004, 26 *HRQ* 932; R. Khan, 'The War on Terrorism', 2005, 45 *IJIL* 1, p. 16.

BIBLIOGRAPHY

Books

Andreassen, Bloed Arie and S. P. Marks (eds) (2006), *Development as a Human Right*, Harvard: Harvard University Press.

Baxi, Upendra (1998), *The Development of the Right to Development*, Paris: Aldershot *et al.* and UNESCO.

Cassese, Anthone (ed.) (1978), *Pour un droit des Peuples. Essais sur la Declaration d'Alger*, Paris: Berger-Levrault.

Dupuy, R. J. (ed.) (1980), *The Right to Development at the International Level*, Alphen aan den Rijin: Sijthoff & Noordhoff.

____(1991), *International Law: Achievements and Prospects*, Mohammed Bedjaoui (ed.), Paris and Dordrecht: UNESCO and Martinus Nijhoff.

Fox, G. H. and B. R. Roth (eds) (2000), *Democratic Governance and International Law*, Cambridge: Cambridge University Press.

Hanski, Raija and Markku Suksi (eds) (1997), *An Introduction to the International Protection of Human Rights: A Textbook*, Åbo: Institute for Human Rights, Finland.

Mehdi, R. (ed.) (2002), *La Contribution des Nations Unies a la Democratisation de l'Etat*, Paris: Pedone.

Sands, P. (2003), *Principles of International Environmental Law* (2nd edn), Cambridge: Cambridge University Press.

Symonides, J. (ed.) (1998), *Human Rights: New Dimensions and Challenges*, Paris: Ashgate and UNESCO.

Tomuschat, Christian (2008), *Human Rights between Idealism and Realism*, Oxford: Oxford University Press.

Weiss, T. G. and S. Daws (eds) (2006), *The Oxford Handbook on the United Nations*, Oxford: Oxford University Press.

Articles in Books and Journals

Donnelly, Jack (1999), 'Human Rights, Democracy, and Development', 21 *HRQ* 608.

Franck, T. (1992), 'The Emerging Right to Democratic Governance', 86 *AJIL* 46.

Hoffmann, P. (2004), 'Human Rights and Terrorism', 26 *HRQ* 932.

Khan, R. (2005), 'The War on Terrorism', 45 *IJIL* 1.

Nowak, Manfred (2006), 'What Practices Constitute Torture?: US and UN Standards', 28 *HRQ* 809.

O'Connell, P. (2007), 'On Reconciling Irreconcilables: Neo-liberal Globalization and Human Rights', 7 *HRLR* 483.

Siehr, A. (2004), 'Derogation Measures under Article 4 ICCPR', 47 *GYIL* 544.

Sinha, M. K. (2006), 'Human Rights and Good Governance', 46 *IJIL* 539.

Tomuschat, Christian (1985), 'Human Rights in a World-Wide Framework', 45 *HJIL* 547.

Udombana, N. J. (2000), 'The Third World and the Right to Development: Agenda for the Next Millennium', 22 *HRQ* 753.
Vasak, Karel (1977), 'A 30-Year Struggle', *The UNESCO Courier*, November 1977.
Wet, E. de (2006), 'The International Constitutional Order', 55 *ICLQ* 51.
Wheatley, S., De. Meeester, and C. Ryngaetrt (2003), 'Democracy and International Law', 51 *ICLQ* 225.
William, Idowu (2005), 'African Legal Values and the Challenges of Globalization', 45 *IJIL* 354.
Zambelli, M. (2002), 'Putting People at the Centre of the International Agenda: The Human Security Approach', 77 *Die Friendens-Warte* 173.

Official Documents/Reports

The Independent Commission on Disarmament and Security Issues, *Common Security: A Blueprint for Survival* (New York: Simon and Schuster), 1982.
'Governance: The World Bank's Experience', World Bank, Washington, 1994.
Oloka-Onynango, J. and Udagama, Deepika, 'Globalization and its Impact on the Full Enjoyment of Human Rights', UN Doc. E/CM 4/Sub 2/2000/13, 15 June 2000.

8

The Place of Capitalism in Pursuit of Human Rights in Globalized Relationships of States

Mohsen al Attar
Ciaron Murnane

INTRODUCTION

From the rubble of the Second World War emerged the Universal Declaration of Human Rights (UDHR), an idealistic—albeit fully attainable—set of obligations to which states committed themselves. This document was followed shortly after by two international covenants, each expanding on the UDHR by articulating a particular set of interrelated and mutually dependent rights, including civil, political, social, and economic rights. It is no secret that, from their inception, controversy has surrounded the concretization of the latter two. Indeed, the modern narrative of international human rights has been coloured by a clash between clusters of predominantly socialist and/or Third World states wishing to promote the universal pursuit of minimum standards of economic and social rights (ESRs), and the largely capitalist and/or First World states primarily concerned with the advancement of civil and political rights (CPRs).

The controversy is rooted in the divergent—potentially paradoxical—priorities of contemporary global society. Whilst the world economy is firmly within the grip of capitalist economic ideology, specifically its competitive predisposition, collective global consciousness is dominated by a unified commitment to social justice and personal freedom through poverty elimination, as expressed via the human rights narrative. The gap between these competing doctrines is vast and wide; a predatory market mentality versus a progressive human mentality; class privilege versus human solidarity. In this chapter, we examine both of these doctrines with a view to explaining the rivalry between them. We begin with an exploration of the theoretical bases of the doctrines but quickly delve into a case study—South Africa—that assists in better explicating the challenges posed by the capitalist economic superstructure to the concurrent actualization of both sets of human rights.

ORIGINS OF THE DIVISION

The First World bias towards CPRs originates in the political, religious, and economic changes experienced in Western states as far back as the sixteenth century.[1] Throughout the Reformation period (1517–1648 CE), struggles were waged to gain freedoms in the domains of religious practice and public expression. Scores of people, disenchanted with the Catholic Church's monopoly on spirituality, fought for the freedom of *publicly* practising a faith of their choosing. Moreover, the commission of gross atrocities by rival Catholic and Protestant sectarian forces during this period sparked a popular movement for the protection of human life.[2] Shortly thereafter, industrial transformation, propelled by earnings from the mercantilist model, inaugurated the capitalist era. This set in motion a series of domestic clashes as an emergent capitalist class—the bourgeoisie—sought to wrest power from the traditional rulers, the nobility.[3] A withered nobility sought to maintain power in the face of the bourgeois challenge by suppressing the industrialists' political voice. Unfazed by this counter-attack and emboldened by their increasing material wealth, the bourgeoisie mobilized peasants and workers alike, prompting a series of revolutions—including the Glorious (English), French, and American revolutions—and seeking the establishment of rights of representation and rights of political participation for all. (In the first of many betrayals to come, once in power, the bourgeoisie sought

---

[1] Ellie Palmer, *Judicial Review Socio-Economic Rights and the Human Rights Act* (Oxford: Hart Publishing, 2007), p. 12.

[2] Micheline R. Ishay, *The History of Human Rights: From Ancient Times to the Globalization Era* (Berkeley: University of California Press, 2004), p. 65.

[3] See, for example, Samuel Clark, 'Nobility, Bourgeoisie and the Industrial Revolution in Belgium', *Past and Present*, 105 (1984): pp. 140–75.

to limit these new rights to members of their own economic class thereby excluding the very peasants and workers who had ensured the revolutions' triumph.)[4]

These socio-political revolutions were accompanied by an industrial revolution—that catapulted off the earlier technical advancements—on a continental scale. The first factories were veritable cesspools of suffering for the retained workers.[5] Long hours, a dearth of worker-safety protocols, dismal wages, and non-existent job security produced instability and insecurity for an emerging proletariat (sadly, not unlike the conditions of workers in modern sweatshops). Discontent with their exploitation at the hands of the bourgeois-capitalists, their former revolutionary allies, workers began to organize themselves into collectives and demanded improved working conditions and a series of related and enabling rights. The rights fought for included rights to join trade unions, to safe working conditions, and to the availability of adequate food, water, and shelter. Demands were also made for subsidized education and healthcare so as to improve the overall living conditions of this new *working* class. These rights were widely regarded as essential to alleviate the immense social and economic plights the working poor suffered during the era of industrialization.[6] They were also necessary to avoid condemning the working class to perpetual second-class status by providing them with the means to advance their status within these transforming societies.

Efforts to attain these rights were repeatedly thwarted by the bourgeois class who, thanks to the earlier revolutions (that transcended class affiliation), now also doubled as the political class and thus both the decision- and law-makers in Western states. The reasoning behind their unresponsiveness towards the formalization of the sought-after rights was their perceived hostility to industrial growth.[7] Capitalists were concerned that worker protections would constrain their operations, hamper entrepreneurial spirit, and, due to costs of implementation, erode profit margins. Moreover, there was

---

[4]   Ishay, *The History of Human Rights,* pp. 73, 74, 81.
[5]   Ibid., pp. 135–45.
[6]   Ibid.
[7]   See, for example; Gaston V. Rimlinger, 'Capitalism and Human Rights', *Daedalus,* 112(4), 1983, pp. 51–79.

great reluctance to allow the state to intervene in the regulation of private business matters. Heightened sensitivity to state intervention was directly linked to the traditional intrusiveness of the nobility and the earlier struggles waged for CPRs. In other words, capitalists believed that ESRs would curtail both individual liberties and economic opportunities by providing the state with regulatory and enforcement authority over the execution of the rights.

Of course, peasants and workers, savvy to the exploitative manoeuvrings of the wealthy elite—whether the nobles or the bourgeois—merely improved on their mobilization methods and persisted with their efforts. Joining them in their struggle were philosophers and socialist activists, people of conscience who were also disturbed by the horrific treatment of the labour class. Hence, even today, there remains a strong popular perception that ESRs are the handmaidens of *socialism*.[8] Gradually, these efforts did come to fruition. After universal suffrage was established throughout the Western states in the nineteenth and twentieth centuries, a cluster of working class parties were elected in these same nations as 'working people' (now also voters) outnumbered 'propertied people' by a staggering ratio. These parties forced social welfare legislation through their respective legislatures, ensuring that all members of society received a minimum level of economic protection.[9]

What is most interesting, from both an industrialist and a worker perspective, is that these protections were anticipated, in fact prioritized, by some of the earlier capitalist thinkers. For instance, the first extended welfare state was inaugurated at the behest of Prince Otto von Bismarck of Germany, to counterbalance the inevitable social strife—class warfare—that capitalist inequality and inequity produce.[10] He passed health insurance, accident insurance, and old age pension bills not because of socialist or social democratic ideology, but instead as a ploy to neutralize the socialist German Social Democratic Party (SPD) by alleviating the worst effects of capitalism they were rallying against.[11] The welfare state, as it is termed,

---

[8] Ishay, *The History of Human Rights*, p. 135.

[9] Ibid., p. 144.

[10] David G. Williamson, *Germany Since 1815: A Nation Forged and Renewed* (New York: Palgrave Macmillan, 2005), p. 115.

[11] Ibid.

was thus a governmental arrangement promulgated specifically to redress the inevitable social dislocations occasioned by capitalism. Through a variety of tax-funded programmes, governments ensure that the well-being of citizens is upheld across their respective societies.[12] To this end, the programmes in question institutionalize minimum equitable standards of living for all; a safety net intended to temper the fall of the victims of capitalism. Examples of these initiatives include subsidized education and healthcare, low-income housing, unemployment insurance, retirement pensions, price controls over food, and labour standards such as minimum wages and maximum work hours. Other social amenities also fall within the purview of the welfare state, including public transportation, libraries, parks, and cultural services (for example, museums and galleries). Nevertheless, despite these important victories, the fact remains that very few of these ESRs were given the same constitutional status as CPRs.[13] Indeed, time and time again, political elites prove themselves readily willing (and quite comfortable) with the slashing of social welfare programmes, whether the move is prompted by an economic downturn, the election of a new government, or simply a desire to re-allocate budgetary provisions towards short-term economic initiatives. As we shall see shortly, from a societal perspective, the second-tier status of ESRs legislation is highly problematic for society in general and for the human rights narrative in particular.

The nature of capitalism is such that it weakens human solidarity by simultaneously providing the means for the production of vast expanses of wealth alongside near limitless expanses of suffering. Whilst free-market exponents, as far back as Adam Smith and Ludwig von Mises and as current as Milton Freedman and the Chicago School of Economics, may laud the improved living conditions in capitalist societies, they frequently omit three important elements. First, through the enactment of regulations and the building of infrastructure, governments have historically played a crucial role in enabling capitalist activities, suggesting that the free market is not so *free* after all. Second, colonialism and the pillaging of the Americas, Africa, and Asia—barbaric endeavours rooted in racialism and greed—were vital

---

[12] Nicholas Barr, *The Economics of the Welfare State* (Stanford: Stanford University Press, 1987), pp. 5–6.

[13] Ishay, *The History of Human Rights*, p. 144.

in establishing the architecture of European industrialization and the conditions for the growth of European wealth.[14] Third, the gross disparity in assets—the wealthiest 10 per cent of world population possesses a staggering 85 per cent of global household wealth, while the bottom 50 per cent barely owns 1 per cent—and, by extension, well-being, that the market has created at the national and international levels, has given rise to a global climate of injustice, one that is sparking much tension and strife.[15] All in all, then, while it remains true that capitalism has contributed to the creation of opportunities for the advancement of human society, it should not be forgotten that this same economic model has also produced a level and type of predation that undermines the human social fabric.

Tellingly, those who favour free-market capitalism also express great disdain for ESRs. To some of them, ESRs (as embodied in the welfare state) are antithetical to personal liberty as they impose a series of welfare measures on the whole of society, whether or not individual members are in support of these measures. In fact, these same free-market advocates go so far as to argue that ESRs run counter to CPRs in that they impinge on individual freedoms. In contrast, many social-welfare advocates argue the very opposite: that the protection of personal liberties above all else ultimately harms collective well-being. Over time, this ideological split was ratcheted up to the global scale (in the context of the Cold War). On one side was the former Soviet Union (the USSR), many Third World states, and a socialist proviso of human solidarity; on the other was the USA, its First World allies (namely Europe), and Western liberalism's championing of all things individual. Their oppositional ideologies resulted in a clash on the subject of human rights.[16] In simplistic fashion,

---

[14] See, for example, Walter Rodney, *How Europe Underdeveloped Africa* (London: Bogle L'Ouverture Publications, 1972). Rodney's analysis of African colonization and exploitation by European powers can be applied to the similar colonization and exploitation of the Americas and Asia.

[15] James B. Davies, Susanna Sandström, Anthony Shorrocks, and Edward N. Wolff, 'The World Distribution of Household Wealth', Discussion Paper No. 2008/03, United Nations University, World Institute for Development Economic Research, 2008.

[16] Yash Ghai (ed.), *Economic Social and Cultural Rights in Practice: the Role of Judges in Implementing Economic Social and Cultural Rights* (London: Interights, 2004), p. 12.

the USA and its allies characterized ESRs as derivatives of totalitarianism and socialism, which committed people to state dependency, inevitable shortages, and the rationing of goods and services. They promoted CPRs as the bedrock of economic freedom, which saw the West flourish, and the necessary preconditions to global societal and human advancement.[17] In an equally simplistic contrast, the USSR characterized CPRs and other individual-oriented rights as a tool of the ruling class to suppress the masses and to preserve their own privileges.[18] They promoted ESRs as necessary cornerstones for the pursuit of collective human well-being and for the attainment of individual human dignity. This clash is illustrated in the negotiations for the two covenants that followed the original document on human rights: the International Covenant on Civil and Political Rights (ICCPR) and the International Covenant on Economic, Social and Cultural Rights (ICESCR).

SPLITTING HUMAN DIGNITY

These two documents expand on the rights expressed in the 1948 Universal Declaration of Human Rights (UDHR).[19] Atrocities committed during the Second World War by states against civilians—*inter alia*, the carpet bombing of Dresden and other German cities by allied forces, the massacre of people belonging to various identity groups (such as the Roma, Jews, and disabled) by the Germans, and the American nuclear annihilation of Hiroshima and Nagasaki—prompted a modern movement for the protection of human life. Religious groups and social activists persuaded states to begin deliberations over a series of *universal* protections intended to underscore—*sanctify*—the importance of human life and human welfare.[20] Of course, the obvious CPRs were included, such as the right to liberty, to life, to be free from torture, to expression, as well as several others. Interestingly, attempts were also made to promote an expansive definition of human welfare. Following the lead of

---

[17]   Palmer, *Judicial Review Socio-Economic Rights and the Human Rights Act*, p. 14.

[18]   Ishay, *The History of Human Rights*, p. 221.

[19]   Rhona K. M. Smith, *Textbook on International Human Rights* (Oxford: Oxford University Press, 2007), p. 27.

[20]   Ishay, *The History of Human Rights*, pp. 214–15.

Panama's Ricardo Joaquin Alfaro, Latin American nations, as Third World representatives (at the time, many African and Asian nations were still European colonies and thus not permitted at the drafting table), proposed a comprehensive model of human rights that also contained ESRs, such as education, health, and labour rights, intended to secure the well-being of the masses. This push was promptly defeated by First World states.[21]

Undeterred by this defeat, Third World nations—far more numerous now that decolonization struggles had spread and were in full swing across the globe—continued their campaign for universal human welfare. Negotiations were quickly launched following the ratification of the UDHR for the production of a *single* covenant that would contain all forms of human rights: civil, political, economic, social, and cultural.[22] Opposition, however, remained. The first sign of a split over implementing all forms within the same covenant occurred in the UN Commission of Human Rights in 1950. It was made clear during the commission's deliberations that Western states were opposed to the inclusion of ESRs alongside CPRs within the same document.[23] For its part, and at this stage, the UN General Assembly emphasized that both sets of rights were 'indivisible and interdependent' and should not be separated.[24] The stance did not last long. One year later, following a variety of persuasion tactics by Western states (military and economic), the General Assembly opted instead for two distinct covenants: the first containing civil and political rights and the second embodying economic, social, and cultural rights.[25]

By 1966, the General Assembly had assented to both covenants and, in time, these were ratified by almost all UN member states. It should be noted, however, that dual-ratification did not translate into dual-legitimacy. Even a cursory review of the human rights movement abundantly demonstrates that both documents

---

21 Vijay Prashad, '"The South Also Exists", as the Third World Once Did', *NACLA Report on the Americas*, 40(5),2007, available at https://nacla.org/node/4554.
22 Smith, *Textbook on International Human Rights*, p. 41.
23 Asbjørn Eide, Catarina Krause, and Allan Rosas (eds), *Economic Social and Cultural Rights: A Textbook* (Dordrecht: Martinus Nijhoff Publishers, 2001), p. 3.
24 Ibid., p. 3.
25 Ishay, *The History of Human Rights*, p. 223.

have not been given the same emphasis in international law. First World dominance of what is considered 'human rights law' has been marred by a preoccupation with the implementation of CPRs, with ESRs being largely neglected (if not discredited). This dominance has occasioned at least two negative outcomes for the realization of ESRs.

First, human rights have become synonymous only with CPRs. One need merely glance at the manifestos and campaigns of international human rights non-governmental organizations (NGOs) such as Amnesty International and Human Rights Watch to conclude that they are predominantly concerned with the implementation of CPRs rather than ESRs. In fact, several have gone so far as to label ESRs 'second generation' rights, suggesting that they come subsequent to the implementation of CPRs and thus can be temporarily shelved until 'first generation' rights are achieved.[26] Lamentably, this privilege is even contained in the ICESCR itself, with Article 2 of the covenant only requiring states to take steps towards the *progressive realization* of these rights, efforts that are to be dictated by available resources and politically fickle budgetary allocations.[27] In contrast, the ICCPR obligates states to give *immediate effect* to the rights contained within it, irrespective of the level of expenditures involved.[28] First World states profess that CPRs are urgent and absolute, and should be unquestionably enforced, either voluntarily by respective states or coercively through the paradoxically labelled measure of humanitarian intervention. ESRs, conversely, are merely 'policy concerns' or 'aims' that are to be realized gradually and without outside influence.[29] The hierarchical stratification of human rights was best (and unknowingly) illustrated by a former US assistant secretary of state, Kenneth W. Dam, who asserted that civil and political rights

---

[26] Mashood A. Baderin and Robert McCorquodale, 'The International Covenant on Economic, Social and Cultural Rights: Forty Years of Development', in *Economic Social and Cultural Rights in Action*, Mashood A. Baderin and Robert McCorquodale (eds), (Oxford: Oxford University Press, 2007), pp. 9–10.

[27] 'International Covenant on Economic Social and Cultural Rights', opened for signature 19 December 1966, 993 UNTS 3, Article 2(1) (entered into force 3 January 1976).

[28] Palmer, *Judicial Review Socio-Economic Rights and the Human Rights Act*, p. 19.

[29] Balderin and McCorquodale, *Economic Social and Cultural Rights in Action*, p. 10.

should not be 'watered down' to the level of economic and social rights.[30]

Second, and this is the crux of the chapter's argument, the dominance of traditional Western liberal values, both as they relate to the individual and to the economy, results in the demonization of any form of state intervention that seeks to promote the protection of ESRs. This hostility is due, as already mentioned, to the alleged trespass on individual freedoms that ESRs occasion, as also to the apparent challenge an expansive definition of human rights poses to the capitalist architecture of the global economy. In other words, ESRs, which place a duty on State Governments to ensure the provision of social services such as education and healthcare, contravene Western liberalism's ideological foundations. First World states have even used their clout within a vast array of international institutions, primarily human rights based but also financial ones, to ensure the perpetuation—and purity—of their economic model and, by extension, their bias towards CPRs.[31]

This bias has also had severe consequences for the human rights movement as a whole. If the human rights narrative were to be reduced to a single word, dignity would likely win the laurels. If we were to develop the point further, we might say that human rights seek to actualize human dignity through the promotion of equitable social relations, the protection of vulnerable individuals and communities, and the championing of collective causes of general human welfare. Western liberalism's athletic defence of personal freedom and state detachment appears to run counter to the dignity narrative as it excludes perspectives (communitarian models) and possible measures (universal social services) that may be needed to promote human welfare. In this instance, ideology appears to trump dignity as the individualist proclivity for capitalism is privileged over the collectivist nature of human rights.

With the launch of the neo-liberal economic model some three decades ago, the clash—and contradiction—between capitalism and human rights greatly intensified. Neo-liberalism is a model of

---

[30] P. Alston, 'US Ratification of the Covenant on Economic, Social and Cultural Rights: The Need for an Entirely New Strategy', *American Journal of International Law*, 84, 1990, p. 373.

[31] Eide *et al.*, *Economic Social and Cultural Rights: A Textbook*, p. 11.

economic relations designed to encourage greater involvement of private actors in the delivery of public services.[32] Within the welfare state, the onus is on governments to ensure the adequate provision of social services to all members of society regardless of status, ethnicity, or gender. By shifting public services over to the private sector, under the guise of the rather nebulous concept of 'market efficiency', corporations are delegated the responsibility of ensuring adequate service delivery. From a human rights perspective, this repositioning of responsibility is highly counter-intuitive and presumptively problematic. Unlike public institutions, private actors such as corporations are motivated not by notions of equity but by desires for economic profit. Accordingly, the delivery of services is restructured not to ensure more universal access but more profitable management and enhanced availability to members of society with the means (wealth) to *purchase* the services. The motivational swing is crucial. No longer is the aim the promotion of human dignity and welfare—in line with the human rights narrative—but the creation of profitable economic opportunities for individual actors—in line with Western liberal economic diktat. Three decades of neo-liberalism have yielded a more polarized world. For instance, while trade and investment liberalization have added between $.5 and 1 trillion respectively to annual income in the USA, average real money earnings over the last decade have fallen for over 96 per cent of American workers.[33] The old adage rings as true today as it did when first spoken: *The rich get richer while the poor get poorer.*

Economic programmes, which produce these levels of inequality (and inequity), undermine human welfare and thus hinder the human rights movement. Though the link may seem tenuous it is, in fact, quite palpable. The hoarding of wealth by one social group *can* provides them greater political and economic clout over other such groups. Decisions are thereafter made according to the desires of the minority rather than the needs of the majority. In the end, entire populations find themselves at the mercy of the wealthy elite as their access to the most basic necessities of life covered by ESRs—including

[32] David Harvey, *A Brief History of Neoliberalism* (Oxford: Oxford University Press, 2005), p. 65.

[33] Kenneth F. Scheve and Matthew Slaughter, 'A New Deal for Globalization', *Foreign Affairs*, 86, 2007, p. 40.

water, food, shelter, and land—diminishes, leaving them vulnerable to the diktats of those in possession of them.[34]

To reiterate, then, the split of human rights into two ostensibly separate categories has been highly detrimental to the movement as a whole. As was recognized by the UN General Assembly nearly sixty years ago, all forms of human rights are interrelated, interdependent, and indivisible.[35] Indeed, it is impossible to fully implement civil and political rights, without also implementing economic and social rights. A person cannot adequately make use of their rights to vote and to democratic participation if they do not have access to an adequate education, let alone access to food, water, and shelter. For the human rights movement to succeed, efforts must first be directed towards redressing the two-tier status that has taken hold of the narrative. Next, human rights advocates must tackle Western liberalism's near-manic emphasis on individual freedoms and economic liberalization. For its part, individualism poses an obstacle to the advancement of collective human welfare while the free-market framework continues to shadow and hamper the development of an economic model that privileges most, not to say all, rather than one that champions the interests of a few.

In the second half of this chapter, we explore the experience of South Africa, one of the few states to experiment with a constitutionalized approach to ESRs. In progressive fashion, human rights sympathizers sought to redress the inequities of apartheid by legislating a series of welfare aims that the state obligated itself to attain. The exercise has not been without its hurdles. As we demonstrate, one of the primary obstacles faced by the South African government was the inherited capitalist economic structure, compounded by the neo-liberal model launched shortly after independence. The capitalist economic framework is proving to be a more formidable foe in the struggle for universal human welfare than the gunboats of the apartheid regime.

---

[34] David A. McDonald, 'The Bell Tolls For Thee: Cost Recovery, Cut-Offs and the Affordability of Municipal Services in South Africa', in *Cost Recovery and the Crisis of Service Delivery in South Africa,* David A. McDonald and John Pape (ed.) (Cape Town: Human Sciences Research Council, 2002), pp. 161–82.

[35] 'Statement by UN Committee on Economic Social and Cultural Rights', UN Doc E/1993/22, Annex. III, [5].

CASE STUDY: SOUTH AFRICA'S SOCIO-ECONOMIC CRISIS

In many ways, South Africa's past and present is a microcosm of the system-wide problems—just outlined—that free market capitalism precipitates. The violent imperialist colonization of this region by European settlers in the nineteenth century stripped the indigenous African population of much of its land and natural resources (particularly gold and diamond). In turn, the wealth generated from these resources was confiscated from the indigenous population and reinvested in Europe to assist with the ongoing industrialization efforts. It was also utilized to provide economic prosperity for the minority populations of Dutch and British settlers in South Africa. The economic and political inequality occasioned by colonialism between the minority white population and the oppressed black majority was perpetuated and reinforced by the brutal apartheid political system. Indeed, the minority white population ruled with an iron fist, denying black South Africans' access to both ESRs and CPRs, while privileging their own access to local resources. Inevitably, this political arrangement exacerbated the wealth gap that was forming between white and black South Africans. In short, despite being the numerical majority within South African society, blacks possessed far less of national wealth than their white counterparts. This situation mirrors present-day global concentration of material wealth in the hands of the First World irrespective, once again, of the Third World's population size that dwarfs that of its correlate.

Sadly, this inequality did not change significantly post-apartheid. For example, at present the unemployment rate among blacks is staggering—23.5 per cent, or 4.18 million South Africans[36]—and one of the key obstructions to South Africans' attainment of a more prosperous life. The health of the masses is another important element, specifically the HIV/AIDS epidemic. Fifteen per cent or approximately 5 million South Africans live with HIV. Of particular concern is the 29.5 per cent of pregnant women who are infected with the virus, which can be transmitted to their unborn children as well.[37]

---

[36] Nasreen Seria and Mike Cohen, 'South Africa's Unemployment Rate Increases to 23.5% (Update2)', *Bloomberg News*, available at http://www.bloomberg.com/apps/news?pid=20601116&sid=aoB7RbcZCRfU.

[37] David Bilchitz, *Poverty and Fundamental Rights: The Justification and Enforcement of Socio-Economic Rights* (Oxford: Oxford University Press, 2007), p. 153.

Even more harrowing is that almost thirty thousand people die annually of AIDS. When combined with other social and health-related challenges, life expectancy for black South Africans is an abysmal 50 years for males and 53 for females, with over half the population perishing between the ages of 15 and 60.[38] Finally, education among black South Africans is especially poor. While 65 per cent of whites over 20 years old and 40 per cent of Indians have high school or higher qualification, only 14 per cent of blacks and 17 per cent of 'coloured' peoples have achieved this level of education.[39]

The end of the repressive apartheid system and the establishment of a democratic system in South Africa in 1994 was rightfully hailed as a momentous leap forward for the whole of humanity. This is indisputable. Over a century of racialized legal and political structures were being overturned and a new era of human dignity and equality inaugurated. Regrettably, however, the fanfare was short-lived. As the world quickly discovered (and the just-mentioned figures corroborate), colonial legacies run deep and, notwithstanding the acquisition of *political* equality by the black majority, the broad-based disadvantages blacks suffered because of *economic* inequality persisted. Access to healthcare, educational institutions, employment, and other basic socio-economic rights continued to be severely constrained for blacks as the establishment of a democratic system did not presuppose the redressing of socio-economic disparities. Of course, from a human rights perspective it is difficult to miss the links between the lack of attention on economic inequality and the division between ESRs and CPRs. So long as poverty and economic oppression are regarded as distinct from democracy and human dignity, the debilitating social and economic inequalities that exist will never be adequately overcome.

The Constitutionalization of Socio-Economic Rights

In an attempt to address these statistics and the socio-economic costs of the apartheid regime, ESRs—alongside CPRs—were included

---

[38] 'World Health Organization: South Africa', available at http://www.who.int/countries/zaf/en/.

[39] 'Education in South Africa', SouthAfrica.info., available at http://www.southafrica.info/about/education/education.htm.

in the newly drafted Constitution of the Republic of South Africa, 1996. The constitutionalization of socio-economic rights placed an obligation on the state to protect and provide the necessary minimum level of economic and social resources for individuals to achieve a life of dignity and respect. These include the rights to such resources as social security, work, food, healthcare, education, and shelter. Not unexpectedly, considering the history of ESRs, the issue of constitutionally recognizing socio-economic rights has been contentious, and fraught with political and legal challenges. The two main objections to judicial enforcement of constitutional ESRs are that the rights themselves are non-justiciable and that their enforcement would be undemocratic.

It is argued that ESRs are non-justiciable because of the 'positive' nature of these rights. A positive duty differs markedly from a negative duty in that the former creates an obligation for the government to *provide* the rights while the latter merely requires *non-intervention* in the exercise of the rights, or *non-prevention* of individuals from obtaining them. A positive duty necessarily implies giving the judiciary authority to issue rulings that would require the legislature or the executive to make changes to resource allocations in governmental budgets.[40] Critics thus assert that since positive rights possess a political quality, in that public opinion is not universal as to how budget allocations should be directed, it is best to leave such discretion with the legislature and executive.[41] The challenge concludes by alleging that judicial review or intervention in resource allocation on the basis of ESRs would therefore be a breach of the separation of powers, which is why it must remain non-justiciable by the courts.[42]

The second argument, that an approach allowing the courts to enforce ESRs would be undemocratic, flows from this. The basic premise is that the legislature should make ESR-related decisions because, in a democracy, political representatives are directly accountable to the electorate.[43] Consequently, to permit unelected judges to

---

[40] Martin Scheinin, 'The Protection of Economic and Social Rights in Domestic Legal Systems', in *Economic, Social and Cultural Rights: A Textbook,* Eide *et al.,* 58.

[41] Palmer, *Judicial Review, Socio-Economic Rights and the Human Rights Act,* p. 26.

[42] Scheinin, 'The Protection of Economic and Social Rights in Domestic Legal Systems', p. 58.

[43] Ibid.

revisit political decisions and force elected officials to change their policies would be undemocratic.[44] This argument reduces democracy to simple 'majoritarianism'[45] rather than a system of collective decision-making in which its institutions and practices treat all individuals, including members of minority groupings, with equal concern and respect.[46] Under the latter definition, allowing judges to rule on cases that affect popular access to ESRs would actually be democracy-*enhancing* as the interests of the frequently-marginalized (such as the poor) may be considered and possibly protected, rather than being provided for simply when it is politically expedient for governments to do so.

At the core of both these arguments, however, is the incompatibility of ESRs with the neo-liberal ideology, protected and perpetuated by corporations and State Governments (as outlined in the first part of this chapter). These entities fear that the creation of a positive duty to provide ESRs alongside judicial powers to ensure governmental accountability would necessitate the setting aside of more resources and tax revenue so as to fulfil these obligations. A potential flow-on effect would be an increase in taxation of both individuals and corporations and, presumably, additional regulation to enable governments to implement this expansion in public welfare services. Notions of increased taxation and heightened governmental intervention *directly* clash with the ideals of free-market capitalism as they are espoused by Western governments and international financial institutions such as the International Monetary Fund and the World Bank. It is this fervent and unyielding belief in market capitalism (and neo-liberalism today) that lies at the heart of the opposition to constitutionally protected ESRs.

Notwithstanding the strong opposition to its inclusion, South Africa elected to constitutionally protect ESRs. However, its constitution has subdivided them into three types. First, there are 'basic' socio-economic rights. These are positive rights the government *must* provide, thus precluding it from relying on a 'progressive

---

[44] Bilchitz, *Poverty and Fundamental Rights*, p. 104.
[45] 'Majoritarianism' equates democracy merely with the implementation of the majority opinion on an issue, instead of also taking into consideration and implementing the views or needs of minority groups.
[46] Bilchitz, *Poverty and Fundamental Rights*, p. 104.

realisation' clause to temper the burden of actualizing the rights.[47] Examples are Section 28 on the rights of children and Section 29 on the right to education.[48] Next, there are 'prohibitive' rights.[49] These rights *prohibit* the government from *refusing or interfering* with a person's attempt to obtain the right. An excellent example is Section 27(3), which prohibits the refusal of emergency medical treatment.[50]

Lastly, there are the 'progressive realisation' rights. These ones are most susceptible to the incompatibility claim of critics and will be the focus of the cases that follow. Like the basic rights, these rights must be provided by the state but the burden is less stringent. Indeed, echoing Article 2 of the ICESCR, the government is only obliged to take 'reasonable ... measures, within its available resources, to achieve the progressive realisation' of the respective rights.[51] Essentially, they have been given the status of the previously described 'second generation' rights, suggesting they are either less important or less urgent. An example of a progressively realizable right is the right to housing outlined at Section 26(2).[52] As will be demonstrated in the following section, the consequence of this categorization is that instead of being guided by the needs of the people in the pursuit of these rights, the duty is fettered with concerns of 'reasonable' allocation of resources. To date this has meant that in judicially reviewed cases, government policy has principally been ruled against only where the requisite increase in expenditures was deemed too small or unreasonable. Even in the latter case, reluctance by the South African Constitutional Court to make positive rulings on these rights has enabled the state to delay the implementation of policies that could assist in the provision of ESRs to a greater extent.

---

[47] Schenin, 'The Protection of Economic and Social Rights in Domestic Legal Systems', p. 61.

[48] *Constitution of the Republic of South Africa*, Sections 28 and 29.

[49] Schenin, 'The Protection of Economic and Social Rights in Domestic Legal Systems', p. 62.

[50] *Constitution of the Republic of South Africa*, Section 27(3).

[51] Schenin, 'The Protection of Economic and Social Rights in Domestic Legal Systems', pp. 61–62.

[52] *Constitution of the Republic of South Africa*, Section 26(2).

Adjudicating Socio-Economic Rights: 'Progressive Realization' Under the South African Constitutional Court

The four major socio-economic rights cases decided by the South African Constitutional Court, *Soobramoney* v. *Minister of Health Kwa Zulu Natal,*[53] *Government of the Republic of South Africa* v. *Grootboom,*[54] *Minister of Health* v. *Treatment Action Campaign,*[55] and *Khosa* v. *Minister of Social Development,*[56] illustrate the court's balancing act. While enforcing its constitutionally mandated jurisdiction over ESRs, it must also face the challenges put to this jurisdiction (as already outlined), including the supposed 'rightful place' of the legislature and executive to make allocation decisions in the struggle towards the 'progressive realisation' of socio-economic rights. This is even more difficult in South Africa's pro-free-market economic context, which is unreceptive to the entire concept of ESRs.

In the *Soobramoney* case, a patient requiring dialysis treatment was refused the service because he fell outside the prioritization criteria established by the government for such treatment.[57] The patient argued, amongst other things, that the refusal breached the right to healthcare guaranteed under Section 27(1) of the constitution. While sympathetic to the patient's predicament, the court asserted that it 'will be *slow to interfere* with rational decisions taken in good faith by the political organs, and by medical authorities who have the responsibility of dealing with such matters'.[58] The implications of this decision should not be overlooked. Essentially, the court was electing to give wider discretion to government authorities when the rights at issue compelled the expenditure of large resources. It did so because the right to healthcare was limited by the 'progressive realisation' clause, under Section 27(2) of the constitution, which makes clear that for certain rights there is a higher threshold to judicial

---

[53] *Soobramoney* v. *Minister of Health Kwa Zulu Natal,* 1998 (1) SA 765 (CC) [hereafter, *Soobramoney*].

[54] *Government of the Republic of South Africa* v. *Grootboom,* 2000 (11) BCLR 1169 (CC) [hereafter, *Grootboom*].

[55] *Minister of Health* v. *Treatment Action Campaign,* 2005 (5) SA 721 (CC) [hereafter, *TAC*].

[56] *Khosa* v. *Minister of Social* Development, 2004 (6) SA 505 [hereafter, *Khosa*].

[57] Palmer, *Judicial Review, Socio-Economic Rights and the Human Rights Act,* p. 43.

[58] *Soobramoney,* p. 29.

intervention.[59] In the end, the prioritization criteria at the heart of the controversy was deemed 'reasonable' and thus not in breach of the right to healthcare.

In the subsequent decision of *Grootboom*, the *Soobramoney* stance was clarified. *Grootboom* concerned homeless individuals (squatters) who had taken up residence in private, unoccupied premises. They were eventually evicted from the property. Following their eviction they took their case before the Constitutional Court, arguing that their eviction was in breach of the right to housing mandated under Section 26(2) of the constitution.[60] The court reconfirmed their application of the reasonableness test. In the words of Yacoob J., '[t]he real question in terms of our constitution is whether the measures taken by the state to realise the right ... are reasonable'.[61] While the government's housing plan was deemed reasonable and thus not in violation of Section 26(2), the court found the lack of emergency housing relief for people in short-term need *unreasonable* and issued a declaratory order requiring the government to rectify the deficiency.[62] While this decision contains elements of a victory in the struggle for ESRs, it is important to note that economic resources still retained primary consideration throughout the court's deliberations, with citizens' rights, needs, and dignity coming a distant second. Moreover, an overly charitable hands-off approach to ensuring governmental compliance with the declaratory order left the state virtually free from accountability for failing to follow court instructions. Finally, the court also rejected the call to replace the reasonableness test with a 'minimum core' obligation to a mandatory basic level of socio-economic rights that would be protected by the constitution, even if there remained 'progressive realisation' limitations.[63] Indeed, with each new ruling, the reasonableness test appears

---

59   Schenin, *Economic, Social and Cultural Rights: A Textbook*, pp. 65–66.
60   Bilchitz, *Poverty and Fundamental Rights*, pp. 139–40.
61   Ibid., p. 133.
62   Schenin, *supra* n. 59, p. 66.
63   The 'minimum core' is the concept that all people should be entitled to a base or minimum level of economic and social rights, regardless of how vague or indeterminate the possible extension of such rights might be. See Katharine G. Young, 'The Minimum Core of Economic and Social Rights: A Concept in Search of Content', *The Yale Journal of International Law*, 33, 2008, pp. 113–71.

to gain a greater foothold in guiding the court's decisions in matters of ESRs. This is even more apparent in the *TAC* and *Khosa* cases.

As per their mission statement, the Treatment Action Campaign (TAC) is a non-governmental organization that campaigns for 'access to treatment, care and support services for people living with HIV'.[64] In 2000, the antiretroviral drug Nevaripine, which prevents the transmission of the HIV virus from mother to child in pregnant women, was being selectively administered in clinics across South Africa. A pharmaceutical company was providing the government with limited supplies of the drug gratuitously. TAC brought a case before the Constitutional Court arguing that by failing to implement the programme nationwide, the government was denying HIV-infected mothers and their children their right to healthcare under Section 27(1).[65] As observed in the *Soobramoney* case, the right to healthcare is a 'progressive realisation' right for which the court would apply a reasonableness test in seeking to determine whether state obligations were being met.[66] The court considered three elements in deciding whether the selectivity of the drug distribution programme was reasonable. First, the court assessed the cost of a nationwide programme and found that this would be minimal as the drug was being provided free of charge. Second, it examined the safety of patients receiving Nevaripine and determined that, on medical evidence, it was safe. Finally, it calculated the potential number of lives that could be saved or even improved by nationwide distribution and concluded that this would prevent HIV infection in thousands of children.[67] In the end, the court ruled that restricting the programme to selected clinics was 'unreasonable'.[68]

In the *Khosa* case, some Mozambican citizens with permanent residency in South Africa were refused social security benefits because they were not *citizens* of South Africa.[69] The applicants argued that

---

[64] 'About the Treatment Action Campaign', available at http://www.tac.org.za/community/about.

[65] *TAC*, pp. 16–17.

[66] *Constitution of the Republic of South Africa*, Section 27(2).

[67] Bilchitz, *Poverty and Fundamental Rights*, p. 154.

[68] *TAC*, p. 81.

[69] *Khosa*, pp. 3–4.

this restriction to citizens only was contrary to their socio-economic rights. Social security is guaranteed under Section 27 of the constitution and, in fact, does not *explicitly* restrict accessibility to citizens only. The applicants further argued, and the court agreed, that denying permanent residents access would have grave consequences, including banishing them to the margins of society and leaving them wholly dependent on family support. They also claimed that there was little substantive difference between their status as permanent residents and that of official citizens, buttressing the unreasonableness of their exclusion. Tellingly, the arguments were still balanced against the effect the expansion of social security would have on governmental budgets and resource allocations.[70] Due to the minimal nature of the increase, the court ruled that the restriction to citizens only was 'unreasonable'.

Although two of the four cases were decided in favour of ESRs—in that the government was found to be in breach of its positive duty because the established plans were ruled unreasonable—we must inquire as to whether the outcomes would have been the same had Nevaripine not been provided free of charge or had an expansion of social security to permanent residents dramatically increased costs to government. The court's dual emphasis on policy processes and an abstract notion of reasonableness directly linked to costs appears to marginalize the interests (sometimes life-or-death) and dignity of the applicants. This suggests that the *TAC* and *Khosa* victories are more likely anomalies—occasioned by the affordability of the measures—rather than progressive moves towards the attainment of universal socio-economic equity. As represented by the negative decisions in the *Soobramoney* and *Grootboom* cases and the tone of the rulings in the *TAC* and *Khosa* cases, the court remains apprehensive of the criticisms levelled against its authority to adjudicate ESRs, particularly its fear of encroaching on governmental responsibility, and thus carries itself with exaggerated caution.

Yet, if the constitutional protections afforded ESRs are to have any meaning, especially in cases more difficult than *TAC* or *Khosa*, the court may need to reconsider its vague and unpredictable 'reasonableness' test as well as its fixation on the economic implications

---

[70] Bilchitz, *Poverty and Fundamental Rights*, p. 171.

of its decisions. The legitimacy of governmental actions and policies must be determined according to their fulfilment of the core indispensable needs of the whole of South African society, particularly the marginalized and vulnerable, as set forth in the nation's constitution. Ultimately, the court must move beyond the paradigm of state resource constraints if it is to play its constitutionally mandated role of furthering human dignity, in this instance via the assessment of claims for socio-economic rights according to the needs of society rather than the goodwill of government. Until this change in mentality is realized, the dominant free market mindset and its knee-jerk opposition to ESRs will continue to obstruct the delivery of socio-economic services to all South Africans, especially those in the most defenceless of positions, and thus to the actualization of human rights.

Governmental Opposition to the Actualization of Socio-Economic Rights

As asserted in the *TAC* case, the orders the Constitutional Court can pronounce to uphold socio-economic rights are, in theory at least, quite wide-ranging.[71] These include, among others, declaratory orders about the unconstitutionality of legislation and the need for constitutionally supported amendments, mandatory orders for specific policy changes, and supervisory stipulations (including deadlines) necessary to monitor governmental progress towards the remedying of a breach. In reality, however, the court has been rather reluctant to make either mandatory orders or supervisory stipulations. In deciding not to impose a mandatory order in the *TAC* case, the court stated that since 'the government has always respected and executed orders of this Court' there appears to be 'no reason to believe that it will not do so in the present case'.[72] In fact, there were several reasons to suspect that the government would not follow the ruling and that a more proactive approach by the court was warranted.

First, the manner in which the South African government's economic policies have been structured and enforced since the ANC

---

[71] Ibid., p. 155.
[72] *TAC*, p. 129.

came to power in 1994—particularly under Thabo Mbeki's stewardship—leaves much to be desired from an ESR perspective. The ANC's Freedom Charter, drafted during the apartheid struggle, promised to implement several measures to universally improve socio-economic conditions.[73] However, much like the bourgeois class following the revolutions in Europe and America, ANC political elites such as Mbeki quickly abandoned the masses who struggled alongside them during the apartheid era. Instead of pursuing the progressive Freedom Charter, as endorsed by the masses during the anti-apartheid movement, the elites opted for a neo-liberal programme formed by their former oppressors. As described in the first half of the chapter, this prompted cuts in social spending (welfare), liberalized labour laws, and calls for the further privatization of state-owned resources.[74] Following the implementation of these neo-liberal policies, the number of people living on less than a dollar a day in South Africa—below which a person is considered to be in absolute or abject poverty—doubled to 4 million. Moreover, although 1.8 million homes were built, 2 million people lost their homes, a sizeable percentage of which came via evictions.[75] While masterminded by Mbeki, support for this programme spread across several ranks of the ANC cadre. In this climate of economic liberalism, it is naïve for the court to believe that without strong oversight the government will happily implement changes that necessitate a redistribution of government expenditures, higher taxation of the wealthy, and a broad-based move towards universal socio-economic equity.

Second, in response to previous rulings, the government has repeatedly proven itself defiant towards the implementation of the court's orders. Indeed, two years after the *Grootboom* decision, the declaratory order had still not been fully implemented. The government has interpreted the order narrowly, arguing that emergency housing relief was only owed to residents of the plaintiffs' neighbourhood. It has also sought to restrict assistance to individuals who lost their homes through either flood or fire.[76] So flippant was the

---

[73] Naomi Klein, *The Shock Doctrine: The Rise of Disaster Capitalism* (London: Allen Lane, 2007), p. 209.

[74] Ibid., p. 209.

[75] Ibid., p. 215.

[76] Bilchitz, *Poverty and Fundamental Rights*, p. 151.

government towards the court's ruling and towards its obligations that a later case, *City of Cape Town* v. *Rudolph*, was brought to compel the local governmental authority to comply with *Grootboom* and, importantly, to provide evidence to the court that they had done so.[77] A full eighteen months passed before the authority finally acknowledged its obligation though it had still not fulfilled the order. Lamentably, despite the vulgarity of the government's intransigence, the court *again* opted for a powerless declaratory order censuring the authority for non-compliance and ordering it to do so.[78] In the *TAC* case, the court was equally laissez-faire in its approach, notwithstanding the grossly inadequate implementation of the *Grootboom* decision, entrusting the government to make Nevaripine available nationwide without the imposition of either a mandatory order or supervisory stipulations. This again proved to be a mistake as the government reluctantly—and ultimately inadequately—made the drug available nationwide. In practise, only a few provinces gave HIV-infected pregnant woman extensive access to Nevaripine, while others that had the capacity to do so could not because of a lack of state support.[79] Given the epidemic nature of the HIV/AIDS virus in South Africa, the government's apathy towards the delivery of vital—and available—medicines is nothing short of negligent and, as some have argued, quite likely criminal. For the court to continue to eschew vigilance towards governmental compliance, particularly in the face of ever-mounting defiance, seems perplexing at a minimum and outrageous at a maximum.

THE WAY FORWARD?

South Africa's story is an inspirational one. In 1994, the black majority chose to forgive the white minority's brutal reign and begin a new chapter in their nation's history, moving forward hand-in-hand with their former oppressors. Of course, generations of xenophobic policies had left human solidarity in tatters and in desperate need of rebuilding. Yet, before this could occur, the social, cultural, and economic gaps between the different ethnic groups needed to be

---

[77] Ibid., pp. 151–52.
[78] Ibid., p. 152.
[79] Ibid., p. 163.

redressed. Figure after figure, statistic after statistic confirmed the obvious: the disparities between blacks and whites, between the poor and the wealthy were enormous as the bulk of state resources had historically been used to uplift the white minority while concurrently suppressing the black majority, One of the earliest actions then of the newly elected (and ethnically representative) legislature was to adopt a constitution that protected the rights of *all* people. As part of the state's metaphorical rebirth, this pioneer—and pioneering— legislature also constitutionalized socio-economic rights, a necessary step if the gaps were to be lessened. With much courage, the South African legislators had stormed onto the world stage by doing what most governments had hitherto been unwilling and afraid to: recognize the interdependence of both sets of human rights and offer each one equal protection under the law. As the foregoing discussion makes abundantly clear, the actualization of these rights has proven far more complex than the mere legislation of them. Granted, there are a number of logistical and infrastructural obstacles to ensuring universal availability of access to healthcare, education, housing, and other necessities of life. This should not be denied. Yet, logistics and infrastructure are mere child's play when considered alongside the challenge waged by capitalist sectors of society.

In the South African case, many of the ensuing battles occurred in the courts. Considering that the judges, some experienced and some not, were treading new ground, their performance to date has been nothing short of remarkable. Technical arguments are routinely made for and against the approach—the 'reasonableness' test—adopted by the Constitutional Court. These perspectives are worthy of their own study. However, and this has been the theme of the chapter, the power of capitalism itself and the world that it has created have produced a particular climate, one that is not conducive to socio-economic rights; and, therefore, one that is not conducive to human dignity. For instance, despite the best of intentions, South Africa has been incapable of actualizing their self-imposed aims. Under pressure from international financial institutions and a political cadre that has bought into the dominant economic ideology, government authorities refuse to expand welfare provisions of their own accord to fulfil their ESR obligations, all of which are crucial to the whole of South African society. For its part, the judiciary, either cheerfully or grudgingly, has been unwilling to enforce the state's obligations to a high standard, also yielding to domestic and international political pressures and giving carte blanche to governmental authorities in matters concerning ESRs. Indeed, the speed with which ESRs have been sidelined in the post-apartheid political programme would be startling *unless* we accept that both governmental recalcitrance and judicial ambivalence take root in the same economic orthodoxy, one that is simultaneously, supportive of CPRs and antithetical to ESRs. Capitalism, it seems, possesses decisive influence over the human rights narrative. We will conclude with a brief comparison of the South African experience with another nation's quest for socio-economic rights to determine what is possible, from a human rights perspective, outside the capitalist model.

The Cubans won their independence in 1959, bringing an end to the reign of petty dictator Fulgencio Batista. More importantly, however, the revolution marked the beginning of a new era for the Cuban people; the year Cuban society took the first steps towards the establishment of, what they termed, a *just* society.[80] Indeed, without wasting a breath, they began the arduous task of rebuilding their nation under the banners of social equality and human solidarity (or, it could be said, under the banner of human rights). One of their first acts was to launch a national literacy campaign. Over a hundred thousand Cubans, mostly high school students, volunteered to relocate to the countryside to teach peasants and labourers to read and write. In just one year, illiteracy was reduced from 42 per cent to 4 per cent as over a million people were taught to read. The literacy campaign quickly morphed into a public education campaign as the state implemented measures to ensure that all levels of education, from primary to tertiary, were fully available for all people. Next, Cubans implemented land reform to break up the oligopolistic power of wealthy landlords. A limit was thus placed on the amount of land any one person could own and compensation was provided to the few affected (including the Castro family!). The land recovered was distributed to landless peasants or parcelled into a series of community-controlled cooperatives. In three years, the number of landowning peasants quintupled from 40,000 to 200,000. By distributing land and nurturing feelings of ownership and belonging, Cubans were able

---

[80] This paragraph quotes extensively from Saney's text. See Isaac Saney, *Cuba: A Revolution in Motion* (London: Zed Books, 2004).

to increase food production to unprecedented levels and strengthen communal solidarity. In this same vein, the island instituted a programme of food subsidization to ensure access to consistent levels of nutrition on a daily basis. Finally, with more doctors per capita than any other country (in the world), Cuba possesses a highly advanced system of healthcare. All medical procedures and all medicines are covered by the state system. In fact, in any given year (and since the early 1970s), Cuba even manages to send tens of thousands of doctors to the poorest neighbourhoods in Latin America, Africa, and Asia to provide free medical care.

Combined, these measures have ensured that, until today, every citizen has adequate shelter, nourishment, and healthcare. We may criticize Cuba for its civil rights record—sometimes justifiably—but we must applaud the nation's commitment to the common good. Despite scarce resources, principles of social equity and human solidarity have helped propel the tiny island to the front of the Human Development Index where the compassion of community trumps the self-interest of the market, consistently outscoring many First World nations in the most relevant UN statistics, including the provision of healthcare, education, social security benefits, food subsidies, and housing. (As to the final element, it should be noted that 85 per cent of Cubans *fully* own their homes, a figure that dwarfs homeownership in most Western nations.) The difference between the South African and Cuban commitments to social and economic justice is that the former came secondary to notions of market liberalism whilst the latter prioritized justice over dominant economic ideologies. The results, as the figures indicate, could not be more different, suggesting that the successful pursuit of human rights is dependent on the curtailing of capitalist excess and the prioritization of human dignity above all else. If South Africans—indeed, if the world—are serious about human rights, it appears that the way forward is to abandon the competitive ideology of capitalism in favour of a collaborationist and solidarity ethos.

This change in thinking is not utopian. Examples of this struggle for social equity abound in the Third World, as the Cuban story, the human rights campaign of Alfaro, South Africa's constitutionalization of ESRs, and the populist reforms brought about by the Bolivarian Revolution concurrently attest to. The First World however has, regrettably, lagged behind. This was not always so. Following the

Depression of 1929, there was political and societal consensus in First World states that a functional society was contingent on the provision of public services to *all* its members. The result was lower unemployment and crime, better health and happiness, and genuine feelings of community and social responsibility. Neo-liberalism took a hatchet to most of these programmes, not to mention the feelings of collaboration and solidarity. All is not lost however and we can, once again, rediscover this mindset. The financial crisis of 2008 created a historic opportunity—not dissimilar to the one of 1929—to re-shift our political focus and economic model from the interests of the capitalists to the interests of the public. A little political imagination is needed to seize this opportunity and to break the spell of capitalist ideological conviction. We may then begin to build a mass movement behind a programme of radical reform, one that allows the whole of humanity to benefit from the technological, economic, and social advances of the modern era. This is entirely plausible but we must first reject the atomizing and divisive principles of free-market liberalism. The next crucial step is to prioritize global human solidarity through the proper enforcement of socio-economic rights and, in the process, underscore the importance of everyone's right to live with dignity and respect. Human solidarity as a precursor to human dignity? Simple. Doable.

BIBLIOGRAPHY

Books

Baderin, Mashood A. and Robert McCorquodale (eds) (2007), *Economic Social and Cultural Rights in Action*, Oxford: Oxford University Press.

Barr, Nicholas (1987), *The Economics of the Welfare State*, Stanford: Stanford University Press.

Bilchitz, David (2007), *Poverty and Fundamental Rights: The Justification and Enforcement of Socio-Economic Rights*, Oxford: Oxford University Press.

Eide, Asbjørn, Catarina Krause, and Allan Rosas (eds) (2001), *Economic Social and Cultural Rights: A Textbook,* Dordrecht: Martinus Nijhoff Publishers.

Ghai, Yash, and Jill Cottrell (eds) (2004), *Economic Social and Cultural Rights in Practice: the Role of Judges in Implementing Economic Social and Cultural Rights*, London: Interights.

Harvey, David (2005), *A Brief History of Neoliberalism*, Oxford: Oxford University Press.

Ishay, Micheline R. (2004), *The History of Human Rights: From Ancient Times to the Globalization Era*, Berkeley: University of California Press.

Klein, Naomi (2007), *The Shock Doctrine: The Rise of Disaster Capitalism*, London: Allen Lane.

McDonald, David A. and John Pape (eds) (2002), *Cost Recovery and the Crisis of Service Delivery in South Africa*, Cape Town: Human Sciences Research Council.

Palmer, Ellie (2007), *Judicial Review Socio-Economic Rights and the Human Rights Act*, Oxford: Hart Publishing.

Rodney, Walter (1972), *How Europe Underdeveloped Africa*, London: Bogle L'Ouverture Publications.

Saney, Isaac (2004), *Cuba: A Revolution in Motion*, London: Zed Books.

Smith, Rhona K. M. (2007), *Textbook on International Human Rights*, Oxford: Oxford University Press.

Williamson, David G. (2005), *Germany Since 1815: A Nation Forged and Renewed*, New York: Palgrave Macmillan.

Articles in Books and Journals/Research Papers

Alston, P., 'US Ratification of the Covenant on Economic, Social and Cultural Rights: The Need for an Entirely New Strategy', *American Journal of International Law*, 84, 1990, pp. 365–93.

Clark, Samuel, 'Nobility, Bourgeoisie and the Industrial Revolution in Belgium', *Past and Present*, 105, 1984, pp. 140–75.

Davies, James B., Sandström, Susanna, Shorrocks, Anthony, and Wolff, Edward N., 'The World Distribution of Household Wealth', Discussion Paper No. 2008/03, United Nations University, World Institute for Development Economic Research, 2008.

Rimlinger, Gaston V., 'Capitalism and Human Rights', *Daedalus*, 112(4), 1983, pp. 51–79.

Scheve, Kenneth F. and Slaughter, Matthew, 'A New Deal for Globalization', *Foreign Affairs*, 86, 2007, pp.34–47.

Young, Katharine G., 'The Minimum Core of Economic and Social Rights: A Concept in Search of Content', *The Yale Journal of International Law*, 33, 2008, pp. 113–71.

Official Documents/Reports

Constitution of the Republic of South Africa.

International Covenant on Economic Social and Cultural Rights (ICESCR), opened for signature 19 December 1966, 993 UNTS 3, Article 2(1) (entered into force 3 January 1976).

'Statement by UN Committee on Economic Social and Cultural Rights (CESCR)', UN Doc. E/1993/22, Annex. III.

Online Documents

Prashad, Vijay, "'The South Also Exists", as the Third World Once Did', *NACLA Report on the Americas*, 40(5), 2007, available at http://nacla.org/node/4554 (accessed 7 August 2009).

Seria, Nasreen., and Cohen, Mike, 'South Africa's Unemployment Rate Increases to 23.5% (Update2)', *Bloomberg News*, available at http://www.bloomberg.com/apps/news?pid=20601116&sid=aoB7RbcZCRfU (accessed 1 June 2009).

'Education in South Africa', available at http://www.southafrica.info/about/education/education.htm (accessed 1 June 2009).

'About the Treatment Action Campaign', available at http://www.tac.org.za/community/about (accessed 7 August 2009).

'World Health Organization: South Africa', available at http://www.who.int/countries/zaf/en/ (accessed 1 June 2009).

Legal Cases

Soobramoney v. Minister of Health Kwa Zulu Natal, 1998 (1) SA 765 (CC).

Government of the Republic of South Africa v. Grootboom, 2000 (11) BCLR 1169 (CC).

Minister of Health v. Treatment Action Campaign, 2005 (5) SA 721 (CC).

Khosa v. Minister of Social Development, 2004 (6) SA 505.

Editors and Contributors

EDITORS

Jeffrey F. Addicott, SJD, LL.M., University of Virginia School of Law; LLM, Army Judge Advocate General's School; JD, University of Alabama School of Law, BA (with honors), University of Maryland. As Distinguished Professor of Law and the Director of the Center for Terrorism Law at St. Mary's University School of Law, San Antonio, Texas, he has published over 20 books, articles, and monographs on a variety of legal topics including forthcoming: *Terrorism Law: Cases, Materials, Comments*, (6th Edition).

Md. Jahid Hossain Bhuiyan teaches law at the Department of Law, ASA University Bangladesh. During his studies in Belgium he gained experience in legal practice with the lawyers of European countries. He has to his credit articles published in reputed journals of Australia, Bangladesh, India, and Malta. He is co-editor of several books, including *International Humanitarian Law: An Anthology*, and *An Introduction to International Human Rights Law* (published by BRILL in 2010).

Tareq M.R. Chowdhury, LL.D., Stockholm University is Professor and Dean at the Department of Law, ASA University Bangladesh. He was faculty at Stockholm University, Sweden. He has participated in several national and international conferences, and made substantial contribution through his papers. He has contributed many research articles. He is the author of *Legal Framework of International Supervision* (published by Stockholm University in 1986).

CONTRIBUTORS

Mohsen al Attar is a Senior Lecturer at the Faculty of Law, University of Auckland, New Zealand. He specializes and publishes in the areas of International Trade Law, First-to-Third World legal relations, and Islamic Law.

Jernej Letnar Černič, PhD (2009) in Law, the University of Aberdeen, Scotland, is a Max Weber Postdoctoral Fellow at the European University Institute, Italy, and a Senior Lawyer at the Law Institute in Ljubljana. He has published in Slovene, English, and Swedish on human rights law, international law, European Law, and human rights and business.

Avinash Govindjee, LL.D. (2005), Nelson Mandela Metropolitan University, is an Associate Professor at the Faculty of Law, Nelson Mandela Metropolitan University, South Africa. He has published chapters in over ten books and twenty articles in accredited South African law journals, focusing mainly on Human Rights, Labor, and Social Law.

M. Abdul Hannan, PhD (2006) in Law, University of Rajshahi, is an Associate Professor at the Department of Law and Justice, University of Rajshahi, Bangladesh. He has published extensively in the area of international law, human rights, and commercial law.

Kamrul Hossain, LL.D. (2007) in International Law, University of Lapland, is a Senior Researcher in the Arctic Centre of the University of Lapland, Finland. He has published extensively in the field of human rights law, international environmental law, and law relating to international peace and security. His forthcoming publication is at press to be published in the Yearbook of Polar Law, 2010.

Edel Hughes, PhD in International Human Rights Law (NUI), is a lecturer in law at the University of Limerick, Ireland. She has published widely on international human rights law. Her monograph entitled *Turkey's Accession to the European Union: The Politics of Exclusion?* was published by Routledge in 2010.

Owen McIntyre, PhD (2005) in International Law, University of Manchester, is a Senior Lecturer in Law at University College Cork, National University of Ireland, Ireland. He has published extensively on all aspects of environmental and natural resources law with a particular emphasis on International Water Resources Law, including *Environmental protection of International Watercourses under International Law* (published by Ashgate in 2007).

Ciaron Murnane is a graduate of the Faculty of Law, University of Auckland, New Zealand and a local barrister. His areas of interest are globalization and human rights.

Elijah Adewale Taiwo, LL.D. Nelson Mandela Metropolitan University, South Africa, is a lecturer at the Faculty of Law, University of Ibadan, Nigeria. His areas of research interest include Constitutional/Administrative Law, Human Rights, and Arbitration. He has published several papers in these areas of law.

Edwin Tanner, PhD (1998) in Law, University of Melbourne, is a practising Barrister-at-Law and Senior Lecturer in Law at Victoria Law School, Melbourne, Australia. He has published extensively in refereed journals in the area of law and linguistics, including *the Statute Law Review, Sydney University Law Review, Melbourne University Law Review*, and *Monash University Law Review*.

Brigit Toebes, PhD (1999) Utrecht University, the Netherlands, is an Honorary Lecturer at the University of Aberdeen, Scotland, United Kingdom, and currently based in Copenhagen (Denmark) as an independent researcher, external lecturer and consultant. She has published widely on the interfaces between health and human rights, including *The Right to Health as a Human Right in International Law* (published by Intersentia/Hart in 1999).

Index